Inequality and Democratization

An Elite-Competition Approach

Research on the economic origins of democracy and dictatorship has shifted away from the impact of growth and turned toward the question of how different patterns of growth—equal or unequal—shape regime change. This book offers a new theory of the historical relationship between economic modernization and the emergence of democracy on a global scale, focusing on the effects of land and income inequality. Contrary to most mainstream arguments, Ben W. Ansell and David J. Samuels suggest that democracy is more likely to emerge when rising yet politically disenfranchised groups demand more influence because they have more to lose, rather than when threats of redistribution to elite interests are low.

Ben W. Ansell is Professor of Comparative Democratic Institutions at Nuffield College, Oxford, and coeditor of *Comparative Political Studies*. His work on education, democracy, and housing markets has appeared in the *American Political Science Review, Comparative Political Studies, World Politics,* and *International Organization*. His book *From the Ballot to the Blackboard* (Cambridge, 2010) was awarded the 2011 William Riker Prize by the Political Economy Section of the American Political Science Association.

David J. Samuels is Distinguished McKnight University Professor of Political Science at the University of Minnesota. He is the coauthor of *Presidents, Parties, and Prime Ministers* (Cambridge, 2010); the author of *Ambition, Federalism, and Legislative Politics in Brazil* (Cambridge, 2003); and the coeditor of *Decentralization and Democracy in Latin America* (2004). His work has appeared in the *American Political Science Review*, the *American Journal of Political Science, Comparative Politics, Comparative Political Studies, Legislative Studies Quarterly,* and the *British Journal of Political Science*. He currently serves as coeditor of *Comparative Political Studies*.

Cambridge Studies in Comparative Politics

General Editor
Margaret Levi   University of Washington, Seattle

Assistant General Editors
Kathleen Thelen   Massachusetts Institute of Technology
Erik Wibbels   Duke University

Associate Editors
Robert H. Bates   Harvard University
Gary Cox   Stanford University
Stephen Hanson   The College of William and Mary
Torben Iversen   Harvard University
Stathis Kalyvas   Yale University
Peter Lange   Duke University
Helen Milner   Princeton University
Frances Rosenbluth   Yale University
Susan Stokes   Yale University
Sidney Tarrow   Cornell University

Other Books in the Series

Ben W. Ansell, *From the Ballot to the Blackboard: The Redistributive Political Economy of Education*

Leonardo R. Arriola, *Multi-Ethnic Coalitions in Africa: Business Financing of Opposition Election Campaigns*

David Austen-Smith, Jeffry A. Frieden, Miriam A. Golden, Karl Ove Moene, and Adam Przeworski, eds., *Selected Works of Michael Wallerstein: The Political Economy of Inequality, Unions, and Social Democracy*

Andy Baker, *The Market and the Masses in Latin America: Policy Reform and Consumption in Liberalizing Economies*

Lisa Baldez, *Why Women Protest: Women's Movements in Chile*

Stefano Bartolini, *The Political Mobilization of the European Left, 1860–1980: The Class Cleavage*

Robert Bates, *When Things Fell Apart: State Failure in Late-Century Africa*

Mark Beissinger, *Nationalist Mobilization and the Collapse of the Soviet State*

Nancy Bermeo, ed., *Unemployment in the New Europe*

Carles Boix, *Democracy and Redistribution*

Carles Boix, *Political Parties, Growth, and Equality: Conservative and Social Democratic Economic Strategies in the World Economy*

Catherine Boone, *Merchant Capital and the Roots of State Power in Senegal, 1930–1985*

Catherine Boone, *Political Topographies of the African State: Territorial Authority and Institutional Change*

Catherine Boone, *Property and Political Order in Africa: Land Rights and the Structure of Politics*

Michael Bratton, Robert Mattes, and E. Gyimah-Boadi, *Public Opinion, Democracy, and Market Reform in Africa*

(*Continued after the Index*)

Inequality and Democratization

An Elite-Competition Approach

BEN W. ANSELL
University of Oxford

DAVID J. SAMUELS
University of Minnesota

CAMBRIDGE
UNIVERSITY PRESS

CAMBRIDGE
UNIVERSITY PRESS

32 Avenue of the Americas, New York NY 10013-2473, USA

Cambridge University Press is part of the University of Cambridge.

It furthers the University's mission by disseminating knowledge in the pursuit of education, learning and research at the highest international levels of excellence.

www.cambridge.org
Information on this title: www.cambridge.org/9780521168793

© Ben W. Ansell and David J. Samuels 2014

First published 2014

A catalogue record for this publication is available from the British Library

Library of Congress Cataloguing in Publication data
Ansell, Ben W., 1977–
Inequality and democratization : an elite-competition approach / Ben W. Ansell, David J. Samuels.
    pages cm
ISBN 978-1-107-00036-0 (hardback)
1. Democracy—Economic aspects. 2. Democratization—Economic aspects.
3. Economic development—Political aspects. 4. Land tenure—Political aspects.
5. Income distribution—Political aspects. I. Samuels, David, 1967– II. Title.
JC423.A578 2014
321.8–dc23   2014018359

ISBN 978-1-107-00036-0 Hardback
ISBN 978-0-521-16879-3 Paperback

Contents

Tables

Figures

Preface

In light of recent experience, the question is not whether democracy will rob property owners of their property, but whether propertied interests will rob common men of their chief weapon of defense against exploitation, democracy.

Benjamin E. Lippincott ([1938] 1974, 238)

Our intellectual journey began with a question Samuels raised to Ansell. Long a student of Brazilian politics, Samuels also taught a graduate seminar on democratization. Reading Boix and Acemoglu and Robinson left Samuels scratching his head, because Brazil confounded the "redistributive" arguments in both books. Brazil is notoriously one of the world's most unequal countries, yet it had democratized at precisely the moment when inequality peaked. Samuels found it hard to reconcile what he knew about Brazil with what these "median-voter" models of regime change were telling him, and he began to hound Ansell for his insights into the political economy literature on redistribution. Was Brazil merely an outlier?

We soon discovered the Vanhanen (2000) data on land inequality and the Bourguignon and Morrisson (2002) data on income inequality, generated Gini coefficients from them, and then correlated those Ginis against Polity IV data and ACLP's regime-type data. To our surprise, we discovered a positive correlation between the level of income inequality and whether an autocracy transitioned to democracy. At that point, we had no explanation for this finding, which would not go away no matter how much we tortured the data. Yet we reasoned at that point that, to the extent that the correlation held up, regime change could not be a function of elites' fear of the poor.

We kept returning to the fact that redistributivist theories seemed to misinterpret what a Gini coefficient looks like in the real world, particularly overlooking the fact that Kuznets (1955) established decades ago—that in a poor but developing society, a low Gini coefficient does not indicate the presence of a large middle class. Quite the opposite. To the extent that high Ginis are correlated with regime change and high Ginis indicate the presence of a sizable middle class, regime change is not a redistributive game between the median voter and the autocratic elite, but a game played between relative economic elites, all of whom have incomes well above the mean.

Once we realized that a high Gini is a proxy for the emergence of sizable "middle" class groups, we also perceived that the correlation between high Gini coefficients and democratization was not so counterintuitive as one might initially think. We also began to see how our argument resembles Barrington Moore's in terms of the importance placed on the role of the relative power of landed elites and the urban upper-middle classes in democratization. Our emphasis began to shift theoretically toward the issue of property rights protection as we came to the conclusion that the connection between inequality and democratization is drawn through rising groups' demands to rein in arbitrary government authority.

In and of itself, the argument that democracy and property are not just compatible but are causally connected is not new. In fact, as we make clear in Chapter 1, the argument's philosophical roots lie with Enlightenment liberalism, which itself provided the original foundation for Modernization Theory. John Locke's "contractarian" liberalism is fundamentally about a need to rein in Leviathan, to protect individual rights to life, liberty, and property. Enlightenment liberals believed that a "modern" government was one that reflected the newly emergent balance of forces in society, with a balance of powers and controls on government power. Only under such institutions would progress endure.

What we found surprising is the near-complete absence of this monstrously influential intellectual tradition in social-science research on regime change. To be sure, neoclassical theories of the state have proven quite influential, but mostly in the study of the political sources of economic growth—and not on the political *consequences* of economic growth. Boix and Acemoglu and Robinson took Meltzer and Richard's median-voter model and applied it to the study of regime change. We do the same for North and Weingast's (and others') institutionalist arguments about the importance of reining in arbitrary government authority for economic growth. Extending the logic, we suggest that democratization is about fear of the expropriative authority of the state, not fear of the redistributive power of the poor.

Our argument is yet another salvo in the debate about Modernization Theory. For decades Modernization Theory focused on the political consequences of aggregate economic growth. As evidenced by the brief and cavalier treatment of the issue in Przeworski et al. (2000), the issue of inequality was largely sidestepped in most research, partly (if not mainly) because no good data existed. Boix and Acemoglu and Robinson brought the issue of the relative distribution of the benefits of modernization front and center, rejuvenating research on the political consequences of economic development. We hope this book makes a similar contribution—but that it also reorients our understanding of the relationship between economic development, inequality, and regime change.

Elements of various chapters from this book were first published in *Comparative Political Studies* Volume 43 #12 (2010), and versions of our argument were presented at the 2007, 2010, and 2011 meetings of the American Political Science Association; the 2008 meeting of the Midwest Political Science Association; as well as at the National University of Brasília, the Federal University of Goiás, the Federal University of Minas Gerais, the London School of Economics, University College London, ITAM and CIDE in Mexico City, and seminars at the following universities in the United States: Wisconsin, Michigan, Minnesota, Columbia, California-Davis, Kentucky, Texas, Stanford, Yale, and Rochester. We thank participants at those seminars for their comments. We would particularly like to thank Margaret Levi for organizing a workshop at the University of Washington, where we received invaluable feedback from numerous participants, and Jonathan Rodden for doing the same at Stanford.

We thank Carles Boix and Sebastian Rosato for data on regime types, and Peter Lindert for his data on social-welfare spending. Two Minnesota graduate students, Kevin Lucas and Henry Thomsen, provided research assistance on Chapters 7 and 8. We would also like to thank John Ahlquist, Allyson Benton, Pablo Beramendi, Nancy Bermeo, Carles Boix, Ernesto Calvo, Bill Clark, Gary Cox, Geoff Dancey, Thad Dunning, Zach Elkins, Jim Fearon, Jennifer Gandhi, Barbara Geddes, Scott Gehlbach, Miriam Golden, Timothy Hellwig, Karen Long Jusko, Herbert Kitschelt, David Laitin, Margaret Levi, Kevin Lucas, Eric Magar, Eddie Malesky, Verónica Michel, Erica Owen, Jim Robinson, Jonathan Rodden, Phil Shively, Hillel Soifer, Sidney Tarrow, Kharis Templeman, James Vreeland, Barry Weingast, Erik Wibbels, and especially David Art, Jane Gingrich, Dan Slater, Joan Tronto, and Daniel Ziblatt for comments on various chapters.

We chose the epigraph at the beginning of this preface not simply because it neatly fits our argument. We wrote this book while at the University of Minnesota, where Ben Lippincott taught more or less continuously from 1929 to 1971. The American Political Science Association awards a Benjamin E. Lippincott Prize every other year, to "recognize a work of exceptional quality by a living political theorist that is still considered significant after a time span of at least 15 years since the original date of publication." We were pleased to find Lippincott's work on Victorian-era politics still relevant after these years, and we gratefully acknowledge support from the Benjamin E. Lippincott and David Larson endowments in the Department of Political Science at the University of Minnesota. Samuels also benefited from a semester's leave at Minnesota's Institute for Advanced Studies.

1

Introduction

What explains the emergence of democracy? Why did some countries democratize in the nineteenth century, while others never have? Which social groups are relatively more or less important proponents of regime change? Does economic growth promote democracy, and if so, how?

Debate about answers to these questions continues. In recent years, scholars have turned away from the question of whether economic development per se fosters regime change, and begun to explore the question of whether the *distributional consequences* of economic development help explain patterns of democracy and dictatorship.

In particular, a set of papers and two influential books by Daron Acemoglu and James Robinson (henceforth "A&R": 2001; 2006) and Carles Boix (2003) have propelled research in this new direction. These books offer what we call *redistributivist* theories of regime change, in that they focus on how economic inequality—the relative distribution of income or assets—impacts voters' demand for redistribution. All else equal, redistributivist arguments suggest that inequality harms democracy's prospects because, in intensifying voters' desire for redistribution of autocratic elites' wealth, it generates a similarly intense reaction by those same elites, who will dig in their heels to maintain the political status quo. In an equal society, demand for redistribution would be weaker—as would elite opposition to liberalization.

In reinvigorating research on the "economic origins of democracy and dictatorship" (the title of Acemoglu and Robinson's book), redistributivist approaches implicitly adopt the fundamental tenet of Modernization Theory—that political change can follow economic change. Yet they add an important new twist, in drawing our attention to the fact that economic development can have very different political consequences, depending on how the growing economic pie is divided up. Such arguments begin with an apparently straightforward contrast between autocracies, which restrict the franchise, and democracies, which allow the poor greater voice and vote. Logically, because there are always more poor people than rich people, franchise extensions lower the average voter's income, which should increase demand for redistribution. When such redistributive pressures are high, economic elites will—out of self-interest—resist granting the poor the vote.

We challenge this purported syllogism between democracy and redistribution, and the concomitant assumption that a natural tension exists between democracy and property. Indeed, it is likely that the tension between *autocracy* and property, due to lack of voice and accountability, is far greater than any threat to property under democracy. We also argue that the threat from the median voter that drives redistributivist approaches is a chimera, and that political-economy theories built on such fear lead scholars down an unfruitful path. Democracy does not emerge when redistributive threats to elite interests are low. Instead, it is more likely when rising yet politically disenfranchised groups demand greater voice in government affairs because *they* have more to lose. Democracy is about fear of the autocratic state, not fear of the poor.

1.2 DEMOCRACY *OR* PROPERTY? THE REDISTRIBUTIVIST THESIS

The notion of "democracy as Robin Hood"—that the poor would use the vote to soak the rich—enjoys an exalted status in contemporary political-economy research. And perhaps for good reason, for it draws on deep and well-known philosophical roots. One can find fear of the depredations of majority rule in Aristotle's *Politics* (Book III, Ch. 10, 14–18), while modern political philosophers as different as Rousseau, Adam Smith, and Tocqueville also all implied in one way or another that democracy and property are incompatible.

Given its philosophical pedigree, the notion that economic equality would inevitably follow political equality has "dominated the hopes and fears attached to democracy" since the earliest days of representative government (Przeworski 2009, 301). Indeed, an intellectual strange bedfellows coalition spanning the political spectrum has long buttressed the redistributivist logic: those on the left have hoped the poor would remain unsatisfied with the mere acquisition of *de jure* political equality, while those on the right have feared universal suffrage would threaten property.

Both sides have had powerful incentives to advance the notion that democracy and property are in tension not just in theory, but in fact. On the left, we find this claim in Marx and Engels, who both believed democracy should precede communism because universal suffrage would undermine property and exacerbate class struggle. Marx emphasized this theme in the *18th Brumaire* and in *Class Struggles in France*, for example. And not surprisingly, the quest for "distributive justice" has long served as the core principle mobilizing leftist political movements.

On the right, one sees the alleged syllogism between democracy and redistribution in a prominent strand of conservative-libertarian thought, which also assumes that politics is driven by a clash between rich and poor. Democracy is a vehicle for the "legalized plunder," in the words of Frédéric Bastiat (1850), of the property and income of the rich through taxation and redistribution. Fear of redistribution, demands for lower taxes, and calls for economic liberty rather than equality have long mobilized conservative movements.

According to Przeworski (1999, 40), the logic of the supposed tension between democracy and property is so intuitively obvious that by 1850 the idea that democracy would inevitably bring about socioeconomic equality was universally accepted. To this day, Przeworski suggests that intelligent observers have a hard time reconciling universal suffrage and economic inequality, believing that under democracy the poor will naturally soak the rich (Przeworski 2010, 85). Hope on the left and fear on the right—and the clashing calls for economic equality or economic liberty—still drive political debate.

The notion of a tension between democracy and property also figures in prominent accounts of regime change. For example, in engaging and critiquing Barrington Moore, Rueschemeyer, Stephens, and Stephens (1992, 6) (RSS) suggest that democracy emerges due to demands for both political *and* economic equality. RSS drew on Marx in suggesting that the working class would be democracy's 'most frequent proponent' (42) precisely because democracy creates opportunities for redistribution.

In recent years redistributivist arguments with intellectual roots on the other side of the political spectrum have gained traction. In 1981, Allan Meltzer and Scott Richard—who can fairly be classified as "free-market" economists—distilled the alleged incompatibility of democracy and property into a simple formal-theoretic rational-expectations argument about electoral politics. Since there are always more poor people than rich people, universal suffrage means that a majority of voters—and most importantly the median voter under majority rule—earn less than average income. Because everyone with below average income should want to raise taxes on everyone with above average income, democracy should always produce pressure for redistribution—and such pressure should increase with inequality, because as the rich get richer the poorer median voter would gain more by continuing to raise taxes.

Meltzer and Richard's model has had enormous impact on the study of political economy. Many have explored its intended application, relating the degree of inequality to variation in redistributive social-welfare spending. Boix and A&R derived their arguments about regime change from Meltzer and Richard's assumption that everyone, from the incumbent dictator down to the lowliest peasant, knows that in a democracy the poor will soak the rich—and that the larger the gap between rich and poor, the worse will be the soaking.

Boix assumes that political regimes aggregate preferences about redistribution from among those who have the right to participate (p.10). Given this, low levels of inequality under autocracy enhance the chances of democratization because redistributive pressure from the poor is low. Acemoglu and Robinson begin similarly, stating that, "Democracy is usually not given by the elite because its values have changed. It is demanded by the disenfranchised as a way to obtain political power and thus secure a larger share of the economic benefits of the system" (p.29).

Although these books differ in their arguments and conclusions to some degree, they begin from and apply similar theoretical principles—that outcomes of political conflict are a function of the preferences of the median voter, who would like high taxes and substantial redistribution to poor people like themselves (see Acemoglu and Robinson 2006, 103–4; Boix 2003, 23–4). The rich, meanwhile, seek the opposite: no taxes and no redistribution. All redistributivist arguments—whether about social-welfare spending or regime change—focus on elites' fear of the relatively poor median voter, highlighting the similarity between conservative fears and leftist hopes that democracy and redistribution go hand in hand.

1.3 PUZZLES FOR THE REDISTRIBUTIVIST APPROACH

In our view, the redistributivist thesis offers a misleading understanding of the relationship between inequality and democratization. Our motivation for developing an alternative explanation of this relationship starts with a question: Is democracy more likely to emerge from an autocracy with a Gini coefficient of income inequality of .24, or one with a Gini of .51?

In principle, Gini coefficients can range from 0 (perfect equality—everyone has the same amount) to 1 (perfect inequality—one person has everything, while everyone else has nothing), but .24 is among the lowest Ginis ever recorded. In contrast, .51 is a highly unequal society, at approximately the 80th percentile of historical estimates. Given this, Boix's answer embodies the conventional wisdom: democracy is more likely to emerge in the equal country. In turn, A&R might suggest that democracy is unlikely in either country, because they predict that regime change is only likely when inequality is at a "middling" level.[1]

Now consider a different question: Which country was more likely to democratize: China in 1880, or the UK in 1867? Everyone knows the answer to this question, but what not everyone knows is that the Gini coefficient in

---

[1] In an earlier paper, Acemoglu and Robinson (2001) suggested that the probability of regime change increases monotonically with inequality, but they abandoned this hypothesis in their book.

China in 1880 was .24, while in the UK in 1867 it was .51.[2] Even if these estimates are somewhat imprecise, no one questions these two countries' levels of inequality relative to each other. This generates a conundrum: all else equal, if Boix's argument were correct, China should have democratized long ago, while the UK might still be an autocracy. For their part, A&R argued that democratization was likely in the nineteenth-century UK, but only because they also suggested that inequality was moderate at that time. However, Victorian Britain's Dickensian chasm between rich and poor suggests that the case does not comfortably fit their argument.

As we will confirm, these cases are not outliers. Many recent examples of regime change—Brazil and South Africa most notoriously perhaps—occurred as income inequality was peaking. Holding all else equal for the moment, the juxtaposition of the UK against China, as well as cases of recent transitions in high-inequality countries, raise questions about the empirical accuracy of redistributivist hypotheses, simply because such examples confound the claim that regime change should occur when the threat of redistribution from the poor is relatively low.

We are hardly the first to question the utility of the median-voter model. Meltzer and Richard offered a seductively parsimonious explanation of redistributive politics, yet empirical support for their argument remains notably weak. Even though the decades since the article's publication have brought better measures of democracy, inequality, and redistribution, scholars have been confounded in their efforts to confirm a relationship between these three variables. Instead, findings have consistently and repeatedly called into question the notions that democracies redistribute more than autocracies and that inequality is correlated with pressures for redistribution.[3] In fact, results have repeatedly found that democracies redistribute less than they "should," and some scholars have even found that redistribution *declines* as inequality increases (e.g., Moene and Wallerstein 2001, 2003; Shelton 2007).

The lack of firm support for the MR thesis has caused endless scholarly head-scratching and has generated a cottage industry of research seeking to salvage the belief that a tension exists between democracy and property. Some suggest the thesis would hold if other factors didn't dilute the impact of voters' natural demand for redistribution, such as elites' ability and willingness to tilt

---

[2] The former estimate comes from Milanovic, Lindert, and Williamson (2011). The latter comes from Bourguignon and Morrisson (2002).

[3] See, for example, Aidt, Daunton, and Dutta (2010); Aidt, Dutta, and Loukoianova (2006); Aidt and Jensen (2011); Banerjee and Duflo (2003); Benabou (1996); Cheibub (1998); Cutright (1965); Dincecco and Prado (2010); Easterly and Rebelo (1993); Haggard and Kaufman (2012); Jackman (1974); Kenworthy and McCall (2008); Lott and Kenny (1999); Pampel and Williamson (1992); Perotti (1996); Putterman (1996); Rodrigiuez (1999); Scheve and Stasavage (2009); Shelton (2007); Tullock (1983). Reviews of the literature include Harms and Zink (2003); Mueller (2003); Roemer (1998).

the playing field by flooding politics with money;[4] elites' ability to shape the poor's political beliefs, particularly through ownership of mass media;[5] or the fact that as the salience of noneconomic issues such as ethnicity or religion increases, demand for redistribution declines.[6]

All efforts to explain the MR model's shortcomings accept its basic premise, that voters' desire for redistribution increases as their incomes decline. However, other attempts to account for the model's weak empirical performance dispense with this assumption. Perhaps relatively poor voters oppose redistributive schemes and believe instead that (1) the market system is fair and the rich should be respected, not envied; (2) structural constraints either do not exist or do not shape one's life chances; (3) people generally get what they deserve in life and shouldn't ask for a handout; (4) expropriating the rich might have unintended and undesirable consequences; or (5) even though they are poor in the present, they might be rich in the future (Alesina and La Ferrara 2005; Benabou and Ok 2001). For any or all of these reasons, most voters might prefer policies that equalize economic opportunity, but not outcomes (see e.g., Hochschild 1996).

No consensus exists as to why democracies redistribute less than they "should," but the empirical point remains: insisting on portraying democracy as Robin Hood makes little social-scientific sense. Still, scholars have been unwilling to abandon their faith in the redistributive model, leading Przeworski to sardonically call it "political economists' favorite toy" (2010, 85). Models that explain a lot using only a little are rare gems—things of great beauty and value, at least to social scientists. Simplicity is seductive, and parsimonious models often become the conventional wisdom. Yet simplicity is not always a virtue, because Ockham's razor can sometimes shave off too much, eliminating vital information.

We call attention to the Meltzer-Richard model's inability to explain redistribution in existing democracies because if it cannot accomplish what it was designed to do, we have little reason to expect it to explain regime change,

---

[4] Critics of democracy have long suggested that elites' informal influence under democracy, which derives from their material wealth and privileged access to those who hold power, overwhelms the masses' numerical advantage. This argument can be traced to Pareto and Mosca, is found in the work of Roberto Michels, C. Wright Mills, and E.E. Schattschneider, and continues—perhaps less as critique of democracy per se than as a call for reform—to hold a prominent place in discussions of American (e.g., Bartels 2010; Gilens 2012; Schlozman, Verba, and Brady 2012) and comparative politics (e.g., Winters 2011). Political economists agree—witness the well-known efforts seeking to explain why most government spending tends to favor the wealthy (e.g., Benabou 1996, 2000; Benabou and Ok 2001; Grossman and Helpman 2002; Justman and Gradstein 1999; Lizzeri and Persico 2004; Ross 2006; Stigler 1970).

[5] One need not be an acolyte of Gramsci to appreciate this point; after all, utilitarianism's avatar J.S. Mill suggested that political equality per se would never drive public spending because most voters lack the necessary self-understanding to cast a vote in their own interest.

[6] See Alesina and Glaeser (2005); Gilens (2000); Grossmann (2003); Huber and Stanig (2009); Lee and Roemer (1998); Roemer (1998, 2005)

especially based on expectations actors have about redistribution in *hypothetical future* democracies. The model's empirical and theoretical weaknesses need to be brought front and center in the study of regime change, because the lack of a clear relationship between democracy and redistribution implies that median-voter models lead scholars down an intellectually unprofitable path.

1.4 DEMOCRACY *AND* PROPERTY?

Our elite-competition approach offers a new theoretical explanation of the process of "endogenous" democratization—of the relationship between economic growth, inequality, and regime change. We start by turning the Meltzer-Richard model on its head. We assume that an elective affinity exists between property and democracy, rather than tension, and that a causal arrow runs from the former to the latter. In our view, regime change does not emerge from autocratic elites' fear that the poor would expropriate their wealth under democracy. It instead results when politically disenfranchised yet rising economic groups seek to rein in the power of autocratic elites to expropriate *their* income and assets.

We will argue and demonstrate empirically that the threat from the median voter under democracy is largely irrelevant to the story of regime change. Instead, we presume that elites who control the autocratic government represent the far greater threat—to the property of those who lack political rights. Typically, economic development brings about the rise of new economic groups, whose members are wealthier than average and who have growing economic interests to protect, but who lack political rights. Given their precarious political position, these rising elites will invest in changing the political regime, in an effort to rein in its expropriative authority.

The roots of this argument lie in Enlightenment liberalism, which connects the rise of commercial society with demands to rein in arbitrary government authority over individual rights, particularly over property. In recent decades, just as Meltzer and Richard were translating the "democracy *or* property" thesis for modern social science, scholars such as Douglas North (1986) were doing the same for the "democracy *and* property" antithesis. Perhaps the best-known modern statement linking greater demand for property rights to greater demand for limited government is North and Weingast's (1989) explanation of the emergence of limits on state authority during England's Glorious Revolution. The emergence of democracy takes a back seat in this tale, which focuses on explaining the sources of economic growth, but the authors' emphasis on the importance of secure contract and property rights is clearly rooted in Enlightenment liberalism (see also Weingast 1997).

Scholars of regime change have largely ignored the implications of these ideas. Indeed, Przeworski (2007, 6) has gone so far as to suggest that North and Weingast's argument would "bewilder" nineteenth-century observers. This

view is erroneous, as is the more relevant notion that it was consensus opinion at that time that the poor would, if given the opportunity, use the vote to
soak the rich. In fact, nineteenth century observers would readily recognize the
influence of John Locke, who not coincidentally published his *Two Treatises*
the year of the Glorious Revolution, in North and Weingast. More importantly, contemporary scholars who write in the spirit of North's "neoclassical
theory of the state" build on a well-known intellectual tradition that draws on
elements of Enlightenment liberalism—a body of thought hardly unknown in
the early nineteenth century.

Enlightenment liberalism was not exclusively concerned with property, but
material interests were always central—and Locke's emphasis on individuals'
material interests and the threat that control over government poses to life,
liberty and property proved intellectually and politically influential.[7] Adam
Smith, for example, drew this connection out explicitly, stating that although
some government involvement in the economy was necessary, oppressive government was an obstacle to economic development and was best prevented
by parliamentary sovereignty and taxation by representative consent. Malthus
agreed, believing the greatest threat to liberty was the growth of executive
power, and that both small landholders and emerging urban middle classes
offered a necessary counterbalance (Jones 1990).

Emerging theories of limited government did not focus on protecting the
rich from the poor, but on protecting property holders from arbitrary and
tyrannical government authority. Utilitarians later built on these ideas. For
example, echoing Hobbes and Madison, in his *Essay on Government* (1820),
Jeremy Bentham's disciple James Mill (father of John Stuart) argued that to
guarantee individuals' security of property, protection against the government
was more important than protection against each other (Krouse 1982, 513).
James Mill harbored a deep suspicion of power held by a narrow elite, and
like Bentham and Montesquieu sought to articulate a theory of the "protective" functions of government. Mill and his Utilitarian contemporaries believed
that autocracy allowed narrow private interests to hijack the public interest
(Collini, Winch, and Burrow 1983, 109)—and the narrower the suffrage, the
greater the influence of private interests.

[margin note:] James Mill

Deriving "democratic conclusions from Hobbesian premises" (ibid., 108),
Mill concluded that suffrage equaled protection against tyranny—and that
logically, the wider the suffrage, the greater the protection. Democracy and
property were compatible for Mill because a broad franchise would remove
wealthy voters' ability to exploit non-voters (Dunn 1979, 24). Although Mill
had little love for the masses, he "hated the few more than he loved the many"
(Thomas 1969, 255) and believed like Bentham (and later, Gramsci) that the
poor posed no danger to the rich because they were ideologically dominated

---

7 A cogent summary of the origins and influence of the liberal idea of "protective democracy"
can be found in (Held 1987, Chapter 2).

by the (conservative) middle classes, and tended to respect property (Collini, Winch, and Burrow 1983, 104; Dunn 1979, 24n).

Mill's argument extended Locke's notion of the protective functions of government, and other prominent liberals shared his views. For example, Malthus' *Ricardo* and Mill's friend David Ricardo, a strong advocate of laissez-faire capitalism, free trade, and minimal taxation, also passionately defended politically liberal causes, including parliamentary reform (Peach 2008). Although he is sometimes mistakenly cited as advocating suffrage limited to property holders (e.g., Collini, Winch, and Burrow 1983, 107; Przeworski 2010, 82), Ricardo also agreed with Mill and other liberals that the poor would not vote to overturn property, stating that fear of the poor was a "bugbear by which the corrupt always endeavor to rally those who have property to lose around them" to oppose suffrage expansion (Ricardo [1824] 1888, 555). He demurred about the benefits of *universal* suffrage but argued that expanding the electorate would nonetheless "substantially secure to the people the good government they wish for" by reducing corruption and rent-seeking (ibid.).

Unlike his father James, John Stuart Mill emphasized government's educa- *J.S. Mill* tive over its protective functions, a more elitist view. However, contrary to what RSS (2) imply, J.S. Mill did not believe democracy and property were incompatible. Instead, he hewed to the liberal notion that the primary purpose of government was "the provision of a legal framework for making and enforcing contracts, and to defending the liberty, rights, and life of persons and property" (Gibbons 1990, 101), and in his *Considerations on Representative Government* he repeated his father's argument that individual security would be maximized under democracy, because autocracy offers opportunities for the ruling class to exploit its narrow interests at everyone else's expense (Krouse 1982, 528).

Ever since Hobbes, political theorists have highlighted the necessity of the state to discourage predation by one private party against another. Yet these same scholars also understood that Leviathan could become the predator; this fear that a government powerful enough to control citizens could also threaten their liberties rests at the very core of Enlightenment political thought. Resolving this tension remains one of liberalism's central concerns. Locke argued that government's primary purpose was to protect individual rights—to life, liberty, and property. And for liberals like Malthus, Smith, Ricardo, and both Mills, democracy offered relatively greater protection than autocracy. Such theories of limited government were comparatively unconcerned with protecting the rich from the poor, and focused instead on protecting property holders from abuse of government authority.

1.5 DEMOCRACY, PROPERTY, AND ELITE COMPETITION

The long appeal of the notion that democracy and property are in tension can be traced to its roots in both radical and conservative political thought.

Yet the intellectual origins of Modernization Theory—and of the notion of "endogenous" democratization—actually lie with the antithetical notion that democracy and property are fully compatible. Building on Enlightenment liberal ideas and more recent neo-institutionalist research, we draw attention away from demands for redistribution, and toward demands for protection of property rights—to the connection between taxation and (the demand for) representation.

Contemporary neo-institutional theories—such as those of North and Weingast (1989), Douglas North's (1990) "neoclassical theory of the state," Mancur Olson's (1993) conception of the state as a "stationary bandit," and Margaret Levi's (1989) theory of "predatory rule" all begin from a similar premise: all else equal, property rights are likely to be relatively more secure under democracy.[8]

Given this, although economic exchange typically occurs within the existing political rules, North suggests that regime change can occur when citizens "find it worthwhile to devote resources to altering the more basic structure of the polity, to reassign rights" North (1990, 47). In particular, citizens may seek to extend third-party enforcement of contracts and property rights in order to "eliminate rulers' capricious capacity to confiscate wealth" North (1990, 51). Bates and Lien (1985) argued similarly that limited government follows from actors' efforts to "wrest control over public policy from revenue-seeking monarchs" (53).

What sorts of political actors will seek to broaden suffrage and impose limits on government authority? And under what conditions will such actors gain sufficient resources to become politically effective? Our understanding of the relationship between economic development, inequality, and regime change differs in two important ways from arguments that focus on the threat from the median voter: (1) in terms of which social actors drive regime transitions and (2) in terms of the nature and political impact of economic inequality.

First, redistributivist arguments focus on elites' relative fear of the median voter—and thus on the mobilizational capacity of everyone who earns less than the median voter. However, redistributivist arguments have ignored the fact that the median voter is typically quite poor, particularly in developing autocracies. That is, one cannot assume that the median voter is—in sociological, cultural, or political terms—a member of the "middle" class. Individuals with incomes and social status we consider middle class are, as we detail in Chapter 2, typically found in the upper quartile—or even the upper decile—of the income distribution. Often, even members of the working classes earn more than the median income.

---

[8] Counter-examples exist, but are historically rare. For example, Barro (1991, 284) found only three modern dictatorships that were not hostile to private property, only one of which has not since democratized (Singapore) (see also e.g., Leblang 1996; Rodrik 2000). Recent work on autocratic regimes has not questioned this view (see e.g., Gehlbach and Keefer 2011).

To the extent that the actors social scientists typically highlight as driving regime change—the bourgeoisie and/or the working class, for example—are located far above the median voter, and to the extent that the median voter in an autocracy is relatively poor, we have good reason to question the empirical accuracy and the theoretical utility of the core redistributivist assumption. After all, Mancur Olson's (1965) theory of collective action suggests that the poor are numerous, possess few resources, have diffuse and diverse interests, and tend to lack self-awareness of their status as politically oppressed—much less have any idea of how to remedy the supposed fact of their oppression.

We offer a more empirically plausible hypothesis about who will organize to promote regime change: political transitions result from the emergence of intra-elite conflict, between a group that controls the state and other relatively wealthy groups that do not. Individuals are far more likely to mobilize when they constitute smaller, wealthier groups with more homogenous and concrete interests—traits we find among both incumbent and disenfranchised economic elites. Intra-elite conflict under autocracy is more likely to emerge when societies experience an imbalance between political and economic power. More specifically, we expect intra-elite political conflict not just when new economic groups emerge that have a growing fear of expropriation, but when their growing numbers and wealth make them a more credible political threat and too costly to repress or co-opt.

Following Dahl (1971) and Knight (1992), the outcome of such conflict will depend on actors' relative bargaining strength, which is in turn a function of the nature and extent of economic development. For example, with modernization, landed elites may find themselves losing ground to new economic groups such as an industrial and/or financial bourgeoisie, a middle class, or the urban working classes, all of whom earn more than the median voter. Such rising groups will demand political concessions and an end to expropriative taxation, in an effort to translate their newfound economic gains into political influence (Bates and Lien 1985; Herb 2003; Levi 1989; Ross 2004).

Focusing on political contestation between economic groups near the top of the income distribution, rather than on conflict between rich and poor, draws attention to the second key distinction between our approach and redistributivist arguments: in terms of the way we conceptualize economic inequality and its political consequences. Unlike redistributivist arguments, we account for the political impact of economic growth across different sectors, distinguishing between inequality in land (historically, predominantly owned by the incumbent autocratic elite) and inequality produced by growing sectors in industry and finance (more likely to be dominated by rising yet disenfranchised groups).

Distinguishing among economic sectors has important ramifications for how we understand regime change. Most importantly, it opens up the possibility that the political impact of land inequality could differ from the political impact of income inequality—as for example when a rising urban financial bourgeoisie lacks political voice relative to a stagnating yet politically entrenched landed elite.

land inequality   In terms of the relative distribution of land, our empirical prediction is conventional: inequality supports autocracy, while equality fosters democracy. However, our causal mechanism differs: High land inequality does not primarily signify elites' fear that the rural poor would vote to expropriate land under a future democracy, or support a government that would do so. It proxies for the relative strength of a conservative landowning elite unwilling to share political power with representatives of rising and competing economic groups.

High land inequality signifies that a relatively small and cohesive group controls agricultural policy and rural labor mobility. In such a context, landed elites prefer autocracy because they need the state's coercive authority to repress wage demands and keep labor in place, working the land. In contrast, low land inequality signifies a relatively greater proportion of smallholders. In such a situation the key theoretical issue is not the relatively lower redistributive threat from landless peasants, but the greater likelihood of economic (and thus political) divisions within the agrarian sector, the relatively weaker political position of large landowners vis-à-vis control over agricultural policy, and the relatively lower political demand for coercive control over rural labor mobility.

income inequality   Turning to income inequality, our prediction is counterintuitive. We suggest that democracy is more likely to emerge when rising disenfranchised groups accumulate a growing share of national income. Yet because such groups are found near the top of the income distribution—not near the middle— democratization will occur when income inequality is relatively *high*. This claim rests on the following fact, which we explore in Chapters 2 and 3: historically, the process of economic development that has led to the emergence of growing but politically disenfranchised economic groups has also been associated with a pronounced *increase* in income equality. To the extent that this is true, land *equality* and income *inequality* will be associated with democratization; other combinations of these variables will be less likely to lead to regime change.

Our argument uses land and income inequality as measures of the relative balance of economic power, and suggests that political and economic change will co-evolve. We recognize that land and income are not, in the real world, perfectly separable goods. Yet for purposes of thinking about the relative fruitfulness of different theories of the relationship between democracy, development, and inequality, it will become clear how important it is to distinguish these two factors. Tables 1.1a and 1.1b set out our baseline expectations for the relative impacts of land and income inequality on the probability of democratization, along with examples of countries that might be considered "ideal types" for thinking through the connection between inequality and regime change.

TABLE 1.1A. *Income and Land Inequality: Probability of Democratization*

	Low Land Inequality	High Land Inequality
Low Income Inequality	Moderate	Low
High Income Inequality	High	Moderate

TABLE 1.1B. *Income and Land Inequality: Example Cases*

	Low Land Inequality	High Land Inequality
Low Income Inequality	Korea 1970	Germany 1900, China 1880
High Income Inequality	UK 1900, Sweden 1900, China 2010	Brazil 1985

In short, in our approach the key actors differ from redistributivist approaches, as does our understanding of the nature and political impact of inequality. We also take the fiscal consequences of control of the state's expropriative capacity more seriously. Median voter models stress the elites' fear that the masses will tax them, but ignore the far more plausible reverse dynamic, that incumbent elites will engage in regressive taxation and impose fiscal burdens on anyone who lacks political rights. Elites who control the state represent a greater threat to the median voter than vice versa because they are more cohesive, have greater resources, and control more effective means of coercion.[9]

Democratization is not about whether the median voter is going to soak the rich, it is about whether all citizens—but particularly rising economic groups who lack political representation—can obtain impartial protection against arbitrary violations of contracts and property rights. Regime change comes about due to divisions within the elite—between those who control the state and those who fear those who control the state. Land inequality may very well retard democracy, but economic development under autocracy has typically meant that while many remain mired in poverty, some proportion of the population is growing wealthy, producing an increase in income inequality. The newly wealthy will be more eager, willing and able to fight to protect their economic interests. In contrast, lower levels of income inequality will be associated with less intense demands for political change. This book elaborates on

---

[9] And in any case, the median voter is not a tax collector—so even if preferences exist for redistribution, it is ultimately the state, vulnerable as it is to capture by the rich, that does the taxing and spending. (We owe this last point to Dan Slater, whose work [Slater 2010] elaborates in great detail on the role of the state in autocratic regimes; see also Smith 2007; Slater and Smith 2012; Albertus and Menaldo 2012).

this argument, providing the basis for a new understanding of the historical relationship between economic and political change.

1.6 PLAN OF THE BOOK

As Coppedge (2012) urges, we have adopted a multi-method approach that combines formal models, quantitative analysis, and brief case studies. Chapter 2 assesses a theoretically critical conceptual issue in the study of the relationship between development, inequality, and regime change. Conventional wisdom—from Lipset (1959) to Boix (2011)—associates development and the emergence of a middle class with increasing economic *equality*. However, the opposite is frequently the case.

As Kuznets (1955) explained, the onset of economic development generates economic inequality, but not simply because the wealthy 1% are distancing themselves from the impoverished 99%. Growth generates inequality because it brings about the emergence of new economic groups, who are leaving the remaining poor far behind. As these groups—the urban bourgeoisie, middle, and working classes—grow larger, economic inequality will actually increase.

The correlation between economic development and income inequality suggests a need to rethink the relationship between income inequality and regime change. Chapter 2 does so by connecting social scientists' primary empirical measure of inequality—the Gini coefficient—to the nature of social-class structures in the real world. As we reveal, in most developing countries members of the bourgeoisie and middle classes—and even most members of the working classes—earn far more than the median voter. This supports our argument's main contention: the median voter is typically poor, politically inert and thus unimportant for explaining democratization, while most of the action occurs in the top 20% of the income distribution, among relative economic elites.

Chapter 3 further explores the descriptive accuracy of the assumptions about key actors' interests in different theories of regime change: ruling elites, the rising bourgeoisie and middle classes, the working classes, and the poor. We question whether actors behave as per redistributivist models and suggest instead that our elite-competition approach offers a more plausible alternative. This chapter connects the dots between the emergence of relatively wealthy new social groups, higher income inequality, and growing demands for regime change: Under autocracy, higher income inequality will be associated with demands for political reforms because more people have more to lose. We illustrate the descriptive accuracy of our argument's assumptions with evidence from Britain's 2nd Reform Act and shorter case studies of nineteenth-century Germany and Sweden and twentieth-century Korea and China.[10]

---

[10] See also Slater (2010) for in-depth case studies from radically different social contexts that jibe with our argument and conclusions.

To move beyond these suggestive case studies, in Chapter 4 we formalize our argument, developing a model that explains how income inequality and land equality generate the most likely conditions for regime change. We identify the problematic nature of redistributivist models' core assumptions and explain how the assumptions of our elite-competition model offer a descriptively more accurate alternative. Rather than focusing on elites' perception of threat from the poor median voter, we focus on rising economic groups' incentives to press for changes in the political rules, to reduce the threat of expropriation.

Formal models are not very useful if they are descriptively accurate but still fail to predict patterns in the data. In Chapters 5 and 6 we test our model's primary implication, that democratization is a function of income inequality and land equality. We conduct a series of cross-national statistical tests, using two different datasets on economic inequality and examining the determinants of regime change between 1820 and 2004, and find consistent support for our hypotheses. The countervailing effects of land and income inequality persist across historical periods and different measures of inequality and democracy, and are robust to a range of estimation techniques and sensitivity tests. We find no evidence for the redistributivist hypothesis that income inequality retards democracy; our elite-competition model provides a much better fit to the data.

If democracy were really hindered by fear of the poor, we would concede that the Meltzer-Richard model is theoretically fruitful: it would have proven its utility beyond its originally intended application of explaining redistribution. Likewise, our elite competition argument would gain credence if we could demonstrate its theoretical fruitfulness—that it too has implications beyond the question of regime change. With this in mind, Chapters 7 and 8 consider extensions to our argument.

Logically, if our model offers a superior heuristic representation of the world, then not only should it generate better predictions of the relationship between inequality and regime change, but it should also be able to account for patterns of government spending. In Chapter 7 we revisit the hypothesis that redistributive social-welfare spending is a function of both democracy and inequality. This exercise emulates Boix's (2003) Chapter 5—and yet, we come to opposite conclusions. To explain why we extend our formal model, highlighting how inequality shapes the relative political influence of elite groups. Under democracy, inequality gives economic elites relatively greater political influence to channel public spending toward themselves. Given this, unequal democracies should spend less on universalistic public goods, but might see targeted public spending toward relatively wealthy groups (Bartels 2010; Ross 2006).

To test this hypothesis, building on Lindert (2004), we created an original dataset of government social-welfare spending from 1880 to 1930 for almost every country then existing. Data from this era obviate many problems of causal inference that plague post-1960 government spending data. In contrast to Lindert, Boix, and many others, we find that democracy, income inequality, and the interaction between democracy and income inequality have no positive effect on redistributive spending. In fact, the effect of inequality is, as our elite-competition argument directly implies, robustly negative. We then replicate this finding with post-1960 data.

In Chapter 8 we turn from "macro" data at the level of individual countries to "micro" data at the level of individual people. A critical assumption in the Meltzer-Richard model is that demand for redistribution increases as individual income declines; the model also directly implies that such demand should also be a function of national-level inequality. Some research has explored this relationship under democracy, but none has explored it in autocracies. Echoing the findings in Chapter 7, using data from the World Values Surveys we again find that cross-nationally, as inequality increases demand for redistribution *declines*. Moreover, we find a positive relationship between income, demand for democratization, and opposition to both redistribution and government expropriation, supporting our argument that relatively wealthy out-groups, not the relatively poor masses, are the key proponents of regime change.

In the book's conclusion we discuss what we have learned, consider the limitations of our findings, and suggest potential theoretical and empirical extensions of our model to the study of democratic survivability and collapse. We also explore the normative implications of the counterintuitive fact that democracy and inequality seem to run together.

The puzzle of democracy's emergence has bedeviled social scientists for centuries, and there are few political questions more important in the world today than whether democracy, "the last best hope of earth," in Abraham Lincoln's famous words, can emerge and thrive. What are the conditions that support government that can preserve individual liberties and prevent tyranny? As he would later argue at length (Olson 1982), Olson's *Logic of Collective Action* reminds us that the problem John Locke and James Mill both identified—that a small minority in control of government have both the means and the motive to impose their interests upon the disenfranchised majority—is central to the question of regime change. Democracy does not emerge because of threats from the poor, but because relatively wealthy yet relatively disenfranchised groups want to live free from fear of state predation. The conditions under which relative economic elites will invest their own livelihoods—and lives, often—in an effort to rein in state authority remains a pressing issue for investigation.

2

Inequality, Development, and Distribution

2.1 INTRODUCTION

The idea that the poor – through their vote – represent a threat to democracy and property has inspired research on regime change for decades. From Lipset (1959, 31) to Boix (2011), scholars have expected growth, equality, and democracy to run together. Although it has gone largely unchallenged over decades, the notion that the poor threaten property and democracy is fundamentally mistaken on both empirical and theoretical grounds.

The roots and persistence of this error lie with a failure to properly connect social scientists' standard quantitative measure of income inequality – the Gini coefficient – to equally standard sociological understandings of class structure, in terms of the relative sizes and incomes of different social groups: the incumbent autocratic elite (which we assumes includes large landowners if they exist), rising (relative) economic elites, including the bourgeoisie and in many cases industrial workers, and the poor.

In this chapter, we show that properly connecting Gini coefficients to social structures supports our contention that competition over regime change tends to occur between relative economic elites. We start from the observation that income inequality is typically very low in preindustrial societies. Historically, the onset of sustained economic growth – a secular shift from agricultural to nonagricultural sectors – tends to generate a rapid increase in income inequality. Simon Kuznets (1955) noted this phenomenon decades ago,[1] but

---

[1] Kuznets assumed that wages and inequality in nonagricultural sectors would always be higher than in agriculture, because wages vary little in the latter but vary greatly in commerce, industry and services. Thus, when agriculture's relative contribution to GDP declines, income inequality rises because (1) income gains accrue more rapidly in the non-agricultural sector, (2) the relative number of people employed in the non-agricultural sector increases, or (3) both. See also Aghion and Williamson (1998); Bourguignon and Morrisson (1998); Fields (1993, 2004); Harris and Todaro (1970); Williamson (2009). Income inequality can derive from other

students of regime change have not teased out this correlation's political implications.[2]

The key theoretical point is that the combination of growth and inequality in a developing autocracy does not imply a growing redistributive threat from the median voter. As Kuznets noted, economic development has the effect of increasing intergroup variation in incomes, which is what the Gini coefficient actually measures. That is, inequality does not increase simply because the rich are further distancing themselves from everyone else, as Lipset and others appear to assume, but because of the emergence and growth of the bourgeois, middle, and working classes. Members of these groups tend to earn far more than the future median voter, who in nearly all historical cases tends to remain relatively poor. And because they have far more to lose, members of these rising economic groups are also increasingly likely to mobilize to press for political reforms.[3]

Economists are interested in the causes of growth and its economic consequences in terms of equality or inequality. Students of regime change, by contrast, are interested in the political consequences of equal and unequal growth. Historically, most democracies tend to be rich, while most autocracies are poor. The challenge has always been to discover whether or not a causal relationship drives this correlation. Progress in addressing this challenge has been hindered by a failure to properly interpret the political implications of an increase in income inequality as a society develops. Growing income inequality does not always follow economic development, but to the extent it does (holding land inequality constant), regime change is more likely – not because it indicates growing redistributivist demands from the increasingly poor median voter, but because it indicates the growth of relatively wealthy groups demanding protection from arbitrary state authority.

sources, such as increased trade openness, capital liberalization, and technological diffusion, but as with the "diverging economic sectors" argument that Kuznets (and Baumol) posited, these factors lead to the same outcome: relative increases in income for the bourgeois and middle classes, and even the working class (depending on whether it is employed mainly in export or import-competitive sectors).

[2] For example, adopting a redistributivist perspective Przeworski et al. (2000, 117) assume that inequality might "stimulate movements attracted by the egalitarian promise of democracy." Empirically, they initially find that "the durability of dictatorships is unaffected by income distribution" (120), but immediately thereafter suggest that both democracies and dictatorships collapse as inequality increases (121), and just a bit later they appear to agree with our conclusion by suggesting (without any explanation) that dictatorships "are particularly vulnerable" when inequality is high (122). The last two statements are particularly puzzling given that the point of the book is to dismiss any potential "endogenous" relationship between economic growth (equal or not) and regime change.

[3] We do not posit a full Kuznets curve, where inequality increases and then decreases with development. All else equal, we simply expect regime change to be more likely if and when income inequality increases. We agree that the right-hand side of the Kuznets curve has less empirical support than the left-hand (upward) side (see e.g., Aghion and Williamson 1998). Indeed, rising inequality in many developed democracies in recent decades also calls into question the notion that democracy and redistribution go hand in hand.

2.2 INEQUALITY AND CLASS STRUCTURE: A THOUGHT EXPERIMENT

To explain the connection between income inequality and the growing strength of relatively wealthy actors demanding political rights, we start by returning to the thought experiment posed in Chapter 1: Are we more likely to see regime change in an autocracy with a Gini coefficient of .24 or one with a Gini of .51? As noted, <u>Lipset</u> or <u>Boix</u> offer the conventional answer to this question: *equal* democratization is more likely in the relatively more equal country. For their part, <u>Acemoglu and Robinson (2006)</u> might suggest that neither case offers *middling* good prospects for democracy because they expect regime change only where inequality is at a middling level.

Our answer differs. To understand the connection between income inequality and regime change, let us illustrate what different Gini coefficients look like in the real world, in terms of social structure. To do so, a brief explanation of the Gini coefficient is necessary. Consider Figure 2.1, which plots the cumulative proportions of income (Y-axis) against the cumulative proportion of individuals (X-axis) in a hypothetical society. The 45-degree line indicates perfect equality (Gini = 0): at each point on that line, the proportion of individuals equals the proportion of income. For departures from this situation, a Lorenz curve plots the cumulative proportion of individuals against the corresponding cumulative proportion of income those individuals hold. The Gini coefficient is the ratio of the area between the uniform distribution line and the Lorenz curve as a proportion of the area of the triangle defined by the uniform distribution line and the borders of the figure. <u>As the area between the Lorenz curve and the uniform distribution line increases, so does the Gini coefficient, to a maximum of 1.</u>

In the society represented by Figure 2.1, the Gini coefficient is .24. To *low Gini* achieve this degree of equality, nearly everyone must earn the same amount. For example, we get this Gini coefficient in a society of 100 individuals if 98 people earn $1/day, 1 earns $7/day, and 1 earns $27/day. This is obviously highly stylized, but the point should be clear: <u>this society may be highly inegalitarian in having a tiny elite, but according to the Gini coefficient it is highly equal simply because nearly everyone is equally poor.</u>

Let us now compare Figure 2.1 against the society represented in Figure 2.2, *high Gini* where the Gini coefficient is .51. As in our first hypothetical, here there is also a huge gap between the richest 1% and the poorest group. In this society, 20 people earn $3/day, 20 earn $4/day, 20 earn $5/day, 20 earn $10/day, 15 earn $15/day, 4 earn $25/day, and 1 earns $275/day. However, the reason inequality is higher is not simply because the ratio of incomes earned between the top 1% and the bottom 20% is 4.5/1 as opposed to 1.35/1 as in our first example, but because there is <u>much greater intergroup differentiation of incomes.</u>

It is true that different income distributions can generate similar Gini coefficients, potentially invalidating inferences about the relationship between inequality and social structure. For example, if we changed the income of the

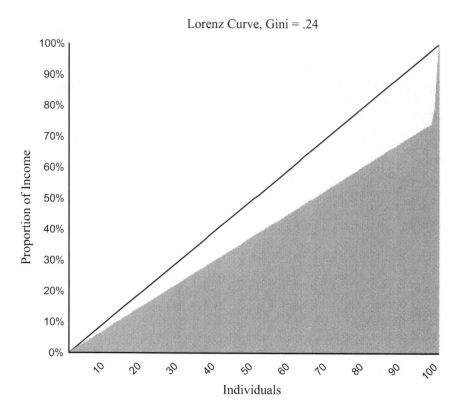

FIGURE 2.1. An Equal Society

top group in Figure 2.1 to $90/day and left everything else the same, the Gini would leap to .48. However, what is possible mathematically and what occurs in the real world are two different things. In truth, real-world distributions of Gini coefficients are highly constrained, giving us confidence in our inferences about the relationship between Ginis and social structure.

For example, if we changed the society in Figure 2.1 in this way, the top 1% would have about 46% of all income (90 units of 195), far above any recorded level (Milanovic, Lindert, and Williamson 2011). By way of comparison, the top 1% share of income in the U.S. peaked at about 20% in the 1920s, although it has recently approached that level again (Atkinson and Saez 2011). In contemporary Brazil, one of the world's most unequal societies, the income share of the top *10%* in 2010 was about 45%.[4]

---

[4] O Estado de São Paulo, "*Mais ricos têm renda 39 vezes maior que os mais pobres, diz Censo 2010*" ["Richest earn 39 times the income of the poorest, according to the 2010 census"]. Accessed at http://www.estadao.com.br/noticias/cidades,mais-ricos-tem-renda-39-vezes-maior-que-os-mais-pobres-diz-censo-2010-,799093,0.htm, April 5, 2012.

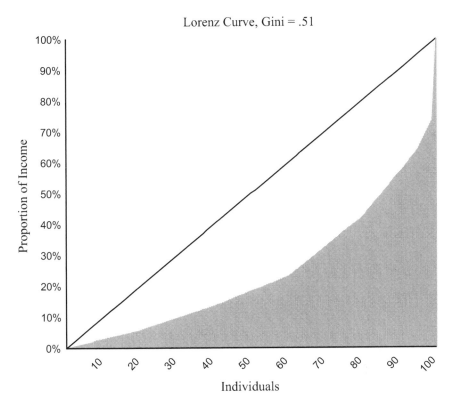

FIGURE 2.2. An Unequal Society

Real-world Gini coefficients of income inequality range only from about .15 to about .70 (Deininger and Squire 1996). They go no higher for two reasons. First, in contrast to calculating land inequality, for example, to calculate income inequality one cannot assume that individuals have zero income. Instead, economists assume that everyone earns enough money to survive – the UN's absolute poverty level of $1.25/day. This means that even in highly unequal countries there is an upper limit to what autocrats can "extract" before their subjects start dying off or leaving (Milanovic, Lindert, and Williamson 2011).

For example, suppose a society consists of 100 people, 99 of whom earn the subsistence minimum of 1 unit/day, and total societal income is 105 units. This means that the single member of the elite earns 6 units/day. This society's Gini coefficient is .05. If total income grows to 200 units but all growth accrues to the single wealthy individual (who proxies for the apocryphal "1%") the Gini coefficient will jump to .50 – but it can go no higher at that level of output because the elite cannot extract more income from the rest of the population without violating the subsistence assumption.

A second reason for the upper limit on real-world Gini coefficients is that in modern economies autocratic elites lack the ability to extract the full surplus potentially available (Milanovic, Lindert, and Williamson 2011). These two factors do not hold for real-world distributions of land, simply because the vast majority of individuals – whether a society is largely rural or urban – do not own land, and because land cannot be hidden or converted to some other form of wealth, which means it is easier to expropriate. Not surprisingly, measures of land inequality reveal a higher average level yet greater variation than for income inequality (Jazairy, Alamgir, and Panuccio 1992); this is one of the reasons why land inequality has different political consequences from income inequality.

The conclusion is straightforward: in the real world, a low Gini coefficient of income inequality indicates very little intergroup income differentiation. In contrast, a high Gini implies greater differences in the incomes across social classes: some people are poor, some are wealthy, and some are in the middle. The sociological implication is straightforward and theoretically salient: *in a developing autocracy, a low Gini coefficient typically means a relatively small middle class.*

In most countries – just as in contemporary China, or the nineteenth-century UK – intergroup income differentiation rises with economic development. The preindustrial level of income inequality in most countries in the world since about 1800 reflected a political and economic equilibrium in which the vast majority of the population survived at or just above subsistence level, economic output was stagnant, and a tiny landed elite concentrated political power and leveraged its control of government to maximize political rents. Such assumptions are standard (e.g., Grossman and Noh 1994; Justman and Gradstein 1999; Kuznets 1955), and are characterized, as Figure 2.1 suggests, by comparatively low income inequality, although the situation could be of either high or low land inequality.

The onset of economic growth upsets this equilibrium by generating massive profits in non-agricultural sectors – and it is this development that tends to increase income inequality. This pattern of development – of the diverging fortunes of different economic sectors – is common enough over the last 200 years to serve as useful heuristic device for thinking about the economic origins of democracy and dictatorship. After all, "modernization" – the consequences of industrialization and the decline of agriculture – served as the basis for Lipset (1959) and Moore (1966), and continues to ground debates about "endogenous" democratization (Boix 2011). Our argument, however, points to an errant turn in research on regime change: Under many conditions modernization is associated with the growth of the middle classes and bourgeoisie – but this indicates a rise in inequality, as measured by Gini coefficients, not equality.

We recognize that rising income inequality (greater intergroup differentiation) is not an inevitable consequence of economic development (Lindert and Williamson 1985) and that politics does not necessarily follow from economics. As noted in Chapter 1, holding the distribution of land constant, some autocracies start off with fairly low income inequality and remain that way whether they grow or not, while others start off as somewhat more unequal – and also never experience regime change, again regardless of the extent of economic development. Likewise, some autocracies are rich and equal; our argument is less likely to explain transitions from such situations. However, our argument echoes Moore's in suggesting that autocracies characterized by a weak landholding elite and rising urban middle and upper classes are relatively more likely to experience regime change as compared against countries where these conditions do not hold.

The next sections explore social class structure in several historical cases, to support our claim about the connection between Gini coefficients and social classes. This exercise is theoretically informative because it allows us to locate the median voter in a country's economic class structure. We show that the groups that have historically fought for democracy – the bourgeoisie, the middle, and even the working classes – are typically wealthier than the median voter, often much more so. Discovering that the median voter is too poor to play a role in democratization strongly suggests that the median voter cannot plausibly represent a credible redistributive threat. Democratization instead must be driven by relative elites.

2.3 INEQUALITY AND CLASS STRUCTURE: HISTORICAL EXAMPLES

To tie growth and inequality to regime change within our elite-competition theoretical framework, in this section we connect inequality to class structure. More specifically, we show that higher levels of income inequality are associated with the emergence of classes that will fight for regime change.

To create a snapshot that simultaneously reveals a country's level of income inequality and its social structure at a particular point in time, we use "social tables." Economic historians develop social tables using census data, to count the number of individuals in different job categories and estimate per capita income within each category. Such information can then be used to calculate a Gini coefficient (Milanovic, Lindert, and Williamson 2011).

We consider several contrasting cases to illustrate our hypothesis that income inequality should be higher (and the middle classes larger) in countries we expect to democratize but lower (and the middle classes smaller) elsewhere. These examples are hardly representative of the universe of autocratic social structures, but they illustrate social classes' sizes relative to the location of the median voter under varying socioeconomic conditions.[5] In general, the

---

[5] Data for most of the social tables in this chapter all come from the "Early Income Distributions" section of Peter Lindert's Global Price and Income History Group website (http://gpih.ucdavis.edu/Distribution.htm, last accessed April 4, 2012). The files on Lindert's website provide citations to the original data sources.

evidence supports the notion that where we expect regime change, the relevant political action occurs well above the median voter's income – indeed, in the top one or two deciles.

China and the UK

To begin our comparisons, let us return to the contrast between the UK in 1867 and China in 1880. Table 2.1 provides Imperial China's relatively simple social table, portraying a society divided between a tiny elite and the rest of the population, who were all largely equally impoverished (Milanovic, Lindert, and Williamson 2007, 47). Little difference existed between the income of the poorest and wealthiest commoners, while the landed elite sat atop the income scale, controlling a state bureaucracy whose purpose was to "pump resources out of the population and into the hands of rulers" (Moore 1966, 175). There were no urban trading or manufacturing classes, partly because the ruling elite discouraged their emergence.

The case of China is instructive. Income inequality increased somewhat in the decades after 1880, but for several decades after the 1949 Communist Revolution it remained quite low in comparative perspective. However, as Figure 2.3 reveals, income inequality has increased dramatically since the 1980s, reflecting the growth of relatively wealthy urban middle classes, even as rural poverty remains widespread (CIA 2014; Wu and Perloff 2005).[6]

The connection scholars have recently come to contemplate – a link between economic growth, rising inequality, and regime change in China (e.g., Bomhoff and Gu 2011; Inglehart and Welzel 2009; Rowen 2007; Thornton 2008) – fits with our argument but contradicts the notion that a threat of redistribution permeates the connection between inequality and democracy.[7] Only in the past few years have scholars begun to consider the possibility that China's growing middle classes might pressure the Communist Party to liberalize – not simply for a desire for greater individual liberties, but out of a growing desire to rein in corruption and for clearer economic and political rules. It may take a century

TABLE 2.1. *Income Distribution in China, 1880*

Social Group	% Population	% Income
Upper Gentry	0.3	15.5
Lower Gentry	1.7	10.1
Commoners	98.0	74.4

---

[6] Recent estimates put China's Gini coefficient as high as .61. *Economist*, "To each, not according to his needs," 12/15/12, p. 74.

[7] On the lack of a redistributive threat in China, see Whyte (2010).

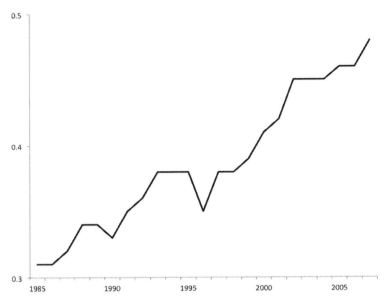

FIGURE 2.3. China's Gini Coefficient, 1985–2010

for a political transition to occur in China – just as long as the UK's gradual transition took – but democracy is certainly more likely today than in 1880, despite the Communist Party's efforts to maintain control. (We explore this case in somewhat greater depth in Chapter 3.)[8]

The comparison between China in 1880 and China in 2010 is suggestive, but we gain much more confidence that a connection between inequality and regime change might exist when we turn to the UK. As readers of Oliver Twist already knew when Charles Dickens first published his tale in serial form, Victorian-era Britain did not have a "middling" level of inequality. Even though the Industrial Revolution brought about the rise of the middle classes, it also exacerbated economic inequalities, which remained persistently high

---

[8] Readers may also wonder about the extent to which other Asian "developmental states" fit our argument. Japan experienced significant increase in income inequality during its initial industrialization in the late nineteenth and early twentieth centuries (Moriguchi and Saez 2006, especially Figure 2). It also had high *land* inequality during that era, which worked against the emergence of democracy. Japan's contrast with other East Asian cases is important. South Korea and Taiwan did not experience substantial increases in income inequality with the onset of development. Yet our argument depends fundamentally on the relative levels of *both* land and income inequality – and the key relevant fact is that both latter countries undertook widespread and extensive land reforms before the process of industrialization began. This left them with comparatively weak landlord classes and comparatively small rural peasant classes – both relatively uncommon factors for poor developing countries. In comparative perspective, the absence of land inequality proved crucial in paving the eventual path toward democratization in both countries. See Chapter 3 for further discussion.

during the nineteenth century and only began to decline noticeably after World War I (Atkinson 2007), for reasons other than mass enfranchisement (Scheve and Stasavage 2012).

Income inequality in the 19th century UK was also higher than in many continental countries; Lindert and Williamson (1983, 96) estimate that in England and Wales the top 5% received 46% of all personal income in 1867, while the same proportion received only 26% in Prussia (1875) and 34% in Saxony (1880), a contrast that echoes the conventional view that the middle classes were relatively weaker in Germany during this era.

Table 2.2 is the social table for the UK at this time. Baxter's (1868) meticulous estimates provide useful insight into the relative size of different social classes. To start with the autocratic elite, the size of the Large Incomes 1 group corresponds roughly to Clark's (1962, 211) well-known estimate that the core of the British ruling class at mid-century contained only about 1,200 men – significantly less than 0.1% of households at that time. This a conservative estimate, although it is not difficult to envision a group this size – about the number of men who sat in the Houses of Commons and Lords – constituting the de facto ruling class.

Nafziger and Lindert (2011, 9) provide a more liberal estimate, suggesting that the Russian, French, and British aristocracies in the seventeenth–nineteenth centuries, defined not by actual wealth but by simple possession of landed title, comprised about 2% of the population. However, as Table 2.2 indicates, this estimate also allows for substantial income differences at the top, implying that it is perhaps too generous. Yet even if we accept this broader estimate of the size of a country's ruling class, the central point remains that an "incumbent autocratic elite" will constitute a tiny proportion of any country's population.

The social tables from the UK and China reveal a key similarity: in both countries the top 2% were extremely wealthy compared to the rest. However, in China the remaining 18% of the top 20% differed little from the bottom 80% of the population, while in the UK the bourgeoisie and middle classes had begun to differentiate themselves socioeconomically from the poor. Yet the country's 1868 social table suggests that in a developing economy, the "middle" classes – not simply for their average income, but for their educational and cultural achievements and status aspirations – are unlikely to sit anywhere near the middle of the income scale, where we find the median voter.

In the UK, middle-class groups were found in the top *two deciles* of the income distribution. We know this because Baxter (1868, 81) lists the occupations in the Small, Middle and Large incomes groups: "All persons of rank and property; officers; agents; learned professions; mercantile men; dealers; tradesmen and persons who buy or sell; owners; masters and mistresses; superintendents; collectors; foremen; measurers; clerks and shopmen." This implies that the *grand bourgeoisie* would be in the top decile (even into the 99th percentile, if we accept Clark's estimate of the size of the ruling class),

TABLE 2.2. *Social Table for the United Kingdom, 1867 (adult males only, income in £)*

Income Group	Cum. Men	Cum Income	Avg. Income
Large Incomes 1 (£5000+)	0.05	13.0	21,069
Large Incomes 2 (£1000–5000)	0.3	23.8	2,998
Middle Incomes (£300–1000)	1.3	35.2	881
Small Incomes 1 (£100–300)	6.8	49.9	200
Small Incomes 2 (< £100)	22.1	65.2	75
Higher skilled manual labor 1: Opticians; watch makers; jewelers, engine drivers	22.7	65.7	59
Higher skilled manual labor 2: Printers; bookbinders; hat-makers; woodworkers; metalworkers, building trades; shipwrights; bakers, butchers	34.2	73.2	50
Lower skilled labor 1: Bargemen/watermen; warehousemen, merchant marine; coaches, machinists, chandlers; tanners; oilmen, blacksmiths, tinsmiths; dockworkers	43.6	78.3	40
Lower skilled labor 2: Coachmen, railway workers; police; chimney-sweeps; servants; colliers; water workers; cotton + woolen workers; sugar refiners; shoemakers; millers; tailors; miners	75.3	91.6	32
Unskilled labor 1: Navy, militia, police; quarries; animal husbandry; dock porters	79.8	93.3	28
Unskilled labor 2: Agricultural laborers, shepherds; farm servants; road laborers; scavengers	97.8	99.4	25
Unskilled labor 3: Soldiers, military pensioners	100	100	21

Source: Baxter (1868); see note 5

while the individuals Marx identified as *petit bourgeoisie* – shopkeepers – would be found near the bottom of the second decile. The UK had higher income inequality than China at this time because these relatively wealthy "middle-class" individuals comprised a much larger relative proportion of the population.

Table 2.2 also lets us locate the "working class" on the income distribution. Such men worked in occupations found in Baxter's Higher and Lower skilled labor groups. A particularly relevant question is where we find the *organized* working class on the income distribution. In this regard, a key bit of contextual information is that prior to the 2nd Reform Act's passage in 1867, about 19% of the adult male population was already enfranchised (Justman and Gradstein 1999, 119) – that is, most of the men up through Small Incomes 2. In contrast, by 1880 about 38% of adult males could vote. This meant that the 2nd Reform Act enfranchised members of Higher Skilled Manual Labor 1, Higher Skilled Manual Labor 2, and about half of Lower Skilled Labor 1, but did not enfranchise the lower ranks of the working class, or any other male worker (let alone women, who lacked the franchise until 1918).

Finally, the social tables tell us that in Victorian Britain, a person with the median income – about £37 for adult men – (about half of mean income, which was around £75) – would be found at the upper end of the Lower Skilled Labor 2 group. Even radical historians' interpretations of the 2nd Reform Act's passage acknowledge that the men in this social class played at best an insignificant role in pushing the reform through. And needless to say, no social group below this level played *any* substantial role at all in pressing for democratization in nineteenth-century Britain.

Other Historical Cases

Finding that the median voter in a case with one of the largest working classes in world history is located well down the income distribution has considerable implications for assessing the relative utility of different theories of regime change. Yet we do not rest our case on the UK example, but instead provide other countries' social tables to shed additional light on the relationship between class structure and different levels of income inequality. These cases confirm that income inequality was lower where the working and middle classes were relatively smaller.

Consider first the historically relevant case of Imperial Germany (1870–1918). Table 2.3, which presents data from the 1882 Imperial occupational census, helps us understand why income inequality was relatively lower in Germany around this time than in the UK: because there was much less income differentiation across social groups, due to Germany's relative delay in industrializing. Note in particular that urban, "bourgeois" workers – those we would identify as sociologically "middle class" – are located in the top 5%

TABLE 2.3. *Social Table for Germany, 1882*

Sector	Workers	% Workers	Per Capita Income	Relative Income
Professionals/Civil Service	1,031,147	5.5	1855	3.1
Printing	69,643	0.4	1198	2.0
Land Transport	352,739	1.9	1018	1.7
Metalworking	528,714	2.8	810	1.4
Mining	431,707	2.3	788	1.3
Construction	946,583	5.0	751	1.3
Commerce	1,133,278	6.0	656	1.1
Woodworking	521,660	2.8	634	1.1
Industry/Trades	3,013,476	15.9	614	1.0
Water Transport	84,301	0.5	604	1.0
Textiles	850,859	4.5	460	0.8
Household Servants	1,722,506	9.1	428	0.7
Agriculture	8,246,246	43.6	407	0.7
Total	18,932,859		597	

Source: Statistisches Reichsamt (1884)

of all incomes – and that this group comprised a far smaller proportion of the workforce than in the UK.

Also worthy of note is the fact that Germany had established universal male suffrage in 1871, even though parliament remained subordinate to the crown and political contestation was tightly constrained. This allows us to locate not just a future but an *actual* median voter, among the group of household servants just above the mass of impoverished agricultural laborers at the bottom of the income distribution. Note that almost 85% of workers earned just 1.1 times the average income or less – indicating far less income differentiation than in the UK.

Imperial Germany usefully contrasts with Victorian Britain. In terms of income distribution, its social structure resembles China's in 1880 more than the UK's in 1867 – and as a result, despite the redistributivist prediction that democracy is more likely under relative equality, the prospects for democracy in 1880 Germany were more like those in 1880 China than in the UK around that time, precisely because Germany's middle and working classes were relatively politically small and weak. And like China, Germany also illustrates the utility of differentiating land from income inequality, because Germany's landed elites retained considerable political influence far later than Britain's.

Let us now consider another historically important case, Russia in 1904. Russia's industrialization occurred even later than Germany's and was even weaker. Consequently, as Table 2.4 reveals, at the turn of the twentieth century Russia's middle classes comprised only about 4% of the population (we include

TABLE 2.4. *Social Table for Russia, 1904*

Social Group	Households	% Hholds	Per Capita Income	Relative Income
Top Incomes	148,343	0.8	11,255	24.5
1st Quartile Industrial Labor	700,166	3.8	826	1.8
Bourgeois Landowners	141,056	0.8	688	1.5
Residual "other"	601,561	3.3	635	1.4
Lesser Nobility	78,937	0.4	631	1.4
3rd Quartile, Industrial Labor	700,166	3.8	616	1.3
Landed Clergy	9,840	0.1	575	1.3
Government Employees	47,498	0.3	500	1.1
"Free Professions"	107,649	0.6	500	1.1
Peasant, Landowning	490,393	2.7	477	1.0
1st Quartile, Landless Peasants	3,242,133	17.7	476	1.0
2nd Quartile, Industrial Labor	700,166	3.8	384	0.8
3rd Quartile, Landless Peasants	3,242,133	17.7	342	0.7
2nd Quartile, Landless Peasants	3,242,133	17.7	290	0.6
4th Quartile, Landless Peasants	3,242,133	17.7	256	0.6
Urban Clergy	30,879	0.2	250	0.5
4th Quartile, Industrial Labor	700,166	3.8	213	0.5
Rural Clergy	85,248	0.5	174	0.4
Servants	774,299	4.2	100	0.2
Total	18,284,899	100	(463)	

Source: Nafziger and Lindert (2011)

"other," "free professions," and "government employees" in this class); skilled workers (the top quartile of industrial labor) comprised another 4%. Nafziger and Lindert (2011, 14) succinctly summarize the crucial take-home point from Russia's social table: "Even though one might have expected" to observe high income inequality on the eve of the Communist Revolution, the evidence "offers no confirmation of this hunch." Russia's lower than average level of income inequality of .36 at this time (the mean of "preindustrial" Gini coefficients in Milanovic, Lindert, and Williamson (2011) is .45) contrasts notably with the much higher contemporaneous levels in Britain (or even Sweden) as well as with higher Gini coefficients in present-day Brazil, China, the US – and even Russia itself.[9] And of course, Russia combined this low level of

[9] Our argument has little to say about the causes of revolution, because we accept Skocpol's (1979) argument that state strength, loss in war and the international climate are more important than the level of income inequality for such rare events. In any case, revolutions are not primarily driven by the poor, nor are they "majoritarian" events; the poor never overthrow a regime. In this regard it does bear pointing out that neither Russia in 1917 nor China in 1949 fit either Boix's or A&R's hypothesis that revolution is more likely at high levels of income inequality.

TABLE 2.5. *Social Table for Peru, 1876*

Social Group	People	% People	Per Capita Income	Relative Income
Taxpayers (Patentes)	27,340	2.1	3670	14.8
Government Employees	19,456	1.5	970	3.9
Poorer Artisans – Lima	11,240	0.9	832	3.4
Other Earners	126,648	9.6	312	1.3
Poorer artisans – Provinces	70,757	5.4	269	1.1
Common Laborers	552,894	41.8	146	0.6
Farmers	513,277	38.8	117	0.5
Total	1,321,612	100	248	1

Sources: Lindert's "Early Income Distributions," http://gpih.ucdavis.edu/Distribution.htm, Accessed May 7, 2012; see Berry (1990)

income inequality with a very high level of land inequality, an inauspicious combination for democracy's prospects.

Now let us consider three less well-known cases to further illustrate the utility of using land and income inequality as decent – if hardly perfect – measures of variation in social class structure. Table 2.5 provides details about social structure in Peru in 1876, which exhibited a middling level of income inequality (.41) (Milanovic, Lindert, and Williamson 2011) alongside a high level of land inequality. Most income inequality was generated by *patentes*, the taxpaying elite; by that group's agents employed in white-collar jobs in government, and by "poorer artisans" working in Lima, who were in fact relatively well-off compared to rural peasants. These three groups comprised only 4.5% of the population, while the potential future median voter was one of the peasants employed in agriculture who comprised almost 80% of Peru's citizens. Peru had more intergroup income inequality than China at this time, but with a tiny middle class, an almost nonexistent urban working class, and extreme land inequality, its prospects for democracy were low. For example, in 1858 artisans (including carpenters, blacksmiths, tailors, and shoemakers) rioted when the government eliminated protectionist measures (Hunt 1985, 285). However, these groups were too small and weak to "stop Peru's rapid march to a new pattern of comparative advantage based on guano," and the number of jobs for both skilled and unskilled urban workers declined in subsequent decades (ibid. 289).

Peru's southern neighbor Chile offers a useful contrast. The social table for Chile in 1861 in Table 2.6 reveals the emergence of incipient middle and working classes, which explains the country's relatively higher income inequality (.64) compared to Peru around the same time (Milanovic, Lindert, and Williamson 2011). However, as in Peru, land inequality in Chile was also extremely high. According to the social table the economic elite – the top

TABLE 2.6. *Social Table for Chile, 1861*

Social Group	Men	% Men	Per Capita Income	Relative Income
Mining Owners	475	0.1	11,579	44.9
Big Landowners	850	0.2	7,498	29.1
Manufacturing Owners	4,499	1.0	4,586	17.8
Commerce	10,232	2.3	1,878	7.3
Middle Landowners	5,359	1.2	1,200	4.7
Professionals	7,226	1.6	1,084	4.2
Employees	5,754	1.3	876	3.4
Workers	3,016	0.7	501	1.9
Functionaries	2,486	0.6	401	1.6
Mining Employees 1	2,139	0.5	374	1.5
Skilled Artisans	13,171	2.9	370	1.4
Railway Workers	1,106	0.3	361	1.4
Sailors	1,672	0.4	301	1.2
Mining Employees 2	6,445	1.4	187	0.7
Conductors	2,049	0.5	180	0.7
Army and Police	6,993	1.6	144	0.6
Mining Employees 3	12,891	2.9	139	0.5
Cobblers	13,106	2.9	137	0.5
Artisans	65,026	14.5	134	0.5
Peasants	132,946	29.6	89	0.3
Household Workers	7,703	1.7	86	0.3
Fishermen	143,640	32.0	59	0.2
Total	448,784	100	(258)	

Sources: Lindert's "Early Income Distributions," http://gpih.ucdavis.edu/Distribution.htm, Accessed May 7, 2012; see Rodríguez Weber (2009)

three groups – comprised just 1.3% of the population. The next three groups ("commerce," "middle landowners," and "professionals") – about 5% of the population – could be considered the middle classes, and the next six groups (down to "skilled artisans" – about 6% of the population) comprised an incipient skilled working class. Below this group about 25% of the population could be considered "lower skilled labor," leaving the median voter to be found in the 63% of the population composed of unskilled rural peasants and fishermen.

Chilean politics in its "parliamentary" era (1891–1925) was characterized by the rise of bourgeois and urban parties challenging large landowners' control of the legislature and supporting wider suffrage. Yet despite these efforts, the relative political strength of the landed elite proved decisive – and for this reason Zeitlin (1984) calls nineteenth-century Chile a case of "aborted bourgeois revolution." Outcomes everywhere are at least partially contingent, but this is generally how we would have expected things to play out: if land inequality remains high even as income inequality increases, democracy is

TABLE 2.7. *Social Table for Java, 1924*

Social Group	People	% People	Per Capita Income	Relative Income
Europeans	61,648	0.2	2,042	42.3
Non-European Foreigners	124,807	0.4	282	5.9
Large Traders + Factory Owners	113,642	0.3	188	3.9
Civil Servants	515,159	1.5	154	3.2
Large Landowners	850,561	2.4	130	2.7
Village Officials	938,005	2.7	97	2.0
Workers in Foreign Enterprises	1,240,296	3.5	81	1.7
Religious Officials	147,158	0.4	63	1.3
Artisans and Small Traders	2,388,629	6.8	57	1.2
Medium Landowners	6,775,218	19.3	49	1.0
"Coolies"	7,373,979	21.0	31	0.7
Small Landowners	9,262,391	26.3	29	0.6
Agricultural Laborers	4,217,247	12.0	29	0.6
Sharecroppers	1,161,886	3.3	25	0.5
Total	35,170,626	100	(44)	

Sources: Lindert's "Early Income Distributions," http://gpih.ucdavis.edu/Distribution.htm, Accessed May 7, 2012; see Booth (1998)

hardly guaranteed. (This problem would haunt both Chile and Peru – and many other countries – until late in the twentieth century.)

Finally, Table 2.7, the social table for Java (part of the Dutch East Indies) in 1924, offers an intriguing contrast with Chile and Peru because income inequality was not only much lower (.32), but also because most income inequality resulted from the extractive capacity of the European colonial elite and the earnings of Chinese resident traders. Among native Javanese, there was very little income differentiation compared to the UK of the 1860s, particularly among the bottom 63% of the population. Although there was a relatively small indigenous middle class upon independence, what distinguished Indonesia – and what may have been relatively more important for its future political trajectory – was the below-average level of land inequality (Booth 1998).[10]

A social table offers a snapshot of a country's social structure at a particular point in time. Such information has been sorely lacking in research on regime change, but provides insight into the location of different social classes in the income distribution, linking Gini coefficients – the standard quantitative measure of intergroup inequality – to qualitative assessments of the relative size and strength of different social classes.

[10] The earliest measure of land inequality for independent Indonesia is 44% "family farms" in 1958; the average for all 83 countries (democracies and autocracies) measured that year was 42%.

2.4 CONCLUSION: IMPLICATIONS OF SOCIAL TABLES

Social tables reveal the connection between income inequality and the existence of sizable middle and working classes. Linking qualitative and quantitative indicators is crucial for assessing the descriptive and predictive accuracy of different theoretical approaches to regime change, as redistributivist models hinge upon the assumption that the median voter is a politically relevant actor, whereas our approach assumes the opposite. Our exploration of social tables suggests that the median voter is typically quite poor, and that most regime contestation occurs between groups near to the top of the income distribution.

The examples we considered are meant to suggest a causal relation between income inequality and regime change, a claim we develop in subsequent chapters. The implications of evidence from social tables should not be surprising, as Barrington Moore intuited these patterns decades ago. Still, these findings help connect the dots from small-N qualitative accounts like Moore's to large-N cross-national studies. The cases we explored varied in terms of social structure and in terms of long-term regime outcomes. The UK most obviously fits Moore's "no bourgeoisie, no democracy" thesis – just as it fits our own, which connects a larger middle class to higher income inequality, and both of these to regime change. Other countries we considered had smaller middle classes and lower income inequality (and often higher land inequality) and did not democratize until decades later, or never have.

Let us summarize the chapter's key points. First, wealthy incumbent elites in any autocracy will compose a tiny proportion of the total population. Second, research on regime change has misleadingly applied the concept of a middle class, laden as it with sociological and cultural meaning. In a developing autocracy the middle class is, historically speaking, almost never located in the actual middle of the income distribution. It is found in the upper two deciles of a country's income distribution, or even in the top decile. This means that arguments that emphasize the democratizing role of the middle class are necessarily "elite competition" arguments, even if that point is not made explicitly.

Third, even if one considers the working class important for regime change – compare, for example, Rueschemeyer, Stephens, and Stephens (1992) versus Collier (1999) – its members also tend to earn (often considerably) more than the future median voter. By extension, in a relatively wealthy autocracy undergoing economic growth like the nineteenth century UK, the future median voter is likely an unskilled worker or rural laborer – and the less developed and more rural the society, the poorer and less skilled the median voter will be.

Fourth, to the extent that the working class is also located above the median voter, we have even more reason to question whether the huge mass of potential future voters under universal suffrage – the rural poor and underclass or lumpenproletariat – are relevant to the causal dynamics of regime change. Marx viewed the rural poor and lumpenproletariat as politically backward;

indeed, of all major social-science arguments pertaining to democratization going back to Marx, *only* the redistributivist approach has ever implied that the poor play a significant role in fomenting regime change. To the extent that all potentially relevant actors are relatively wealthy compared to the median voter *and* all individuals with below-median incomes are not politically relevant actors, democratization cannot be about elites' fear of redistributive threats from the poor.

Very poor autocracies have low Gini coefficients of income inequality because everyone is equally poor. Demand for regime change should increase with economic development as growing middle classes demand political rights and protection from expropriation, and as landed elites lose political sway. Ironically, Boix ultimately agrees that democracy is more likely as the middle class grows wealthier – but he assumes this is a situation of increasing economic equality, affirming that democracy emerges only when "a considerable amount of equalization has already taken place" (Boix 2003, 54). This misdiagnoses both the nature of income inequality in the real world and the relative income of key political actors. A growing middle class in a developing autocracy signifies rising income inequality, and democracy is likelier when a considerable amount of *inequality* has appeared.

If higher income inequality is associated with greater demand for political change under autocracy because more people have more to lose, then it is imperative to rethink our assumptions about relevant social actors' political interests – the autocratic elite, the bourgeoisie and middle class, the working class, and the poor. In the next chapter, we assess the extent to which autocratic elites fear redistributive threats from the working class and the poor versus the extent to which rising socioeconomic groups fear elites' extractive potential.

3

Actors and Interests

3.1 INTRODUCTION

The previous chapter revealed that in developing autocracies income inequality grows with the emergence of new non-agricultural groups – an industrial and commercial bourgeoisie, and the middle and working classes. In such societies the median voter typically remains quite poor and is located nowhere near the sociologically defined "middle" class – and even below the organized working class – on the income scale. Social tables strongly support the notion that most of the action in cases of regime change takes place well above the income of the median voter – among relative economic elites – and suggests that the median voter is unlikely to be a relevant actor in struggles for democracy.

Having located different social groups on the income distribution, in this chapter we lay out our argument's theoretical expectations about key socioeconomic actors' preferences, interests and likely political behavior. This provides support for our argument's key proposition: that competition over regime change occurs between groups near the top of the income scale and concerns fear of the state's expropriative power, not fear of the poor's redistributive threat.

The question of realism of assumptions is a difficult one for social-science theories. All theoretical assumptions are necessarily descriptively false, as they are heuristic devices employed to simplify, represent, and hopefully explain reality. Still, to assess different theories' relative fruitfulness, we should evaluate the relative descriptive and predictive accuracy of their assumptions.

We consider the interests of four groups: (1) incumbent elites, (2) the urban bourgeoisie and middle classes, (3) the working classes, and (4) the poor.[1] After

---

[1] When we formalize our argument in Chapter 4 we consider three groups: (1) incumbent elites; (2) a challenger elite that can include the bourgeoisie, middle classes and the organized working class, and (3) the poor majority.

discussing our assumptions in the abstract, we illustrate the fruitfulness of our approach with evidence from the passage of the Second Reform Act in the UK, as well as with brief discussions of other cases – Imperial Germany, late 19th-century Sweden, 20th-century South Korea and contemporary China – that vary on both the dependent variable and on our key independent variables, in addition to obviously embodying different cultural and historical contexts.

3.2 INEQUALITY, INCOME, AND INTERESTS

Given the evidence in Chapter 2 about different classes' relative sizes and incomes, we can now draw out the hypothesized connection between the emergence of relatively wealthy new social groups, income inequality, and the emergence of political demands for reform. In this section, we compare the expectations of redistributivist and elite-competition approaches about what members of different social groups want from politics as economic development proceeds. We start with incumbent elites and work our way through the goals of the bourgeoisie and middle classes, the poor, and the working class.

Incumbent Autocratic Elites

If the redistributivist argument were true, we would certainly expect incumbent elites to proclaim that mass enfranchisement would bring ruin. Yet such hysterical rhetoric offers insufficient evidence supporting the descriptive accuracy of redistributivist arguments' assumptions: we need direct evidence that elites (1) fear a concrete redistributive threat to landed wealth and/or income from organized groups representing the actual future median voter, and (2) strategically permit franchise expansion only to head off such a threat.

By contrast, if the assumptions of our elite-competition approach were more descriptively accurate, we would not expect incumbent elites to worry primarily about threats from the poor. Instead, they would most fear the prospect of having to share rents derived from control over the state with rising yet politically disenfranchised groups.

This latter idea derives from the neoclassical theory of the state, which presumes that control over the means of coercion is instrumentally valuable. Given a political regime of restricted franchise in which the rich have more influence than the poor, incumbent elites will impose policies that redistribute wealth upward (Boix 2001; Knutsen 2011; Levi 1989; McGuire and Olson 1996; Niskanen 1997; Olson 1993). This notion contradicts a core assumption of the Meltzer-Richard model, that under autocracy the tax rate equals zero. We suggest that it is safe – far more descriptively accurate – to assume that under autocracy rent extraction (which does not necessarily equal and may even be greater than the tax burden) is a perpetual and very real threat to the income and property of anyone outside the incumbent elite.[2]

To flesh out what incumbent elites fear, we must skip ahead a bit and describe the interests of these rising yet politically disenfranchised groups – the bourgeoisie and middle classes, primarily. Stated most simply, our core assumption is that these groups object to taxation without representation. Income inequality under autocracy signifies the growth – in terms of numbers and political influence – of such groups, who will demand (1) limits on the state's expropriative authority over property rights; (2) changes in the nature and incidence of taxation; (3) greater efforts to control corruption; (4) changes to who gains and loses from public subsidies, trade policy, grants of monopoly, labor laws and other club goods; and (5) government investment in infrastructure, particularly to promote commerce and industry. Changing such policies involves winners and losers – and it is likely that expanding the franchise will result in less regressive (even if not fully progressive) fiscal policy. That is, under autocracy, elites' fear of having to share power – and rents – is obviously about "redistribution," but not in the sense that median-voter theories suggest.

land inequality

Given our distinction between the political consequences of land and income inequality, let us explain what we expect to observe from autocratic landowners. As Mahoney (2003, 146) observes, qualitative-comparative research on regime change confirms that labor-dependent landlords are the "most consistently anti-democratic force." The pertinent theoretical question is why? In both the redistributive and our elite-competition approaches, land inequality is a proxy for conservative landowners' relative political power. The two arguments generate the same prediction – high land inequality is bad for democracy – but for theoretically distinct reasons. The former draws no distinction between the political effects of land and income inequality; land inequality is a threat to democracy because landless peasants want to redistribute land. Where land is equally distributed, fewer peasants demand redistribution and transitions to democracy are more likely.

We make the same prediction but the causal mechanism is distinct. Land inequality is bad for democracy not because landowners fear redistribution per se, but because they control agricultural policy – wages, prices, subsidies, tariffs, import restrictions – and want to limit agricultural labor mobility (Rueschemeyer, Stephens, and Stephens 1992). Under high land inequality, landed elites are more likely to be politically and economically unified, which fosters control over these policies and, thus, over the political (and thus by implication, economic) rights of rural labor. Landed elites prefer autocracy because they require the state's coercive tools to keep peasants on the land and under their thumbs. By contrast, in an autocracy with low land inequality, there are more family farmers. The key theoretical issue is not the relatively

---

[2] And is a greater threat than under democracy, see, e.g., Treisman (2000); Montinola and Jackman (2002); Slater (2010).

lower redistributive threat from landless peasants, but the greater likelihood of political and economic divisions within the agrarian sector, the relatively weaker political position of large landowners vis-à-vis control over agricultural policy, and the relatively lower demand for control over rural labor mobility.

A second pertinent theoretical issue in terms of the political consequences of land inequality is that our approach assumes a two-sector economy. When the industrial sector is growing relatively faster than the agricultural sector in terms of contribution to GDP, poor rural laborers are likely to seek out higher wages in urban areas. This challenges landed elites, because out-migration weakens their control over revenues from land, reducing not just their incomes but also their political power (Ardañaz and Mares 2012). In such a situation, increased income inequality signals that economic development primarily benefits urban groups – not just the bourgeoisie but also the working classes – at the expense of those who derive their income primarily from agriculture – *both* landowners and peasants. Redistributivist arguments cannot incorporate this dynamic because they do not differentiate the political consequences of land and income inequality.

The Bourgeoisie/Middle Classes

Let us now turn to the groups that challenge incumbent elites for power, first exploring the political interests of the bourgeoisie and middle classes. Here we are including the *petit* through the *grand bourgeoisie*, as well as white-collar workers. The "middle" class was so named historically because it emerged between the two classes that had always existed – landed elites and the poor. The notion of a middle class has both economic and sociological connotations: its members not only earn more than the poor, but also have higher social status. Yet as our social tables indicated, in developing countries (and even many industrialized countries), the median member of the middle class is typically not found near the middle of the income distribution. Members of the culturally defined middle class may not be as wealthy as incumbent elites, but they do earn between twice and ten times the average.[3] In contrast, the median voter always earns less than average.

The location of the middle classes on the income distribution has important ramifications for theories of regime change. If the future median voter in a democracy is a member of the middle class under autocracy, he or she would set the tax rate under universal suffrage. Evidence from Chapter 2, however, suggests that this is an unsafe assumption. Instead, in a developing autocracy the median voter is likely to be quite poor, with an income far below middle

---

[3] This corresponds to the way economists classify middle classes in developing countries today (Easterly 2001; Banerjee and Duflo 2008, Table 1).

class levels. The formal models we develop in the next chapter always assume that the poor outnumber the bourgeoisie and middle classes.[4]

It is a category error to export our contemporary presumptions about the size of the middle class in the world's wealthiest democracies such as the United States or the UK – where the middle class does encompass more than half of the population – to less wealthy, developing autocracies. Even in many middle-income democracies in the world today, members of the sociocultural middle class earn much more than the median voter and are far less numerous than the poor.

This fact turns our attention to a second way that our argument's assumptions about the middle class differ. We recognize that the bourgeoisie might trade the right to rule for the right to make money, to paraphrase Marx. However, redistributivist models ignore the possibility that as the middle class grows, its fear of the very palpable expropriative threat from the State may dominate the far less certain redistributive threat from the poor.

Demands for the protection of property rights are at the core of our elite-competition approach. Even if not every autocrat is a revenue-maximizer, rising yet politically disenfranchised groups have a legitimate and often pressing fear of expropriation. Moreover, the State represents a far greater threat than the median voter because it is more cohesive, has greater resources, and controls more effective means of coercion. Given this, as out-groups grow wealthier, their expected losses from expropriation or taxation will increase. Yet at the same time, their increased wealth enhances their relative bargaining power, because economic resources can translate into mobilization and political pressure. Resource-rich citizens will invest in political reform to protect against expropriation, demanding political concessions and offering tax compliance in exchange, in an effort to capture political power commensurate with their growing economic power.

In terms of empirically testable hypotheses, we expect to find little evidence that members of the middle classes fear the redistributive threat from the poor.

---

[4] Boix's and Acemoglu and Robinson's three-actor games *require* that the median voter comes from the middle class, implying that it is more numerous than the poor. These models consider scenarios in which the poor and middle class ally against the rich. Such an outcome is likely, for example, when when the median voter is a member of the middle class and the distance between the poor and middle class is low but overall inequality is high (A&R 261; Boix 47). Yet if there are no plausible real-world situations in which the middle class encompasses the median voter, then there are no conditions in redistributivist models in which the middle class and the poor would ally. Indeed, under the far more plausible assumption that the middle class is wealthier and less numerous than the median voter, both Boix (2003, 52) and Acemoglu and Robinson (2006, 260) acknowledge that a three-actor game collapses to a two-actor game in which the role of the middle class as a separate actor disappears and the outcome turns on incumbent autocratic elites' fear the redistributive threat from the poor. If by contrast, we presume that what drives regime change is not fear of the poor but the fear of expropriation held by both the middle classes and the poor, then an alliance between these two groups is possible under certain situations.

Instead, we expect them to promote reforms that strengthen the parliamentary representation of industrial capital and urban groups, particularly suffrage expansion and reapportionment. Such reforms are certainly about political rights, but have an instrumental purpose: to advance their groups' economic interests. Demands for democracy should be associated with demands to control corruption, strengthen property rights, and end autocratic elites' control over trade, finance, taxation, labor laws, and public subsidies and investments. "No taxation without representation," rather than fear of the poor, encapsulates rising economic groups' interests.

The Poor

Before we consider the organized working class, we will examine the interests and potential political relevance of the poor. The underclass consists of rural landless peasants or tenant farmers, and unskilled urban and rural workers. Although its size is difficult to estimate precisely, evidence from social tables suggests that in most developing autocracies the poor includes at least 50% of the population. And in many countries – where the social structure resembles 1880 China, 1876 Peru, or 1904 Russia – the poor constitute an even larger majority.

The size of the underclass in the real world has important implications for theories of regime change, because redistributive approaches explicitly *require* that (1) the median voter favors greater redistribution as inequality increases, and (2) regime-change outcomes are a function of the capacity of the median voter *and everyone below him or her* to pose a credible redistributive threat. Yet qualitative-comparative scholars have focused scant attention on the poor because they assume that this social class lacks either the interest and/or the capacity to mobilize for democracy (Collier 1999, 97–98).

A necessary but insufficient condition of median voter models is that the poor favor redistribution. If the political interests of the poor do not lean this way, the argument falls apart. In this regard, recall Marx's condescension toward the peasantry, which he believed exhibited counterrevolutionary tendencies; he felt similarly about the *lumpenproletariat*, the mass of poor urban workers. We agree that one should not assume that the poor favor redistribution. They might instead want to preserve or restore rather than radically transform the political-economic status quo.[5] In fact, sizable swaths of urban workers, as well as the vast majority of the rural poor around the world have historically exhibited sociocultural deference to wealth and respect for property and law and order. If the poor are conservative, they constitute no redistributive threat.

---

[5] See, e.g., Slater's (2010) discussion of Indonesia, Malaysia, and Thailand, or Luebbert (1991a) on interwar Europe.

Our argument does not rest on proving that the poor are indifferent to redistribution. It rests on two other, more important, demonstrable propositions: (1) the poor are unlikely to act, whatever their preferences, and therefore pose no credible direct threat to elite interests; and (2) the middle classes have powerful instrumental reasons to fear the State *and* are more likely to act on their preferences, and thus constitute a relatively more credible threat to elite interests. No matter their political preferences, the poor are unlikely to play a leading role in contestation over regime change because they tend to be relatively uninterested in national politics, possess few resources, and have low political efficacy (Olson 1965; Verba, Schlozman, and Brady 1994). In this regard, it is useful to note that even in wealthy democracies with decades of electoral experience, inequality tends to *depress* turnout among the poor (Anderson and Beramendi 2012).

We are not assuming that the poor consent to their own exploitation. However, there is a difference between engaging in localized everyday forms of resistance (Scott 1985) and acting as an organized, credible redistributive and revolutionary threat. Contemporary scholars of "subaltern studies" acknowledge that if poverty alone were a typical cause of peasant rebellion, we would see far more violence around the world than we do (see also Collier, Hoeffler, and Sambanis 2005). Redistributivist models require that everyone below the median voter shares a desire for redistribution and represents a credible threat "from below." Yet even if the first assumption were true, the latter is more important for understanding the dynamics of regime change.

The Working Class

If the poor do not represent a credible threat to elite interests, does the working class? Comparative-historical research has advanced this hypothesis (e.g., Rueschemeyer, Stephens, and Stephens 1992), but debate continues about the nature of working-class interests and about the working class's relative importance for regime change (Collier 1999; Mahoney 2003).

Like their assumptions about the poor, redistributivist models that give the working class a key role assume that (1) the median member of the working class is located at or below the median voter on the income distribution, and (2) all members of the working class want redistribution à la the Meltzer-Richard model. In our view, it is safer to assume that: (1) the median member of the working class is located *above* the median voter, and (2) members of the working class favor redistribution *to themselves*, but not to the poor.

The size and location on the income scale of the working class are important sociological questions, because in a developing society most people who are not part of the elite or the bourgeoisie are not part of the organized working class – they are members of the unorganized urban or rural poor. For example, for all intents and purposes, societies such as China in 1880 have no organized urban working class. Of course, the size of the working class will increase as an

TABLE 3.1. *Size of the Working Class*

Country	Census Year	Manual Workers as a % of Adults
Belgium	1900	30.2
Denmark	1900	22.4
Finland	1910	22.2
France	1900	36.0
Germany	1895	31.6
Norway	1900	28.4
Sweden	1900	19.2
Average		27.1

economy develops. Adding up our estimates from social tables, in a developing autocracy the elite will compose about 1–2% of the population, the middle classes at most the top two deciles, and the poor at least half. This leaves about 30% (again, at most) as members of the working class. This proportion corresponds to figures from Western European countries in Table 4.1 from Przeworski and Sprague (1986, 35), who used census data from the turn of the twentieth century – a time when industrialization and inequality were rising, as was demand for democracy.

It is worth noting that apart from the United State and UK (neither of which Przeworski and Sprague included in their calculations), these are the countries with the largest working classes in world history. Elsewhere workers composed a much smaller proportion of the population and exerted far less political influence – points that Rueschemeyer, Stephens, and Stephens (1992) concede. It is also worth noting that these percentages are not of the size of the *organized* working class, which would be significantly smaller as a proportion of the population, but include all manual workers (Przeworski and Sprague 1986, 35).

The descriptive and predictive accuracy of our elite-competition approach does not depend on whether the working class plays a role in regime change or not. We are making a more fundamental point. Strangely, the question of what working-class organizations actually demand as part of a call for suffrage reform has gone largely unexplored in studies of regime change.[6] In terms of their political interests, to the extent that members of the working class earn more than and are outnumbered by the poor, it is not obvious why they would mobilize in cross-class solidarity with those less fortunate than themselves to demand both political rights and the sort of progressive economic

---

[6] For exceptions, see Haggard and Kaufman (2012); Slater (2009), and several entries in the special issue of *Comparative Political Studies* devoted to the "Historical Turn" in Democratization Studies (Capoccia and Ziblatt 2010).

redistribution that median-voter models imply – a lump sum payment to *all* voters.

Instead, workers should favor redistribution to themselves, through targeted government social-welfare spending programs such as social security, job training, and education-even if such programs tend to regressively transfer income upward, *from* the poor, as is often the case (Justman and Gradstein 1999; Lizzeri and Persico 2004; Moene and Wallerstein 2001; Ross 2006). It is hardly a stretch to suggest that organized labor is primarily interested – as are those with even higher incomes – in protecting its own interests, not in universalistic government redistribution.

A counterintuitive yet testable implication follows: because the rise of an urban working class is often associated with a rise in income inequality, to the extent that the working class favors redistribution to itself but not to those who earn less and to the extent that the poor do not or cannot effectively demand redistribution but members of the working class can and do (because they are better-organized and have relatively more resources to engage in lobbying), we should observe a *negative* relationship between income inequality and "progressive" (universalistic) social-welfare spending. We confirm this hypothesis in Chapter 7.

In sum, we assume that the organized working class (1) is wealthier than the median voter and thus shares an interest with relatively wealthy groups in reining in the state's expropriative authority; (2) is never large enough to win a contest over the political regime with "paper stones" – votes (Przeworski and Sprague 1986); (3) will demand redistribution to itself, not to those further down the economic ladder; and (4) may not even seek substantial redistribution at all. After all, many working-class parties were reformist rather than revolutionary (Lipset 1983; Marks, Mbaye, and Kim 2009) and made no redistributive demands (and sometimes even sought to protect the economic status quo) as part of their efforts to promote political change. For this reason, even if the working class is cohesive and large, it is unlikely to constitute a threat to elite economic interests in the way redistributivist models suppose. Instead, it is more likely to behave as our argument predicts.

In the remainder of this chapter, we briefly consider evidence about the size, political interests, and political relevance of different social classes from a range of historical examples, which vary on both our independent and dependent variables.

3.3 INEQUALITY, INCOME, AND INTERESTS AND THE 2ND REFORM ACT

The British 2nd Reform Act of 1867, which expanded the country's electorate from about 20 to 35–40% of men, has the status of a classic, theoretically crucial case – and not simply because both Moore and A&R used it to illustrate the logic of their own arguments. Although the evidence we present is necessarily suggestive, the case serves two important methodological purposes: it highlights the descriptive accuracy of our assumptions about actors' motivations, and it illustrates how our argument's causal mechanisms operate – something that the cross-national statistical analyses that we undertake in later chapters cannot do.

The Bourgeoisie/Middle Class

We expect to observe a connection between political and economic reforms – between representation and taxation – in the demands middle-class groups articulate. This was clearly the case by the early nineteenth century in the UK, where Polanyi (1944, 137) noted that the nearly simultaneous passage of the 1st Reform Act (1832) and the abolishment of Poor Relief (1834) reflected the efforts of urban industrial capital to advance its interests against landed elites (Boyer 1986, 116).

Rising urban interests' demands for reform also congealed around the promotion of free trade and opposition to the Corn Laws (Moore 1976, 355), which artificially supported grain prices at the expense of urban consumers and their employers, who had to pay inflated wages (Fraser 1976, 238). Urban interests connected their political underrepresentation to the ability of landed interests to control economic policy – and as the century progressed issues of political and economic reform became intertwined, if not indistinguishable.

Opposition to the Corn Laws was clearly a "rationalization of selfish middle-class urban interests" (Fraser 1976, 240), but arguments for free trade transcended the notion that British society would benefit from lower grain prices, as they also implied that repealing the Corn Laws would promote international harmony and reduce the chances of war. This associated repeal with pacifism and with reductions in defense spending, which also advanced urban interests to undercut traditional elites' power over the means of coercion, as military officers typically came from the landed elites. In short, the "ambition for bourgeois social and political predominance" underpinned moral arguments against the Corn Laws (Fraser 1976, 241).

The Corn Laws were eventually repealed in 1846, reducing large landowners' income and influence. Still, the connection between the rise of new middle-class groups and demands for parliamentary reform intensified as the century advanced (Smith 1966, 39–40). Liberal efforts at parliamentary reform often concentrated on reapportionment rather than suffrage, to give urban areas a fairer share of seats. Fair representation of urban versus rural interests was so critical because of parliament's growing power over taxing and spending.

In the years immediately prior to the 2nd Reform Act, the growing middle classes pressed classically liberal demands to eliminate corruption and sources of royal patronage, rein in government spending and waste, and control executive power-all of which served to politically weaken the aristocratic elite, and all while exhibiting scant fear of the poor (McClelland 2000, 84). For example, Hoppen (1998, 48–49) writes that the influential "shopocracy," the shopkeeper's lobby – characterized by a "special kind of tight-fisted mean-ness" – organized and lobbied to demand ever-tighter controls over local government expenditures. The mid-nineteenth-century shopocracy embodied middle-class demands at the time for less government spending, especially on the poor. Members of this *petit bourgeois* movement also had both the motivation and the opportunity to organize, as they possessed an "acute political consciousness, heightened by their marginality in the class struc-ture" (Nossiter 1975, 146), and had considerable and growing resources. Thus, they formed the bulk of membership of urban ratepayer and sanitary associations – supporting reining in corruption but also spending on public works.

The shopocracy also illustrates the self-interest of middle-class groups, who persistently sought government protection of their economic interests. As Polanyi was keen to point out, such efforts sometimes hypocritically advocated "anti-liberal" regulations that served to shield capitalists from the vagaries of capitalism – an insight that still resonates today, as it describes the dynamic at work in contemporary models of special-interest lobbying (e.g., Grossman and Helpman 1996). Such demands for government regulation never came from the median voter, nor do they reflect fear of the median voter, but instead reflect the bourgeoisie and middle classes' fear of the state's expropriative power.

Although Moore (1966) highlighted the importance of the bourgeoisie, he took its economic interests for granted. Scholars have paid insufficient atten-tion to the concrete interests of the bourgeoisie and middle classes in the study of regime change – specifically, to the importance of the relationship between taxation and representation. One does not need to swallow Whig his-tory whole to recognize that this issue was front and center in the paradigmatic case of the nineteenth-century UK. Moreover, this case is hardly unique. Schol-ars should focus on the nitty-gritty of debates about political reforms – even failed ones, and even in relatively well-studied European cases. In the UK, lib-erals' demands for political reform were inseparable from their demands for economic reform. Elsewhere, liberals were often politically weaker, and their efforts on both fronts were for naught. Nonetheless, the point remains: such groups' demands focus not on fear of the poor, but on the relationship between taxation and representation – on the fear of state expropriation.

The Poor

Median-voter models assume that the poor favor redistribution and constitute a credible threat. We suggest that the poor tend to be conservative, and lack the resources and organizational capacity to mobilize on their own behalf. In nineteenth-century Europe, the poor's deferential passivity and fragmentation frequently reassured conservatives that mass enfranchisement would pose little danger to the economic status quo. Indeed, the notion that it was consensus opinion among elites that the poor would soak the rich if given the vote is impossible to reconcile with the Victorian-era view that the poorer the man, the greater the ignorance and cultural deference.

Consider a quote from John Stuart Mill, who famously stated during Parliamentary debate that the Conservative Party was "the stupidest party." He made sure to clarify that he "did not mean that Conservatives are generally stupid," but rather that "stupid persons are generally Conservative."[7] Conservatives never endeavored to refute Mill; indeed, Disraeli was one of many Tories who not only agreed with him (Cowling 1967, 54; Himmelfarb 1966, 113, 127), but understood that the poor were generally friendly to conservative interests (Welshman 2006).

In his *The English Constitution*, Walter Bagehot, the long-time editor of the *Economist*, described the conservatism of the poor in the following terms:

The most miserable . . . do not impute their misery to politics. If a political agitator were to lecture the peasants of Dorsetshire and try to excite political dissatisfaction, it is much more likely that he would be pelted than that he would succeed. Of parliament these miserable creatures know scarcely anything; of the cabinet they never heard. But they would say that, "for all they have heard, the Queen is very good;" and rebelling against the structure of society is to their minds rebelling against the Queen . . . the mass of the English people are politically content as well as politically deferential (Bagehot 1865, 327).

The views of Mill, Disraeli and Bagehot reflected deep skepticism that an expanded electorate would change British society significantly. Indeed, many in the UK (and elsewhere) believed that suffrage reform would *reinforce* landholders' power.

It is significant that qualitative-historical scholars rarely argue that the poor play a significant role in regime change. The reason is simple: the assumptions underlying redistributive arguments are unfounded as general principles. There is no evidence of any redistributive threat from "the poor" in the nineteenth-century UK; and good reasons to believe that the same holds in other times and places.

The Working Class

Historians have long debated whether the working class played an important role in Britain's gradual democratization, and its interests and political behavior in the 2nd Reform Act demand a bit more attention. Let us first recall that, since organized workers typically earned far above the median, even if

---

7 House of Commons, Committee Adjourned Debate, May 31st 1866. This quote can be found at http://hansard.millbanksystems.com/commons/1866/may/31, page 1592. Accessed March 23, 2012.

they did play a key role it is not obvious that this would support a redistributivist framework. In any case, even a superficial exploration of urban workers' organization, interests, and goals suggests that economic redistribution was an unimportant – perhaps nonexistent – part of their agenda.

Just before the 2nd Reform Act passed, the *Times* of London suggested that Bagehot's breezy dismissal of any threat from the poor also applied to the working class. The newspaper noted that most men who would be enfranchised seemed wholly indifferent to the fact that they were being "presented with a very considerable slice of the British Constitution" (Himmelfarb 1966, 103), and it ridiculed the notion that workers would want to "divide among them the land and the incomes of their more fortunate neighbors" (ibid., 130).

Why did this mouthpiece of the establishment, which typically had nothing but contempt for working people (McClelland 2000, 76), offer this view? The answer harkens back to our discussion of the interests of the rising middle classes and bourgeoisie: as the *Times* pointed out, the two main working-class organizations agitating for electoral reform in the 1860s – the Reform Union and the Reform League – were funded by wealthy industrialists, who already possessed the franchise (Cowling 1967, 12, 246–248). This suggests that "popular" mobilization at that time was less a product of autonomous working-class agitation than a demonstration of the ability of capitalists to mobilize public opinion in their favor (something that should not seem far-fetched to observers of contemporary American politics, for example). It also certainly implies that key members of the bourgeoisie had no fear of workers' "redistributivist" demands!

In any case, neither the League nor the Union made redistributive demands of any sort. The League, based in London, principally agitated for manhood suffrage and the secret ballot (Cowling 1967, 246; see also McClelland 2000, 89–90). It did not campaign to raise taxes on the rich or increase spending on the poor – yet even so it had trouble fundraising beyond its few wealthy patrons, partly because advocacy of manhood suffrage marked the group as extreme for its day, and partly because the group's membership came from the lower end of the "higher skilled labor" group (Baxter's "Manual 2" in the (1868) UK social table). Britain's fine-grained social class distinctions tended to ostracize League members within the world of London trade unionism, and no other important labor group would join its press for political reform (Cowling 1967, 260).

For its part, the Reform Union, which had a strong presence in northern industrial cities but little initial presence in London, deliberately positioned itself as more moderate than the League. It also advocated for the secret ballot, as well as for reapportionment (the elimination of rotten boroughs) and triennial parliaments (parliament could sit for seven years between 1716 and 1911 without an election; the term was then changed to five years), but its main demand was for *householder* suffrage – for extending voting rights to "heads of households," men who owned or rented an entire house. This excluded all lodgers who rented a room and sons of householders who lived at home, no matter their age.

Reform Union leaders believed that householder suffrage was more politically palatable to parliament than manhood suffrage (Cowling 1967, 243). Given the group's moderation, it should come as no surprise that the Union also made no redistributive demands of any kind. Even more than the League, the Union was the creation of wealthy politicians and northern merchants and manufacturers – "an attempt by a self-conscious bourgeoisie to provide leadership and exert power in the determination of public policy" (Cowling 1967, 243). Given this, the purpose of the many large public protests it organized was to "demonstrate the power of industrial radicalism to an aristocratic Parliament and [to] the Whig elements in the Liberal party that it too had more effective, more impressive, and more articulate followers than the mute agrarian legions on which territorial power depended" (ibid., 244). In an important sense, "working class" interests were really "bourgeois" interests – for political reform, not for redistribution.

Even so, because the Union and the League drew members from the working classes, upper- and middle-class Britons tended to view them as upstarts and outsiders. This social, economic and particularly cultural divide is a key element in understanding working-class interests. Formally, both reform groups' demands were political, not economic. Yet just as wealthy members of the bourgeoisie funded these working-class groups to advance their own political and economic interests, workers also had instrumental reasons for agitating for reform – reasons that support our elite-competition argument.

Working-class activists in the nineteenth-century UK not only posed no redistributive threat, they *deliberately and actively supported the economic status quo*. Indeed, workers who supported the League and the Union had aspirational – even classically liberal – political and cultural values. They did not identify economically, politically, or socially as poor or with the poor. Thus, their interests do not conform to the assumptions in Rueschemeyer, Stephens, and Stephens (1992) or in redistributivist models.[8]

Instead, many believed that their economic interests aligned more with their managers' and employers' than with those beneath them. Skilled workers had prospered as the UK had industrialized, so they tended to favor the economic

---

[8] The discussion here echoes debates about the existence of a "labor aristocracy," skilled workers who constituted a working class elite (see, e.g., Hobsbawm 1985; Katznelson 1985). In fact, according to Hobsbawm (1978, 281), Engels had suggested that the success of British capitalism had made much of the working class "relatively comfortable and ideologically moderate," which explained its lack of class solidarity and status-quo enhancing preferences. In a similar vein, Lenin argued that working-class quiescence was fruit of European imperialism. Debate continues as to precisely which workers were "aristocrats" and which were "commoners," so to speak. We only suggest that many manual workers – in the UK and elsewhere – had aspirational values and that income was a good proxy for the likely strength of such values (Moorhouse 1978, 63).

status quo, supporting "the advantages of free trade and the necessity for econ-omy in public business and the keeping down of rates" (Smith 1966, 13). This quote embodies our argument perfectly: at the height of the Industrial Revo-lution, in the country with the largest manual working class in world history and with a comparatively small mass of peasant/agricultural laborers, the most organized and politically self-aware members of the working class enshrined and embodied classically liberal values.

This claim does not originate with conservative historians such as Cowling or Himmelfarb, whose work deliberately diminishes the role of labor agita-tion for the passage of the 2nd Reform Act. Even Royden Harrison's (1965) *Before the Socialists*, the classic neo-Marxist effort to highlight workers' role, ironically supports the view that "radical" Reform League leaders rejected redistributivist notions. Harrison quotes the League's president, Edmond Beales, as affirming that workers were "deeply interested in the preserva-tion of law and order [and] of the rights of capital and property," precisely because they were "daily becoming capitalists and land-owners" (Harrison 1965, 114). After the Reform passed, Beales advised the League's newly enfran-chised working-class members to "vote for candidates who promised to reduce taxes and government spending" (Smith 1966, 235).

When we hear the leader of the most important and supposedly radical working class reform organization pressing for reduced government spending, we know the foundations of redistributivist arguments are shaky. Workers' own leaders made clear that conservative alarmism had no basis in fact.[9] Like members of the bourgeoisie and middle classes, workers wanted taxation with representation. They also wanted laws permitting unions to organize and equal rights before the law – but in terms of economic goals, their demands focused primarily on reducing regressive tax burdens and eliminating corrup-tion (McClelland 2000, 92). Attacking corruption and high taxes rhetorically allied workers with the bourgeoisie and middle classes and fit with classical liberal notions that enfranchisement would ameliorate rather than exacerbate class conflict, uniting workers with the wealthy to promote British prosperity.

Incumbent Autocratic Elites

The perception among the elite that the working class was respectable rather than menacing gained traction as debate about franchise reform advanced, and many Tories, who had just months earlier fretted about the dangers of

---

[9] Not surprisingly, workers' reformism deeply frustrated leftist radicals and revolutionaries. In a letter to Marx, Ernest Jones (a supporter of the Chartists, the Reform League and other British socialist groups) bemoaned workers' deference. "What is to be done with the English working classes?" he complained (quoted in Wright 1970, 128). "At Leeds they rise en masse because the son of an old Whig lord condescends to address them. At Manchester, Bolton, Nottingham and all about they unanimously pass resolutions for a £6 franchise or less – Manhood Suffrage is not even mentioned!"

enfranchising workers, suddenly reversed course and began to argue that these very same men were the backbone of British stability and prosperity.

Consider the example of Lord Elcho, an aristocratic Liberal Party dissenter. As Acemoglu and Robinson (2000, 1190) note, Elcho opposed his own party's proposed reform in 1866 because it was "well understood" that allowing the working classes to vote "would lead to redistribution" at the elite's expense. And yet when the Conservative Party's proposal came up for a vote the next year, he crossed party lines to vote "aye," proclaiming his faith in the deference and reasonableness of the British working class.[10] His Liberal Party colleagues denounced this cynicism and treachery, but Elcho's false change of heart was not unique. Several other formerly ardent opponents suddenly converted to the cause of reform, cheering Disraeli's vision of "Tory Democracy," which predicted that both the poor and the working class would behave conservatively (Smith 1966, 232–233). Such reversals are inexplicable within a redistributivist account, but fit our argument that hysterical reactionary rhetoric is merely tactical, rather than based on evidence.

In the end Disraeli's intuition hit the mark, as the poor and working classes "proved themselves 'safe'" (Smith 1966, 235) – subsequent election results revealed the Conservatives to be "much stronger among the urban working classes than most contemporary Tories realized, and most historians have believed" (ibid., 237). Moreover, due to Disraeli's clever combination of enfranchisement with reapportionment, the growth of the working-class vote in cities like Manchester or Sheffield (where Liberals were already strong) did nothing to alter the balance of power in Parliament, because increased turnout in smaller, rural boroughs worked in Conservatives' favor.[11]

Case Summary and Implications

It is true that the British working class was moderate in comparative perspective, but workers elsewhere shared similar interests. Consider Przeworski and Wallerstein's (1982) "class compromise" explanation for the evolution of mixed economies. Starting from redistributivist first principles, the authors seek to resolve the paradox of why democracy and property are so clearly compatible. Their explanation requires abandoning the parsimony of the median-voter model and assuming that workers understand that a tradeoff exists between attempts to reduce inequality and efforts to increase economic growth. Class compromise emerges when (1) workers know that they cannot win power on their own and believe that growth will bring increased wages,

---

[10] See "Debate on the Representation of the People Act," July 15th 1867, at http://hansard.millbanksystems.com/commons/1867/jul/15/, accessed March 29, 2012.

[11] See Berlinski and Dewan (2011) on the lack of evidence that Liberal gains in 1868 resulted from changes in the franchise rules.

and (2) when capitalists are assured that they will retain control over investment decisions. If both conditions hold, working-class reformism – which entails limiting redistributivist demands – is rational.

From here, it is but a step to Moene and Wallerstein's (2001) explanation for why so much social-welfare spending around the world fails to benefit the poor and instead favors those who earn far more than average. Moene and Wallerstein abandon the assumption that workers care about the aggregate tradeoff between equality and growth and instead assume that workers mobilize on their own behalf, attempting to target government spending to themselves instead of demanding (as in the Meltzer-Richard model) a lump sum distributed to all voters. A key implication of their argument is that welfare spending on the poor should decline as inequality increases.

In Chapter 7, we build on Moene and Wallerstein's insight, showing that progressively redistributive social-welfare spending around the world in the late nineteenth and early twentieth centuries did actually decline as income inequality increased. This finding utterly confounds median-voter models. However, our elite-competition argument can explain it, as we assume that rising and self-interested groups will be willing to spend government money on themselves but unwilling to support universalistic social-welfare programs that primarily benefit the poor.

The assumptions of our elite-competition model describe the interests and actions of key actors in Britain's gradual democratization in the nineteenth century. Political competition did not hinge on the interests of the median voter, but rather occurred between relatively wealthy economic groups – incumbent elites and rising outsider groups who demanded political voice. Specifically, the bourgeoisie and middle classes feared the expropriative power of the state more obviously than the redistributive threat from the poor, who were disorganized and disinterested. Meanwhile, the organized working class did not demand redistribution – its demands were also rather "bourgeois," focused on the connection between taxation and representation.

3.4 OTHER CASES

To what extent does the logic of our argument extend across time and space? In this section, we offer brief examples, drawn from various cells of the 2X2 of land and income inequality in Table 1.1b, to further illustrate the logic of our argument.

3.4.1 Imperial Germany

Imperial Germany represents a case of high land inequality and (relatively) low income inequality. This combination of structural conditions is less auspicious for democracy, as it implies a relatively strong landed elite and relatively weak bourgeois/middle classes.

Income inequality was relatively lower in Germany than in the UK prior to *low income inequality* World War One. Alexander Gerschenkron (1943) used Imperial Germany as an example of a "backward" or late-industrializing nation, and lower income inequality was primarily a function of the country's lower level of economic development. In particular, in 1882 almost half the population still worked in agriculture. Urbanization was lower too – even as late as 1905 over half of Germany's population lived in towns of less than five thousand (Anderson 1993, 1460). With such a large proportion of the population employed in agriculture, income inequality is likely to be lower due to the relatively uniform returns to labor within that sector. Income inequality was higher in urban areas, where a more diversified economy granted differentiated returns to labor, but even there it was still much lower than average levels in Britain (Grant 2002, 2005).

Relatively low income inequality did not lead to democratization, as Boix (2003) might predict, because it signified relatively small and politically weak middle classes (Luebbert 1991b; Moore 1966). The German Liberal Party – supported by urban bourgeois and professional classes – wanted what liberals elsewhere wanted: taxation with representation. Yet although the Reichstag lacked fiscal authority under the Kaiser, Liberals did not even attempt to push for reforms that would have enhanced parliament's political influence (Blackbourn and Evans 1991; Eley 1991). Instead, given their weakness and relatively small numbers, they were at times cornered into supporting repressive policies, such as the Antisocialist Laws, as well as the government's tariff bills that protected heavy industry and large-scale grain production in the politically crucial province of Prussia – actions that only served to tighten the links between the government and the aristocratic and anti-democratic Junker landed aristocracy (Hunt 1974; Pack 1961; Stürmer 1974; Tipton 1979).

The power of rural elites can be seen in the comparatively high concentration of land ownership (Eddie 2008), particularly in Prussia. Agricultural *high land inequality* census data from 1882 on the size and distribution of landholdings across the Empire generate landholding Gini coefficients of 0.77 for the Empire as a whole, and 0.81 for Prussia (Thomson 2012). These figures are far higher than those in contemporary OECD countries but similar to those in the Middle East or Latin America today (Vollrath and Erickson 2007).

Prussian aristocrats' large estates not only provided them with social positions akin to feudal lords (Anderson 2000), but also made them the dominant political force within Prussia – and, thus, a veto player in the Empire as a whole (Gerschenkron 1943). The Junkers stopped any reform that would have undermined their dominant social position, such as stronger property rights guarantees for small farmers, and they famously preserved their socioeconomic status by enacting protectionist grain tariffs after 1878. Their determination to block any moves toward democratization succeeded until Germany's loss in World War I (see Puhle 1975; Rosenberg 1967).

The relative levels of income inequality in Imperial Germany and the nineteenth-century UK represent puzzles for redistributivist accounts. The UK had a higher level of income inequality, but it democratized. Our theoretical approach, which incorporates the political implications of land inequality and interprets income inequality differently, can explain this outcome. Higher land inequality signaled a relatively stronger landed elite in Germany, while higher income inequality in the UK suggested that British urbanization and industrialization nourished stronger and more politically influential middle classes.

3.4.2 Nineteenth-Century Sweden

Nineteenth-century Sweden is useful to compare with the nineteenth-century UK because both countries exhibit similar values on the independent and dependent variables, confirming that the UK's process of "endogenous" democratization is not unique. Early on, Sweden politically trailed the UK, in that an electoral reform in 1866 increased the proportion of enfranchised men to only about 20%, about half of the UK's electorate after the 2nd Reform Act a year later. Yet by 1909 all tax-paying men had the right to vote in lower-chamber elections.[12]

As in the UK, the struggle for democratization in late nineteenth-century Sweden was not about redistribution, either of land or income. Instead, demands for reform focused on limiting the Crown's authority to conscript men and to levy taxes. Rural smallholders initially led the charge. For example, in the 1880s the government sought to increase military spending and lengthen military service (conscription was universal at the time). Smallholders, who had gained influence after 1866 because most paid sufficient tax to vote in lower chamber elections (Rothstein 1998), opposed both proposals – and also demanded reductions in property taxes and greater property-rights security (Oakley 1966, 212). Disputes over taxation and representation – not a fear of redistribution – dominated the struggle from the beginning.

As the nineteenth century wore on, urban interests joined the battle to rein in the state's authority. Sweden industrialized later than the UK or Germany; in 1871, 72% of the population worked in agriculture, fishing, or forestry. Yet from 1870 to 1900, while this proportion declined to 54%, the proportion employed in industry, mining, and crafts doubled to almost 30% (Tilton 1974, 563). Because urban wages dramatically increased while rural incomes stagnated (Soderberg 1991, 86), income inequality increased during this era to levels higher than in Germany. In 1903, the decade in which income inequality peaked, the top 10% of earners garnered 46% of the income (Roine and Waldenström 2008, 370) – the same proportion as Brazil in 2010.

---

[12] Income-based plural voting in the upper chamber remained in place until 1921, when universal suffrage was introduced (Tilton 1974, 562).

Just as in the UK, industrialization, urbanization, and income inequality went hand in hand with the economic and political rise of a bourgeoisie and then a working class – and, as in the UK, these groups couched their political demands in terms of the connection between taxation and representation, with the issue of conscription added to the mix. The mantra of those fighting for the franchise was, "If a man had to pay taxes, he should have voice in how the funds were distributed; if he had to serve in the army he should be able to participate in policymaking"(Scott 1988, 403). Throughout this era, Swedish Liberals and later Social Democrats consistently demanded limits on the Crown's control over taxes, the budget, and government administration (Verney 1957).

Arrayed against these groups, Sweden's autocratic elites consisted of an alliance of large landholders (who resembled German Junkers) and conservative government officials, who did not want to share power with other classes (Scott 1988, 403). Yet in contrast to Germany, Sweden's growing bourgeois liberal and working class interests were arrayed against politically *weak* landed interests – an auspicious combination for democracy (Rustow 1970). Land ownership was never highly concentrated (Tilton 1974), and policy differences between grain producers and livestock farmers split the Ruralist Party in 1888 over the tariff. Grain producers joined the Conservatives, while livestock farmers joined liberal urban representatives, who were opposed. Rural out-migration in the last half of the nineteenth century (to cities, as well as to places like Minnesota) also helped ameliorate rural hardship.

Sweden's experience echoes the UK's in that relatively low rural inequality combined with relatively high income inequality. Landed elites were relatively weak, and demands for democracy came from rising economic groups with incomes well above the future median voter (Soderberg 1991). Reformers did not ask for redistribution but instead demanded limits on state authority – elimination of conscription, lower taxes, and combat against corruption. Moreover, as in the UK, despite high levels of income inequality, universalistic social welfare spending did not increase substantially as the electorate expanded. Indeed, redistributive public spending remained minimal until the Depression era – and even then, most government spending was highly targeted, not universal and progressively redistributive (Lindert 1994).

3.4.3 Twentieth-Century South Korea

The case of South Korea, which democratized in 1987, presents a challenge for our elite-competition argument, primarily because income inequality was relatively low for the entire post-1953 period. This suggests that the simpler explanation may be best: low demand for redistribution paved the path to democracy. Low income inequality does imply that rising commercial and industrial elites who opposed the autocratic regime were relatively weak, in comparative perspective. However, the key to this case is the absence of landed

elites who would have *supported* the autocratic regime. The crucial endogenous causal factor, in our view, is not the relative political weakness of urban
bourgeois, middle, and working-class interests, but that landed elites were even
weaker than in cases such as the UK or Sweden.

South Korea remained a Cold War flashpoint long after the end of the
war with the North in 1953. The country did not simply leave the conflict
behind and proceed down the path of endogenous economic and political
development. The United States kept the country's economy afloat with bil-
lions of dollars in aid, stationed tens of thousands of troops on its territory,
and provided diplomatic cover for a series of authoritarian governments, all of
which used fear of communism to rationalize repressive rule. The geopolitical
context makes South Korea an extremely unlikely case for endogenous democratization. And yet, an argument can be made that domestic socioeconomic
conditions contributed to regime change, and in the way that our argument
suggests.

When South Korea's industrial sector started growing rapidly in the 1960s,
urban middle-class interests gained strength and demanded political reforms
(Koo 2002, 109) – students, intellectuals, church groups (Lie 2000, 25–27) and
white-collar workers (known as the "necktie corps") composed of government
bureaucrats and private-sector professionals (Choi 1993, 37). Labor unions
also gained strength in the 1970s and frequently took to the streets in protest
(Haggard and in Moon 1993, 74; Koo 1993, 140, 2002, 111; Kim 2000,
55; Lie 2000, 135). However, redistributivist demands were never central.
Instead, fear of the state's coercive authority and calls for greater participation
in policymaking motivated demands for democracy (Choi 1993, 35).

These political forces were undoubtedly important in tipping the scales
toward democracy in 1987. Nonetheless, pressures from industrial, financial, and commercial elites were weaker than in other countries at that time.
Korea's state-led development meant wealthy economic interests had reason
to ally with the regime – or at least remain neutral. In comparative perspective, this likely served to weaken middle- and working-class opposition groups'
efforts.

However, what many scholars of democratization have missed about South
Korea's path is the dog that did not bark – how the country's lack of a powerful
landed elite weakened the autocratic regime and facilitated democratization.
In 1946, North Korea undertook a massive land reform, which it exploited
as propaganda in its effort to undermine the government in the South (Kang
2000, 201). The South Korean government made this propaganda noncred-
ible by simply implementing its own massive land reform program, which
dramatically reduced rural inequality (Amsden 1992, 38; Hwang 1985, 285;
Jang 1985, 332; Jeon and Kim 2000, 266; Kang 2000, 237; Kim 1990, 459)
and almost completely eliminated large landholdings: in 1944 3% of landowners held 64% of the land, but by 1956 the top 6% owned only 18% (Lie 2000,
11). Small farmers did not grow rich, but the country's quasi-feudal rural social

[handwritten margin note: low land inequality]

structure was completely destroyed (Kohli 2004, 71–73; Pak 1956, 1021; Shin 1998, 1314).

An underappreciated irony of South Korea's political trajectory is that in the long run, the military regime's land reform eliminated a social class that would likely have stood by it through thick and thin. By destroying the traditional ruling elite and eradicating farmers' fundamental source of discontent (Lie 2000, 38), land reform initially deflated leftist anti-regime appeals and generated widespread support among smallholders (who constituted a majority of workers throughout the 1950s) for President Syngman Rhee, who remained in office until 1960 (Cho 2001, 351; Jang 1985, 333; Jeon and Kim 2000, 266; Kang 2000, 303–304; Kim 1990, 458–462). Farmers' gratitude eventually dissipated, because land reform by itself could not promote rural development, and government policy consistently favored the industrial sector (Kang 2000, 259). To advance their economic interests, farmers eventually shifted from quiescence to organized opposition to the regime (Lie 2000, 117). By the late 1970s, rural interests were no longer safely in the pro-government camp.

South Korea actually fits long-held ideas about the sources of democracy, but the impact of the absence of a conservative rural elite to its political trajectory has attracted relatively little attention. In this case, the political consequences of low land inequality fit our theoretical expectations: not only in the absence of a landed elite fearing redistribution, but because of the presence of a large class of property holders conscious that the only way they could gain influence over public policy would be by obtaining the vote.

3.4.4 Contemporary China

Contemporary China embodies the sort of social structure that should generate pressure for democratization: low land inequality and rising income inequality. Moreover, despite rapid economic growth and rising living standards in recent years, tens if not hundreds of thousands of anti-government protests occur every year. Participants are not simply demanding greater freedom of expression, but are pressing demands for controls on corruption and rent-seeking. That is, demands for political reform in contemporary China focus on issues of property rights.

The Chinese Communist Party has confounded predictions of its imminent demise following the 1989 Tiananmen Square massacre (Nathan 2003). In the early 1990s the government implemented economic reforms that spurred immediate and rapid growth, which provided the government with widespread popular support. Growing wealth meant the Party could ignore calls for political reform. However, the frequency of anti-government protests highlights the paradox all modernizing authoritarian regimes confront: rising living standards form the basis for the regime's performance legitimacy, but also generate social forces – a growing middle class and an increasingly independent civil society – that are most likely to demand democracy (Diamond 2012, 12).

*low
land
inequality*

China confronts this paradox acutely, given that it combines high income inequality with low land inequality – meaning that, like South Korea, it lacks a rural landed elite, and the key political question is whether the government can continue to forestall political reforms by combining co-optation when possible with repression when necessary. Social structure in 1989 China still reflected the aftermath of the 1949 revolution, which had eliminated traditional rural and urban economic elites and made the country into one of the world's most egalitarian (Kung, Wu, and Wu 2012). Both land and income inequality remained comparatively low up through the late 1980s. For example, during 1977–1986 China's Gini coefficient of income inequality averaged .29 – lower than all but 11 of the 116 countries for which estimates are available for that period of (University of Texas Inequality Project 2008). As for land inequality, in 1987 its Gini coefficient of land ownership stood at .37, lower than the average for Scandinavia (.41), the world region with the most egalitarian land distribution (Benjamin 2008; Frankema 2010).

This socioeconomic structure suggests that despite the outbreak of protests in more than 80 cities in 1989, the pro-democracy forces at that time were too small and weak (Gold 1990; Goldman 1990). Quite simply, the pro-democracy movement could not count on middle-class support because at the time there was no real Chinese middle class. Similarly, low levels of land inequality mean that rural workers were largely indifferent to calls for democracy (O'Brien 2009). The state faced few claims from rising economic elites, and so the party retained its grip on power.

Rapid growth since Tiananmen has brought hundreds of millions into a newly-emergent middle class (Béja 2009). However, the Chinese government has hardly relied exclusively on the pacifying effects of a rising living standard. As of 2010, government spending on "maintaining social stability" exceeded spending on national defense (Wang 2013, 50). A key explanation for why the government feels the need to circle the wagons lies with the political consequences of rapid increases in income inequality. Since the 1990s China has followed the dynamic we highlight, in which rising income inequality accompanies rapid economic growth. Hundreds of millions of Chinese have entered the middle class within the span of a generation, but they have left behind even more of their compatriots, whose incomes have not increased nearly as rapidly.

*high
income
inequality*

Although land inequality remains low by international standards, since 1989 China has experienced what may be the fastest increase in income inequality the world has ever witnessed. Official government figures provide a Gini coefficient of income inequality of .47 in 2012 (Fang and Yu 2012; Yao and Wang 2013), although some observers contend that it is even higher.[13]

---

[13] An independent survey conducted at Chengdu's Southwest University of Finance and Economics estimated China's Gini coefficient in 2010 as .61 – a figure that is higher than all but one of the 129 country estimates contained in the UNDP's 2011 Human Development Report (Times 2013; Liu and Chen 2012; UNDP 2011; Yao and Wang 2013).

A Gini of .47 highlights the extent to which income inequality has skyrocketed as a consequence of two decades of economic growth. The main source of income inequality is the country's large and growing urban – rural income gap,[14] but perceptions of growing intra-rural and, more importantly, intra-urban income gaps have generated growing resentment, leading to a dramatic increase in what are known as "mass incidents" (Liu and Chen 2012), episodes of anti-government protest. Wang (2013, 50) reports that while there were fewer than 9,000 protests against authorities in 1993, there were 87,000 by 2005 – and 280,000 in 2010.

These protests occur in both rural and urban contexts, revealing that today, rural smallholders share concerns with urban middle classes about corruption, taxes, and property rights. In recent years, observers have begun to question the sustainability of both the Chinese government's spending on maintaining social stability and the Party's capacity to continue to co-opt rising economic groups, particularly as the expansion of white-collar jobs fails to keep pace with the increasing numbers of college graduates (Diamond 2012; Pei 2012). Even the author who coined the phrase "authoritarian resilience" to describe the party's ability to retain its grasp on power by adapting to changing economic and political circumstances now writes that "the consensus is stronger than at any time since [1989] that the resilience of the authoritarian regime ... is approaching its limits" (Nathan 2013, 20). While it is uncertain when a transition to democracy might occur, recent studies suggest that the Chinese middle class is more skeptical about the party's policy promises, more critical of government corruption, and more concerned with the growing power of state-owned enterprises than are other social groups. This suggests that middle-class actors seeking to protect their economic gains are likely to be key protagonists in any transition that might occur (Li 2012).

3.5 CONCLUSION

Income inequality in developing autocracies is associated with the growth of rising yet disenfranchised economic groups – the bourgeoisie and middle classes primarily, but also the working class. Social tables reveal that these groups' incomes place them well above the median voter, which suggests that political competition in struggles for endogenous democratization occurs between relative economic elites.

An elite-competition understanding of the dynamics of regime change suggests that incumbent elites' primary fear does not emanate from the poor, but from rising economic groups. In turn, these groups have good reason to fear the expropriative threat from those who control the state – but less reason to

---

[14] Between 1985 and 2008 the ratio of urban to rural mean income rose from roughly 1.6 to 3.3 (Ravallion and Chen 2007, 19).

fear the poor. As income inequality increases, so will rising groups' demands for taxation with representation.

The underclass almost never plays a relevant role in regime change, not because its members may be politically conservative, but because they lack the resources and organizational cohesion to present a credible political threat. As for the working class, social tables revealed that its members also typically earn more than the median voter. Partly for this reason, workers' interests may align with those who earn even more – for equality of opportunity and low taxes, rather than equality of outcomes and higher progressive and universalistic redistributive spending. We also expect workers to demand government programs that benefit their own group, rather than those who earn less.

Any theoretical model's assumptions will necessarily be descriptively inaccurate. Yet when weighing competing theories, assumptions' *relative* plausibility matters greatly. Our argument suggests that there is little reason to believe that the poor and working classes will naturally soak the rich if given the opportunity. Some lament this fact, while others cheer it. Either way, the implication is clear: elites do not always and everywhere believe workers and the poor covet property and privilege. Instead, they may believe that workers and the poor share their own materialistic, aspirational goals.

This chapter connected the conceptual dots between income inequality, social structure, and the relative strength of demands for regime change. Higher levels of income inequality will be associated with growing demands for political reform because it indicates that more people have more to lose under autocracy. This discussion of actors' motivations grounds our argument's theoretical logic, which we formalize in the next chapter. It also serves a crucial methodological purpose, illustrating the descriptive accuracy of our theory's assumptions and providing detail about how its causal mechanisms work. The argument also offers suggestions for future qualitative-comparative research on regime change, beyond what secondary sources currently offer. Our assumptions about actors' motivations should hold across cases, but actors' causal importance will vary, depending on socioeconomic structure – in particular of land and income inequality.

4

An Elite-Competition Model of Democratization

4.1 INTRODUCTION

This chapter develops a formal model connecting inequality to regime change. We first spell out assumptions that redistributivist models share, and then offer our alternative assumptions about actors, their interests, and their likely actions in different contexts. The resulting theory connects land and income inequality to competition between elites from different economic sectors for control over the state – and lays out the likely conditions for such competition to lead to regime change.

Redistributivist models rely on five problematic assumptions: (1) a one-sector economy, (2) two-group politics between rich and poor, (3) the absence of taxation and expropriation under autocracy, (4) particularly high taxation and spending in unequal democracies, and (5) a disconnect between groups' economic resources and their likelihood of prevailing in struggles over political regimes. Although some redistributivist models alter one or more of these assumptions, all share several, and all share the core assumption that democratization is driven by conflict between the rich and the poor.

Our model alters each assumption. First, we consider an economy with two economic sectors, with differential growth rates. Second, our model has three groups: the incumbent elite, a rising economic elite, and the masses. Third, we presume that taxation under autocracy is regressive, transferring resources to the incumbent elite from the other groups. Fourth, we suggest that rising economic elites may prefer partial democracy, which may have *lower* taxation than autocracy. And finally, instead of assuming that the likelihood of a group prevailing is exogenous, we assume that this probability depends on the ratio of resources between groups, meaning that higher-income groups are more likely to win.

After laying out assumptions, we develop our theoretical model in two steps. We first explain the economic fundamentals that determine inequality, and then we explore how various forms of inequality impact the likelihood of expropriation and redistribution under different political regimes and, thus, how these same factors shape disenfranchised groups' incentives to rebel or not ("democratization from below") as well as incumbent elites' incentives to either repress their opponents or to relinquish control over the regime ("democratization from above"). We split our analysis into the case where only the bourgeoisie can credibly rebel ("partial democratization") and the case where the masses may rebel separately or join the bourgeoisie in rebellion ("full democratization").

The chapter concludes by summarizing informally the claims made in previous sections. An appendix to the chapter provides a short extension of the model of partial democratization to include the effects of varying levels of asset mobility.

4.2 THE REDISTRIBUTIVIST APPROACH

4.2.1 Introduction

Redistributivist models of regime change build on Meltzer and Richard's hypothesis about the relationship between inequality and redistributive government spending in democracies. In these models, the median voter sets a tax rate so that everyone pays the same proportion of their income in taxes: the more you earn, the more you pay in absolute terms. However, redistribution is achieved through a uniform lump sum transfer: everyone receives the same amount from the government, regardless of how much they paid in taxes. By implication, those who earn less than the mean income pay less in taxes than they receive, while everyone else pays more than they get in return.

This setup has two pertinent implications. First, tax rates will always be greater under democracy than autocracy. In an autocracy the individual who decides on the tax rate is a member of a tiny, wealthy elite. Because transfers go to everyone, members of the elite would pay far more in taxes than they would receive in transfers and so impose a tax rate of zero. Yet because under universal suffrage the median voter's income will always be below the mean income, the median voter will impose a positive tax rate.

Second, inequality impacts both the tax rate and, consequently, the amount of redistribution. Low inequality means that there is relatively little difference between the income of the median voter and mean income. By contrast, high inequality means that the median voter earns far less than average. Since the size of redistributive transfers depends on mean rather than median income, as (median-preserving) inequality increases, the median voter should prefer more redistribution, and under democracy he or she can vote to impose a higher tax rate to achieve that end.

Redistributivist theories of regime change draw upon this model. Regardless of the level of inequality, the wealthy prefer the tax-free environment of autocracy, while the poor favor democracy. As inequality increases under autocracy, the rich know regime change would mean higher taxes, and so dig in their heels – as do the poorer masses in the opposite direction, demanding democracy precisely to implement the policies the wealthy fear. To what extent is this a fruitful approach? In what follows, we describe Boix's and Acemoglu and Robinson's (A&R) models, discuss five assumptions these models share, and consider their limitations.

4.2.2 Boix's Argument

Boix's extension of the Meltzer-Richard (MR) model is straightforward, focusing primarily on the preferences of the rich and the poor over tax rates under autocracy and democracy. He then adds a second dimension said to influence the probability of regime change, asset specificity.

As in the MR model Boix assumes that individuals' income varies along one dimension, in this case their share of the aggregate capital stock.[1] The poor outnumber the rich but have below mean incomes and, therefore, prefer a positive tax rate, and always prefer democracy over autocracy. In contrast, the rich are willing to pay the costs of repressing the poor to prevent democracy and its redistributive consequences.

Democracy only emerges in Boix's model when the elite decide to grant it rather than repress, not when the masses force elites' hand. For Boix, the effect of inequality is uniformly negative: as it increases, regime change becomes less likely. This is because in making their decision, elites weigh their utility of maintaining autocracy (paying the costs of repression and risking revolt by the poor) against that of the higher taxation that comes with democracy. Elites are relatively more likely to grant democracy when inequality is low because the costs of repression are likely to outweigh the costs of being taxed. Yet as inequality increases, the costs of democracy may exceed the costs of repression.[2] At extremely high levels of inequality, elites always choose to repress.[3]

Boix also incorporates the impact of asset specificity, the relative ease by which elites can move their assets across borders.[4] This echoes Hirschman's (1970) mechanism of "exit" – under certain conditions, if elites do not like the political regime they can leave the country and take their assets with them. However, different assets entail different degrees of mobility. Land is highly immobile ("specific"). Because elites cannot threaten to pick it up and

---

[1] Boix briefly examines capital versus land ownership, but not inequality within each sector.

[2] Boix (2003, 26–7) adds a wrinkle to the model in that the costs of repression for the rich vary exogenously.

[3] In this situation the potential gains to the poor of revolt are so large that revolution may occur. However, this path does not lead to democracy but to a different form of autocracy, a "dictatorship of the proletariat."

[4] We examine the effects of asset specificity on our own model in this chapter's Appendix.

leave, land is highly susceptible to taxation under democracy. Elites with highly specific assets, Boix argues, are unlikely to willingly concede a democracy.

In contrast, assets such as capital are relatively more mobile and are, therefore, less subject to high rates of taxation. By implication, democracy poses less of a threat to holders of mobile assets – because if tax rates rise too high, asset holders can simply pick up and leave. Elites who hold mobile assets are, according to this logic, more likely to concede democracy.

For Boix, asset specificity and inequality impact the probability of democratization separately. However, Boix does not consider the possibility that assets with different degrees of specificity might be distributed more or less equally within countries, nor that the relative distribution of such assets might have more substantial political consequences than their degree of specificity. In any case, the core of his argument and empirical analysis rests on the median-voter logic, in which higher inequality works against democratization.

4.2.3 Acemoglu and Robinson's Argument

A&R's argument is similar to Boix's in some respects. Their core model has two actors: a pro-democracy poor majority and an autocratic wealthy minority, they consider inequality along one dimension, in this case income, and democracy comes from above, when the elite decide to grant it rather than repress. In addition, for the most part, A&R also model an economy with a single productive sector.

The central intuition driving A&R's argument also follows Meltzer and Richard: rising inequality intensifies the poor's demand for redistribution and heightens the elite's fear of both redistribution and democracy. However, A&R's argument differs from Boix's in that they suggest that the relationship between inequality and democratization takes the form of an inverted U: regime change is most likely at middling levels of inequality, but unlikely at either low or high levels. Let us explore how they derive this hypothesis.

When inequality is low regime change is unlikely because the poor have few incentives to threaten elites with revolution. Revolutions destroy a proportion, μ, of national income, and if the amount of destroyed income exceeds the share of national income owned by the rich, θ, then the costs of revolution outweigh its benefits. When inequality is low, the costs of destruction may outweigh the benefits of redistributing the elite's assets.

This logic suggests that as inequality increases, the poor have greater incentives to revolt – because the quantity of elites' resources available for redistribution would exceed the costs of revolution. Elites understand that their losses to redistribution under democracy increase with inequality, and so have incentives to head this outcome off by offering concessions.

However, a credible commitment problem undermines elite offers. This is because A&R assume that the poor's ability to credibly threaten revolution is transitory and independent of the level of inequality. That is, A&R assume that the destructive costs of revolution vary exogenously from period to period – and only when μ is sufficiently low would the gains from revolution actually exceed its costs. The poor's threats are therefore only credible when μ is low. Yet because μ is also transitory, elites' promises of concessions when μ is low may not be credible, because costs may be high in a future period – and when μ is high, elites have incentives to renege on any past concessions because they know the poor cannot credibly revolt. The poor may therefore decide to revolt when μ is low, precisely because they understand that elites' concessions lack credibility.

At middling levels of inequality, democracy can resolve this credible commitment problem. In this situation, the rich agree to be taxed and lose some of their assets permanently, rather than risk a revolution and lose everything. This satisfies the relatively poor median voter enough to forestall the possibility of revolution. Yet as inequality continues to increase, so do the costs of democracy to the elite. Although the rich prefer to pay nothing, when inequality is low relinquishing control over the tax rate imposes a relatively low cost. But when inequality is high, taxes under democracy are likely to be high, giving elites powerful incentives to oppose regime change.

One option remains open to autocratic elites: repressing the poor and retaining autocracy. The cost of repression reduces all citizens' income by a proportion, κ, – and where κ is large, repression may prove too costly for elites. The decision to repress or concede democracy depends on the relationship between economic inequality (θ) and the costs of repression (κ). As inequality rises elites' opposition to democracy increases, and they will be willing to bear greater costs to repress.

This last mechanism explains the downward slope of A&R's inverse U relationship between inequality and democratization. The upward slope of the inverse U reflects the masses' increasing demand for democracy as inequality increases, while the downward slope reflects elites' increasing fear of redistribution under democracy as inequality continues to increase, and their greater willingness to pay the costs of repression. Hence, autocracies will be stable at both low *and* high levels of inequality. Only at middling levels is democracy likely to emerge.

This is the core argument of Acemoglu and Robinson's 2006 book. However, in later chapters they extend this basic model. For example, in Chapter 8 they introduce a middle class, which prefers a "partial democracy" in which they share power with elites, and in Chapter 9 they divide groups by their factor endowments, examining the difference between capitalist and landowning autocratic elites. However, these extensions do not alter the posited inverse U relationship between inequality and democratization.

4.3 RETHINKING ASSUMPTIONS

In this section we question five assumptions that undergird redistributivist models. Some apply Ockham's Razor too readily – sometimes, parsimony entails considerable costs in terms of explanatory power. Others are descriptively inaccurate – they lack of empirical support. We discuss the relative importance of each assumption for each author's argument, why the assumption is problematic, and how we alter each assumption when developing our own approach.

Assumption 1: A Stagnant One-Sector Economy. The first questionable assumption in redistributivist models is that the economy is static and one-dimensional. Assuming the economy is static means that economic change can be conceived simply as changes in the division of a pie of fixed size.

Assuming the economy is one-dimensional means that political contestation occurs between rich and poor over the distribution of a single good – basically, national income. Since there is only one good to be divided, inequality can be understood as the relative disproportionality of the ratio between population shares and income shares – increasing if more resources go to a fixed population of the rich, or decreasing if more resources accrue to a fixed population of the poor.[5]

By contrast, we assume a two-sector economy (agriculture and industry), and allow economic dynamism by presuming that one sector is growing while the other stagnates. We also assume that what distinguishes incumbent from rising elites is whether they earn the bulk of their income from the stagnant or the growing sector. This means that elites can differ not only by the source of their income but by the current and expected future ratio of their resources. This situates our argument in the spirit of classic two-sector models of economic development such as Lewis (1954), Kuznets (1955), Baumol (1967), and Jones (1971), as well as more recent political economy research such as Rebelo (1991), Lizzeri and Persico (2004) and Rajan (2009).

Having two sectors also means that in our model, overall societal inequality is a function of two components: inequality *between* the two sectors and inequality *within* each sector. Overall inequality might increase if one sector grows faster than the other, especially if income is unequally distributed *within* the faster-growing sector. (This is the story Kuznets told.) Yet overall societal inequality might also increase if inequality *within* either sector worsens, regardless of whether that sector is stagnating or growing. This approach

---

[5] Boix briefly considers two economic sectors, but does so informally, and focuses on relative asset specificity across sectors rather than on the relative distribution of resources within each sector. For their part, Acemoglu and Robinson (2006) mostly work with θ, the share of national income held by the rich, to represent inequality. In Chapter 9, they consider a model of the economy in which national income is produced by three inputs: land, labor, and capital, but they assume away intra-elite conflict by not modeling landowners and capitalists as potentially distinct groups who might struggle for power with one another. They also do not consider the potentially distinct impact of inequality across the agricultural and industrial sectors of the economy, or the possibility that overall national inequality could be a function of changes in inequality *within* each economic sector or changes in average wage rates *across* sectors.

hews closely to standard growth models, but – as we detail in the following material – carries distinct implications for how we understand the political consequences of economic growth and inequality.

Assumption 2: Two-Group Politics. Redistributivist models lean heavily on the assumption that political conflict occurs between two groups: rich and poor. This setup generates many of these models' core insights: political regimes reflect different groups' policy preferences; redistribution is a zero-sum game between groups; taxation is absent in autocracies; revolution by the poor is a pervasive threat. A two-group model of politics also makes thinking about the economy simple, since inequality can be viewed as a simple ratio of group incomes, adjusted for population size.

In these models, the two groups are assumed to be unitary actors, eliminating the possibility that regime change might be driven by intra-elite conflict rather than by pressure from the poor. A two-group model also *requires* that inequality be one-dimensional. Even if redistributivist models were to incorporate a two-sector model of the economy, with two groups changes in inequality in each sector are interesting only insofar as they change the overall ratio of income between rich and poor. An increase in land inequality would presumably enrich the already wealthy, but so too would an increase in inequality derived from ownership of industry.

Finally, a two-group model precludes the analysis of coalitional politics, which can only occur with more than two groups. Both Boix and Acemoglu and Robinson do extend their models to consider three groups. For example, Acemoglu and Robinson (2006) introduce a middle class in Chapter 8, with a larger share of income proportional to their population than the poor but a smaller share than the rich. The middle class acts as a buffer between the other two groups, and whether it allies with the elites or the masses depends how far it is from each group in terms of income.[6]

However, their predictions about the impact of an increasingly wealthy middle class are indeterminate. On the one hand, they suggest that as the middle class grows wealthier it is cheaper for the autocratic elite to buy it off and retain autocracy (Acemoglu and Robinson 2006, 266). Yet just a few pages later they suggest that a "large and affluent middle class may make democracy less costly for the rich" (Acemoglu and Robinson 2006, 278). These contradictory predictions derive, we suggest, from the difficulty of thinking about three groups in a one-sector economy.

---

[6] Boix (2003, 47–53) also includes a middle class in his analysis. As it gains income "limited democracy" becomes more likely, a finding we share. However, the specific effects of the middle class's income on overall inequality are not clearly spelled out, making it difficult to derive empirical predictions. In any case, Boix never departs from the assumption that all groups derive their income from the same source, or from his hypothesis linking low inequality to regime change.

In any case, the key issue is the relative plausibility of the threat from the poor compared to the impact of intra-elite competition over resources and political power. We argue that a three-group model incorporating a landed elite, an industrial/commercial bourgeoisie, and the masses is superior to a two-group elite/masses model. In terms of plausibility, the three-group model resembles Kuznets' classic model of inequality and development in introducing an urban bourgeoisie, which derives its income from capital, in potential opposition to the *ancien regime*, which derives its earnings primarily from land. Initially, the bourgeoisie are both individually and collectively poorer than landed elites, but as the industrial sector grows, they can become economically preeminent. Meanwhile, the bulk of the population comprise the poor masses, whose incomes from both agriculture and industry lie at near subsistence levels due to wage competition and the existence of a "reserve army" of rural labor (Lewis 1954).

Not every country has experienced this pattern of industrial development, but that hardly invalidates the heuristic value of a three-sector approach, which can apply to any economy with one economic sector dominated by an incumbent elite that is stagnating relative to a growing economic sector dominated by disenfranchised rising groups. For example, modern regimes based on natural resources, state-owned enterprises, or protected import–competing sectors may produce similar intra-elite conflict.

Regardless, scholarship on democratization – whether focusing on long-term (Collier 1999; Moore 1966; Rueschemeyer, Stephens, and Stephens 1992) or short-term processes (Haggard and Kaufman 1995, 2012; O'Donnell, Schmitter, and Whitehead 1986) – has rarely entertained the notion that regime change is driven mainly by battles between rich and poor, simply because the idea is strikingly implausible. Instead, has highlighted the theoretical and empirical relevance of intra-elite splits.

In our model the crucial division between elites is economic: groups differ based on their factor endowments, and do not share a set proportion of income relative to population. This allows us to distinguish between rising and established elites, who earn income from different sources, have different sizes in terms of shares of the national population, and who may have different shares of the national income.

We do not ignore the masses. As we explain later, their poor's decision whether or not to ally with the bourgeoisie against the autocratic elites can play a key role in determining the nature of the resulting regime. More importantly, starting with three instead of two social groups helps us concentrate the theoretical focus on intra-elite conflict. This approach is more descriptively plausible than a two-group model, as it allows us to consider a wider range of paths of economic development as well as a wider range of forms of inequality. It also, as we demonstrate later in this chapter and in the chapters that follow, provides a more accurate explanation for empirical patterns of regime change.

Assumption 3: Tax-Free Autocracy. The third assumption in redistributivist models that we question is that autocracies do not tax. As noted, the Meltzer-Richard model constrains elites to a particular type of fiscal system: tax rates are proportional to income, but government transfers come in the form of a uniform lump-sum payment. This means that the rich pay more than the poor, but since everyone receives the same amount in return the wealthy always incur losses from any positive tax rate and, therefore, always prefer a tax rate of zero.

This assumption is empirically implausible. As North and Weingast (1989), Tilly (1990), Olson (1993) and countless others have detailed, autocracies regularly predate on their citizens. It is far more plausible to assume that autocracies are fiscally predatory than to assume that they can commit to *not* being predatory by establishing a tax rate of zero.

The Meltzer-Richard framework is also problematic because it is not obvious why autocracies should be constrained to choose only whether or not to adopt a progressive tax system. Redistributivist models variously assume that autocrats can repress citizens, block unrest, and renege on promises to redistribute, so there is no reason why they cannot also consider various ways to manipulate the fiscal system to suit their own interests. Progressive taxation might be anathema to the rich, but regressive taxation would not be. Elites are Robin Hood's enemies; they employ the Sheriff of Nottingham to pursue Robin and his merry band, collecting taxes from the poor and middle class alike to fill their purses. Regressive taxation can expropriate wealth from anyone outside the incumbent autocratic clique.

Incumbent elites' threat to tax or expropriate the wealth of other members of society must be incorporated into models of regime change. Redistributivist models assume that the masses demand democracy because they want to redistribute the income of the wealthy. The masses might be dissatisfied with the existing economic order, but history suggests that revolts against autocracy are more likely to emerge out of anger at more specific oppressive impositions, such as seizures of property or onerous taxes. In short, it makes sense to assume that autocracies are predatory "grabbing hands" (Frye and Shleifer 1997; Gurr 1970; Moselle and Polak 2001; Shleifer and Vishny 2002) that impose regressive taxation, rather than assuming that they impose no taxes at all.

Assumption 4: Redistribution under Democracy. The redistributivist assumption that taxing and spending under democracy can be viewed as a straightforward transfer from rich to poor confronts both empirical and theoretical challenges. First, it is not obvious that democracies impose considerably higher overall tax burdens than autocracies (Mulligan, Gil, and Sala-i Martin 2004). Moreover, taxation under democracy may not be progressive; tax incidence may be neutral or even regressive (Kenworthy 2008).

In addition, on the spending side of the equation, many supposedly "public" goods that democracies provide – especially in new or poorer democracies – are actually targeted toward relatively wealthy citizens, not the median voter and below (Ross 2006). For example, in seeking to explain the sources of franchise extension, Lizzeri and Persico (2004), argue that urban bourgeois elites particularly benefit from public spending, relative to landed elites. Revenue spent on sanitation, infrastructure, education, and other public investments raise returns to industrial capital but are of little use, and indeed may be detrimental, to landowners' economic interests. Consequently, some elite groups may benefit from taxation and government spending but others may oppose it.

This insight supports our decision to model intra-elite conflict. If public spending is zero in an autocracy controlled by landed elites, rising urban elites may prefer to pay the costs of higher taxation under democracy in order to fund public goods that an autocratic regime would not provide.

Much of the regressive character of public spending under democracy is due to relatively wealthy groups' lobbying efforts to target spending toward themselves. Indeed, nowhere is social-welfare spending purely progressively redistributive. The benefits vary widely across social classes. However, the Meltzer-Richard framework cannot capture this diversity or its political roots.

Redistributive politics under democracy differs substantially from what the Meltzer-Richard model implies. Tax rates may not be particularly progressive, and public spending may not be purely redistributive. Instead, it may favor those with political connections and economic assets. To the extent that taxes and spending are regressive under autocracy, yet not particularly progressive under democracy, wealthy autocratic elites have much less to fear from regime change than redistributivist models suggest.

Assumption 5: Exogenous Power.　The final assumption we consider is Acemoglu and Robinson's approach to modeling elites' and masses' relative strength. Specifically, they model political opportunities as following the logic of a Markov chain: at each point in time, the poor either have organizational capacity or not – and such capacity may change in the next period, with an exogenously given probability.

This assumption suggests that the likelihood of victory by one group or another varies from one period to the next, *independently* of the balance of resources across groups. That is, it implies that the likelihood of regime change is *not* directly related to the level of societal inequality. This setup is crucial to the book's emphasis on the dynamic inconsistency of promises and threats and for the hypothesis that political institutions can solve credible commitment problems. However, it also implies that the level of inequality is paradoxically disconnected from the question of how political struggles are won and lost.[7]

---

[7] There is an indirect connection between inequality and the chance of prevailing, in that the wealthy can choose to spend some of their resources to repress the poor when they are in the

One might expect groups' chances of winning a political conflict to be a function of the relative balance of material resources. If this were true, the threat of mass revolt would lose credibility as inequality increased, simply because the wealthy would be much more likely to prevail. That is, as per Boix (2003), democracy would become less likely as inequality increased. Yet recall that Acemoglu and Robinson posited their inverted U shaped relationship between inequality and democracy not as a simple function of the relative balance of resources between groups, but as a function of the relative credibility of threats to rebel or repress. As noted, such threats are only indirectly related to the level of inequality; the exogenously determined organizational capacity of the poor in any given period is more important.

Assuming that group strength is determined exogenously deeply complicates how one models political conflict. We suggest that it is reasonable to assume that group strength is determined endogenously, and that a group's likelihood of prevailing in conflict is proportional to the resources it holds.[8] This approach allows changes in inequality to directly impact changes in groups' relative power.

4.4 AN ELITE-COMPETITION MODEL OF DEMOCRATIZATION

4.4.1 Introduction

This section formalizes our elite-competition model. We assume an economy with two economic sectors – land and industry – and three groups: a landholding autocratic elite, an industrial bourgeoisie, and the masses.[9] Both sectors can have varying levels of inequality, and both contribute to overall societal inequality.

We show that increases in landholding inequality tend to retard democratization but that increases in overall inequality, holding rural inequality

---

exogenously-given state where the poor can organize. If their incomes are relatively higher, they may be more willing to pay this cost.

[8] In this way, our approach borrows from Hirshleifer's well-known work on contest models (Fearon 2008; Hirshleifer 1995, 2001).

[9] We do not extend the model to include a fourth, working class, group. We argued in the previous chapter that in income terms such a group often resembled the bourgeoisie and hence their preferences are subsumed into that group's. An alternative approach would be to split the masses into "rural" and "urban" groups. In many developing countries where the rural population is large, urban wages are typically pushed downwards by the "reserve army" of agricultural labor, meaning that, in this case, the working classes could be thought of as subsumed into the masses. Given this, only in the case of a very sizable working class with wages substantially different from both the masses and the bourgeoisie is a four-group setup warranted. In this case, growing rural inequality retards the chance of an "urban alliance" of the working class and the bourgeoisie rebelling against autocracy, whereas growing intersectoral inequality increases it, along the lines of our main model.

constant, tend to increase the probability of regime change. This latter relationship emerges because overall inequality can increase either when the
bourgeoisie takes a growing share of income from industrial output (relative
to the masses) or when the industrial sector grows more rapidly than the agricultural sector. Either way, a newly enriched but disenfranchised bourgeoisie
increasingly chafes under autocratic taxation and decides to rebel, either on
its own, producing partial democracy, or jointly with the masses, producing
full democracy. As we shall see, rebellions are not necessary for regime transition. In our model democracy can emerge both from below or from above –
even the threat of rebellion may encourage the autocratic landed elite to grant
democracy.

4.4.2 The Economic Model

We begin by discussing our model's economic fundamentals: groups' relative
size and shares of land and industrial output; our measures of *land inequality*,
industrial inequality, and *intersectoral inequality*, the last reflecting the relative
sizes of the industrial and agricultural sectors, and the conditions under which
increases in any of these measures increase *overall inequality*.

Overall Structure of the Economy.   We begin by considering a country with
two sectors – land and industry – and three groups: the incumbent elite (E);
the rising elite, who we will term the bourgeoisie (B); and the masses (M). The
incumbent elite earn income from land, the bourgeoisie from industry, and
the masses from both, through wage labor. Under autocracy the landholding
elite hold power and have a share β of the population, while the combined
bourgeoisie and masses have a population share of $1 - \beta$. The bourgeoisie have
π of the population of those outside the incumbent elite and the masses have
$1 - \pi$. Thus, the population of each group is as follows: the elite have $\sigma_E = \beta$,
the bourgeoisie have $\sigma_B = (1 - \beta)\pi$ and the masses have $\sigma_M = (1 - \beta)(1 - \pi)$.

The Agricultural Sector.   The total amount of agricultural production is normalized to equal one and has constant returns to scale, meaning that returns
to land are directly proportional to landholdings. The elite as a group gain γ,
while the masses as a group gain $(1 - \gamma)$ in income from land. The bourgeoisie
have no land. The implication is simple: As γ rises for a fixed β, land inequality increases.[10] We assume that the population share of the elite β is constant,
allowing us to use γ as our baseline *land inequality* parameter.

---

[10] We might also interpret γ as reflecting the ability of the elite to contain rural wages such that
for a given inequality in the ratio of landholdings, a higher γ reflects rural wage repression
(Ardañaz and Mares 2012).

The Industrial Sector. Formally, the distinction between the agricultural and industrial sectors in our model is that the former has a fixed size, while the latter can vary in size, and potentially generates a larger and larger share of overall economic output. Thus, while we set the agricultural sector to have a total output of one, the size of the industrial sector is $k > 0$. Changes in k will alter overall inequality by changing what we refer to as *intersectoral* inequality.

We assume that income generated from the industrial sector is divided in the following manner: a share ϕ goes as return on capital to the bourgeoisie, and a share $1 - \phi$ goes as wages to the masses. We refer to ϕ as the *industrial inequality* parameter. Both total income to capital and total wages increase in the size of the industrial sector, but will bias toward the bourgeoisie provided that $\phi \geq \pi$; in other words, the share of industrial sector income accruing to the bourgeoisie is always at least as large as the bourgeoisie's population share. We assume throughout that this relationship does in fact hold: that is, industrial development disproportionately benefits the bourgeoisie vis-à-vis the masses. The autocratic landholding elite do not receive any direct returns from the industrial sector, although they may use the tools of government to redistribute some of these gains to themselves through taxation.

Individual Earnings. To establish individual earnings we simply take group income and divide by group population. The earnings for individuals belonging to the elite are simple, since they come only from their agricultural earnings, adjusted by the population size of the elite.

$$y_{Ei} = \frac{\gamma}{\sigma_E} = \frac{\gamma}{\beta} \tag{4.1}$$

The earnings from industry for each individual belonging to the bourgeoisie come from their earnings from industry ϕk, divided by their overall population share $\pi(1 - \beta)$:

$$y_{Bi} = \frac{\phi k}{\sigma_B} = \frac{\phi k}{\pi(1 - \beta)} \tag{4.2}$$

The earnings for individuals who are members of the masses come from both sectors, with $(1 - \gamma)$ from agriculture and $(1 - \phi)k$ from industry, divided by their share of population $(1 - \pi)(1 - \beta)$.

$$y_{Mi} = \frac{(1 - \gamma) + (1 - \phi)k}{\sigma_M} = \frac{(1 - \gamma) + (1 - \phi)k}{(1 - \pi)(1 - \beta)} \tag{4.3}$$

Economic Inequality. In their baseline models, Acemoglu and Robinson (2006) and Boix (2003) posit that inequality is the relative share of income pertaining to each group, adjusted for their relative population. In contrast, we posit three salient groups, and either of the two "elite" groups could have higher income than the other. Consequently, we must develop a different measure of overall societal inequality.

To measure *overall inequality*, which includes both rural and industrial inequality, we must develop inequality measures that reflect the aggregate distribution of both land and industrial income among the three groups and incorporate individual earnings. Our model employs an intuitive measure, used broadly in the literature: the ratio of mean to median income. Mean income is simple to define: since we set total population equal to one, mean income equals total income or $\bar{y} = 1 + k$. We assume that the masses comprise over fifty percent of the population and, hence, that median income equals the per capita income of the masses $y^{med} = y_{Mi}$.

The ratio $I = \bar{y}/y^{med}$ is our measure of inequality: as overall mean income rises for a given per capita income of the masses, inequality rises, as it does when the per capita income of the masses declines for a given overall mean income.

$$I = \frac{\bar{y}}{y^{med}} = \frac{(1 + k)(1 - \beta)(1 - \pi)}{(1 - \gamma) + (1 - \phi)k} \tag{4.4}$$

How is overall inequality affected by changes in land inequality γ, industrial inequality ϕ and the relative size of the industrial sector vis-à-vis the agricultural sector k?

$$I_\gamma = \frac{(1 + k)(1 - \beta)(1 - \pi)}{[(1 - \gamma) + (1 - \phi)k]^2} = \frac{I}{y^{med}} > 0 \tag{4.5}$$

$$I_\phi = k\frac{(1 + k)(1 - \beta)(1 - \pi)}{[(1 - \gamma) + (1 - \phi)k]^2} = \frac{kI}{y^{med}} > 0 \tag{4.6}$$

$$I_k = \frac{(1 - \beta)(1 - \pi)[(1 - \gamma) - (1 - \phi)]}{[(1 - \gamma) + (1 - \phi)k]^2} \gtrless 0 \tag{4.7}$$

As defined, increases in both rural and industrial inequality will increase overall inequality. This is to be expected. However, the effects on overall inequality of a growing industrial sector (relative to agriculture) can be positive or negative. To be precise, a growing industrial sector will increase overall inequality if $(1 - \phi) < (1 - \gamma)$, that is, if the share of income the masses obtain from industry is smaller than what they obtain from agriculture. Equivalently, a growing industrial sector will increase inequality when $\phi > \gamma$, that is, when the bourgeoisie earn a relatively larger share of industrial production relative to the masses than the share of proceeds from land earned by the incumbent elite relative to the masses.

Put simply, industrial growth increases overall income inequality when the distribution of gains from industry is more unequal than the distribution of income from agriculture. If this condition holds, a rise in k will increase overall inequality I. Accordingly, if we see pre-fiscal overall inequality I increase – holding constant rural inequality γ – then there has been an increase in either the relative size of the industrial sector k or in the degree to which the bourgeoisie control the returns from the industrial sector, ϕ.

The idea that differential growth rates across sectors can increase overall inequality is of considerable interest for thinking about the assumed relationship between industrial growth and inequality. In particular, it provides a reduced form account of Kuznets' hypothesis that the onset of industrialization can generate increased income inequality. This occurs due to the inherent constraints on inequality in subsistence agriculture. In countries where most people live in rural areas and produce just enough to sustain themselves and their families, there is little remaining surplus to be distributed unequally (see Clark 2008; Milanovic, Lindert, and Williamson 2007). Consequently, in societies dominated by agriculture, an upper bound exists on economic inequality.

The onset of industrialization alters this equilibrium by generating a vast new economic surplus, which can be (and typically was) distributed unequally. This can occur, for example, when the wages of the urban masses are held flat due to a "reserve army" of labor in rural areas (as in Lewis 1954). Once rural-urban migration slows, urban wages will rise with industrial growth. However, industrialization will still produce heightened inequality provided the bourgeoisie take in a disproportionate share of industrial earnings due to a large absolute gap between their incomes and urban workers' wages.[11]

More broadly, our model is generalizable to any economy in which the income of one elite group is relatively stagnant compared to the income of the other elite group. This might occur if the incumbent elite control fixed natural resources, such as oil, or control favoured but stagnating sectors such as state-owned enterprises or highly protected industries.

4.4.3 The Political Model

We now discuss how these three forms of inequality affect the probability of transitions from autocracy. We do so in two steps. First, we set out the implications of inequality for taxation and public spending in three different political regimes: autocracy, partial democracy, and full democracy. We then examine the determinants of political action by different groups, exploring transitions from autocracy to partial democracy and then transitions from autocracy to full democracy. In doing so, we discuss the incentives of the bourgeoisie and / or the masses to rebel, what determines whether rebellion will succeed, and the elite's incentives to grant democracy or to repress.

---

[11] Thus, our model is consistent with standard dual sector analyses of wage-setting and migration. See Harris and Todaro (1970) and Fields (1993, 2004). In the model this amounts to setting a fixed subsistence wage for the masses in the industrial sector: $\bar{w}_i = m(y_{Mi})$, where m reflects the markup on rural wages. We presume, following Harris and Todaro (1970), that the rate of rural-urban migration μ is increasing in the economic size of the industrial sector k. If m is fixed, this implies that industrial inequality ϕ is fully determined by k and that $\partial\phi/\partial k > 0$ for any concave migration function $\mu(k)$. Put simply, industrial inequality rises with development, through the migration channel. Our baseline model, as it stands, allows the masses to benefit somewhat in terms of individual income from a rising industrial sector: that is, it permits ϕ to vary non-deterministically with respect to k.

Taxes and Public Spending in Various Regimes.   To examine preferences for
different political regimes, we must stipulate the implications of each regime
for each group. Political regimes grant the right to tax and spend to different
groups. We assume that the nature of taxation and the use of tax revenue
differ dramatically across three political regimes, each controlled by a different
group: elites control autocracy, the bourgeoisie control partial democracy, and
the masses control full democracy.

Under autocracy, the elite set an expropriating tax rate of t_A on the income
of the other two groups and redistribute the revenue entirely to themselves.
Consequently, the tax system is fully regressive. t_A is bounded at some upper
value $\bar{t}_A$, whereafter the bourgeoisie and masses are able to evade taxes (as in
Boix 2003). Since the elite's utility increases with the tax rate, their optimal
choice is $t_A^* = \bar{t}_A$. This tax is constant across economic sectors, meaning that
the masses' earnings from land and industry are taxed at the same rate.

It is worth considering what t_A proxies for empirically. Autocratic elites
often engage in direct and regressively redistributive transfers of income from
relatively poorer citizens such as tithing, feudal dues, consumption taxes on
basic needs (e.g., salt taxes), and other forms of "tribute" (this was Polanyi's
(1944) original conception of a "redistributive" state, a far cry from the
Meltzer-Richard notion). Jared Diamond refers to this form of rule as "klep-
tocracy" (Diamond and Ordunio 1997). Other forms of regressive transfers
include compulsory work, conscription (Levi 1989), non-negotiable demands
for credit (North and Weingast 1989), poorly monitored tax-farming (Kiser
1994), and various forms of kickbacks and side payments for access to markets. Expropriation can also be indirect, through market-distorting policies
that privilege existing elites and harm rising elites or the masses – a clear
example is trade protectionism, which often benefited rural elites at the expense
of urban groups (Schonhardt-Bailey 2006).

Under partial or full democracy, the situation differs. In our baseline model,
we assume that in these systems taxation must be at least minimally progressive and that tax revenue is spent on universal public goods, g.[12] Since partial
and full democracies are controlled by different groups, they will likely choose
different tax rates: t_P and t_D, which fund different amounts of public goods.

In partial democracy, total taxes are $t_P \bar{y} = t_P(1+k)$, where $\bar{y}$ is total / average
income. Tax revenues are spent fully on g: consequently $t_P \bar{y} = g$. While all
individuals receive the same amount of each public good, different groups vary
in the benefits they receive from public goods. Each member of a group receives
$V_{Ji}(g)$ in benefit from the public good, where $V_{Ji}'(g) > 0$ and $V_{Ji}''(g) < 0$.[13] We
presume, following Lizzeri and Persico (2004), that the masses and bourgeoisie

---

[12] This means we are assuming the bourgeoisie do not engage in regressive taxation nor in rent-
  seeking from the elite. In other words, there is no "bourgeois dictatorship."
[13] All citizens benefit from public goods but do so with diminishing marginal returns.

value public goods at least as much as the landed elite: consequently, $V_{Mi}(g) = V_{Bi}(g) \geq V_{Ei}(g)$.[14]

We assume that under partial democracy the bourgeoisie control taxing and spending and will choose the tax rate that maximizes their utility:

$$\max_{t_P} U_{Bi}(t_P) = (1 - t_P)y_{Bi} + V_{Bi}(t_P\bar{y}) \tag{4.8}$$

This produces the following optimal tax choice for partial democracy of t_P^*:

$$V'_{Bi}(t_P^*\bar{y}) = \frac{y_{Bi}}{\bar{y}} \tag{4.9}$$

Similarly, we assume that under full democracy, the masses control taxes and spending and will choose the tax rate t_D^* that maximizes their utility according to:

$$V'_{Mi}(t_D^*\bar{y}) = \frac{y_{Mi}}{\bar{y}} \tag{4.10}$$

Since we have assumed that the bourgeoisie and the masses benefit equally from public spending, taxes will be higher in full democracy than in partial democracy since the masses have lower income than the bourgeoisie.[15] This implies we are not entirely abandoning the Meltzer-Richard model when comparing partial and full democracies. When the tax system is constrained to be minimally progressive, as in both of these regimes, then the poorer the median voter the higher the taxing and spending. However, core differences remain between political regimes – autocracy entails regressive redistribution in which the elite avoid taxation entirely, while taxation is progressive in both forms of democracy.

How do these preferred tax rates in different regimes vary in response to changes in land inequality, γ, industrial inequality, ϕ, and intersectoral inequality, k? Since the preferred tax rate of the elite under autocracy t_A^* is always $\bar{t}_A$ – that is, the elite face no "costs" of taxation and, thus, choose the highest feasible rate – their tax rate choice is constant and unaffected by changes in inequality.

However, the two democratic regimes produce tradeoffs for the group choosing tax rates since they must pay any taxes they impose. The bourgeoisie's preferred tax rate is increasing in rural inequality but decreasing in industrial and intersectoral inequality. The masses' preferred tax rate is also

---

[14] A simple way to write this is $V_{Mi}(g) = V_{Bi}(g) = bV_{Ei}(g)$, where $b \geq 1$. This implies for concave utility functions $V_{ji}(.)$ that $V'_{Mi}(g) = V'_{Bi}(g) \geq V'_{Ei}(g)$, that is, the marginal benefit of public goods is at least as high for the bourgeoisie and the masses as for the elite at any given level of provision. In Chapter 7, we alter these assumptions further to include the case where the bourgeoisie may benefit more than the masses from a given amount of spending by targeting public spending toward themselves through "club goods."

[15] To see this, note that V_{ji} is concave, so lower levels of V'_{ji} imply higher levels of spending and hence taxation.

increasing in rural inequality but, unlike the bourgeoisie, it is also increasing in industrial inequality. The impact of intersectoral inequality on the masses' preferred tax rate depends on the levels of industrial versus rural inequality; as stated earlier, if $(1 - \phi) < (1 - \gamma)$, then higher intersectoral inequality increases overall inequality and leads the masses to demand higher taxation under full democracy.

Given (1) how taxing and spending are structured in different regimes, (2) how which group holds power determines who sets the tax rate, and (3) how changes in different forms of inequality affect preferred tax rates, we can now describe each group's expected political behavior. We examine in turn regime transitions from (a) autocracy to partial democracy and (b) autocracy to full democracy.

Political Action (a): From Autocracy to Partial Democracy. We begin by considering a game played solely between the incumbent landed elite and the rising bourgeois elite. Figure 4.1 sets out the structure of the game. The incumbent elite make the first decision, whether to grant partial democracy (PD) and relinquish control of government to the bourgeoisie. Should the elite decide to retain control, the bourgeoisie then must choose whether to rebel and try and seize control themselves.

We model the struggle between the elite and bourgeoisie as a simple contest model, where the probability of bourgeois victory p_B is related to each group's relative income. We use the reduced form $p_B(y_B, y_E)$, which is increasing in its first term – the total income of the bourgeoisie – and decreasing in its second term – the total income of the elite. For fixed population shares, this is tantamount to assuming that as bourgeois individuals become wealthier vis-à-vis the members of the elite, their chances of prevailing and imposing partial democracy rise.

The probability of winning is not the only factor that the bourgeoisie must take into account should they rebel – they must also pay an individual cost of

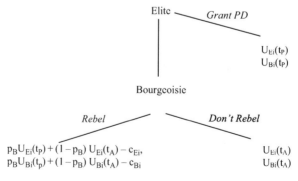

FIGURE 4.1. The Partial Democracy Game

fighting, c_{Bi}. Fighting is also costly for the elite who must pay (a potentially different) individual cost, c_{Ei}. We are implicitly assuming here that the cost for individual members of the masses, c_{Mi}, is too large to make rebellion by their group worthwhile ($c_{Mi} > y_{Mi}$). We alter this assumption in the next section. Still, it is worth analyzing briefly what the level of costs represents. There are two ways of interpreting costs: one is as an individual parameter representing the ease with which individuals in each group can devote time and resources to political rebellion. For the bourgeoisie, with incomes far above subsistence, it may be less individually costly to devote time to political activities than for members of the masses on the breadlines. The other interpretation is to view individual costs as per member representations of overall group costs for organizing. Groups that find collective action easier will have lower costs of organization both in total and per member.

We begin by examining the case where the elite have not granted partial democracy and hence the bourgeoisie have to choose whether to rebel. After examining that case, we can then move back up the game tree to examine the elite's choice to grant partial democracy peacefully or not, conditional on the bourgeoisie's choice should autocracy be maintained.

Bourgeois Rebellion. Taking the probability of winning and the cost of fighting into account, the bourgeoisie decide whether to rebel or not by comparing their expected utility of rebelling to that of not rebelling. The expected utility of rebelling is a weighted average of the bourgeoisie's utility under partial democracy, U_{Bi}^P, and their utility remaining under autocracy, U_{Bi}^A, with the weighting being the probability of victory, p_B, net of the cost of fighting. The expected utility of not rebelling is simply a continuation of autocracy, with a guaranteed utility of U_{Bi}^A. We can establish a "rebellion" function R_i that measures this tradeoff for individual members of the bourgeoisie: when $R_i > 0$ they will choose to rebel.

$$
\begin{aligned}
R_i &= p_B(U_{Bi}^P) + (1 - p_B)(U_{Bi}^A) - c_{Bi} - U_{Bi}^A \\
&= p_B(U_{Bi}^P - U_{Bi}^A) - c_{Bi}
\end{aligned}
\tag{4.11}
$$

Having discussed taxation and spending under each type of regime, we can establish the utility of members of the bourgeoisie under each regime type and then spell out the rebellion function fully:

$$
U_B^A i = (1 - t_A^*)y_{Bi} = \frac{(1 - t_A^*)\phi k}{\pi(1 - \beta)}
\tag{4.12}
$$

$$
U_{Bi}^P = (1 - t_P^*)y_{Bi} + V_{Bi}(t_P^* \bar{y}) = \frac{(1 - t_P^*)\phi k}{\pi(1 - \beta)} + V_{Bi}(t_P^*(1 + k))
\tag{4.13}
$$

$$
R_i = p_B\left(\frac{(t_A^* - t_P^*)\phi k}{\pi(1 - \beta)} + V_{Bi}(t_P^* \bar{y})\right) - c_{Bi}
\tag{4.14}
$$

We can now think about how changes in various forms of inequality change the bourgeoisie's incentives to rebel and, if victorious, install a partial democracy. We examine, in turn, the effects on R_i of changes in rural inequality, γ, industrial inequality, ϕ, and intersectoral inequality, k. The effects of each work through changing the probability of bourgeois victory (where $p_B = p_B(y_B, y_E)$ implies $\partial p_B / \partial \gamma < 0$, $\partial p_B / \partial \phi > 0$, and $\partial p_B / \partial k > 0$) and through changes in taxation and spending under different political regimes.

Effects of Land Inequality on the Bourgeoisie's Decision to Rebel

$$\frac{\partial R_i}{\partial \gamma} = \frac{\partial p_B}{\partial \gamma}\left(\frac{(t_A^* - t_P^*)\phi k}{\pi(1 - \beta)} + V_{Bi}(t_P^* \bar{y})\right) < 0 \qquad (4.15)$$

Increases in land inequality make revolt by the bourgeoisie less likely, because a richer landed elite decreases the likelihood of victory by the bourgeoisie. This means that the bourgeoisie will remain taxed by the landed elite under autocracy and not set their preferred tax rate under partial democracy.[16]

Effects of Industrial Inequality on the Bourgeoisie's Decision to Rebel

$$\frac{\partial R_i}{\partial \phi} = \frac{\partial p_B}{\partial \phi}\left(\frac{(t_A^* - t_P^*)\phi k}{\pi(1 - \beta)} + V_{Bi}(t_P^* \bar{y})\right) + p_B\left(\frac{k(t_A^* - t_P^*)}{\pi(1 - \beta)}\right) > 0 \qquad (4.16)$$

Higher industrial inequality, by contrast, makes rebellion more likely. This works through two mechanisms. First, a *probability* mechanism reverses the impact of land inequality. As industrial inequality rises the bourgeoisie grow wealthier, making them more likely to prevail in struggle with the landed elite.

Second, there is an *expropriation* effect, whereby higher industrial inequality means that the bourgeoisie's losses from expropriation by the incumbent (landed) elite increase with their incomes. This effect will be positive provided that the tax rate experienced by the bourgeoisie under autocracy is higher than that experienced under partial democracy ($t_A^* \geq t_P^*$), which we assume to be the case.[17]

---

[16] As $t_A^* > 0$ and the bourgeoisie choose t_P^* so that its benefits are no less than its costs ($V_{Bi}(t_P^* \bar{y}) \geq t_P^* Y_{Bi}$), the bourgeoisie are strictly better off under partial democracy than under autocracy.

[17] There are two other effects that cancel one another out. These both work through negative changes in the bourgeoisie's preferred tax rate, that is, through $\partial t_P^* / \partial \phi < 0$. On the one hand, higher inequality will be beneficial by reducing the direct costs of taxation to members of the bourgeoisie since it leads to a lower tax rate: $-(\partial t_P^* / \partial \phi) y_{Bi} > 0$. On the other hand, this means fewer valuable public goods will be provided $(\partial t_P^* / \partial \phi) \bar{y} V'_{Bi}(t_P^* \bar{y}) < 0$. We know that at the bourgeoisie's optimal tax choice $V'_{Bi}(t_P^* \bar{y}) = y_{Bi} / \bar{y}$; consequently, these two forces will cancel one another out. This is a demonstration of the well-known "envelope theorem" – since t_P^* is the bourgeoisie's optimal tax rate it already adjusts for changes in industrial inequality. This also applies in the analysis of the effect of intersectoral inequality k on t_P^*.

Effects of Intersectoral Inequality on the Bourgeoisie's Decision to Rebel

$$\frac{\partial R_i}{\partial k} = \frac{\partial p_B}{\partial k}\left(\frac{(t_A^* - t_P^*)\phi k}{\pi(1-\beta)} + V_{Bi}(t_P^*\bar{y})\right) + p_B\left(\frac{\phi(t_A^* - t_P^*)}{\pi(1-\beta)} + t_P^* V_{Bi}'(t_P^*\bar{y})\right) > 0$$

$$(4.17)$$

Finally, higher intersectoral inequality also makes bourgeois rebellion more likely. As with industrial inequality, this works through *probability* and *expropriation* effects, as well as through a *public goods* effect. This latter effect occurs because higher k means higher mean income and hence, for a given tax rate, greater provision of public goods that benefit the bourgeoisie. This effect is similar to that suggested by Lizzeri and Persico (2004), in that the benefits the bourgeoisie would obtain from public goods under partial democracy make them more likely to rebel.[18]

These findings produce the following proposition regarding the effects of different types of inequality on rebellion by the bourgeoisie.

Proposition 1 (Bourgeois Rebellion) *The impact of economic fundamentals on the bourgeoisie's likelihood of revolting and – with probability $p_B(y_{Bi}, y_{Ei})$ – prevailing and establishing a partial democracy are as follows:*

  (i) land inequality γ makes the bourgeois less likely to rebel.
  (ii) industrial inequality ϕ makes the bourgeoisie more likely to rebel.
  (iii) intersectoral inequality k (i.e., an industrial sector growing vis-à-vis the agricultural sector) makes the bourgeoisie more likely to rebel.

Granting Democracy. We noted above that the choice of the elite whether to grant partial democracy peacefully depends on whether the bourgeoisie would choose to rebel if autocracy is maintained. Clearly, if the bourgeoisie do not rebel, it is never in the interest of the elite to grant democracy.[19] However, if rebellion is likely then the autocratic elite need to compare the costs of maintaining the status quo and facing rebellion versus a peaceful transition to partial democracy. As with the bourgeoisie's decision to rebel, we can compare the elite's expected utility if they choose to grant partial democracy versus their expected utility if the bourgeoisie choose to rebel. The landed elite will choose to grant partial democracy if $G_i > 0$:

[18] Moreover, the effects of both industrial inequality and intersectoral inequality on rebellion are complementary (i.e., $\partial^2 R_i/\partial\phi\partial k > 0$) – a highly unequal process of industrialization is likely to produce the greatest chance of rebellion.

[19] That is, we do not need to compare the elite's expected utilities for granting or not granting partial democracy if the bourgeoisie choose not to rebel since in this case the elite will always decide to retain autocracy. Since all parameters are known to both the bourgeoisie and the autocratic elite, there is no uncertainty inherent in this choice.

$$G_i = U_{Ei}^P - p_B(U_{Ei}^P) - (1 - p_B)(U_{Ei}^A) + c_{Ei} \qquad (4.18)$$

$$= (1 - p_B)(U_{Ei}^P - U_{Ei}^A) + c_{Ei} \qquad (4.19)$$

As before, we need to know the derivation of U_{Ei}^A and U_{Ei}^P in order to write out this expression more fully:

$$U_{Ei}^A = y_{Ei} + t_A^* \frac{y_B + y_M}{\beta} = \frac{\gamma + t_A^*(1 - \gamma + k)}{\beta} \qquad (4.20)$$

$$U_{Ei}^P = (1 - t_P^*)y_{Ei} + V_{Ei}(t_P^* \bar{y}) = (1 - t_P^*)\frac{\gamma}{\beta} + V_{Ei}(t_P^* \bar{y}) \qquad (4.21)$$

We can, thus, write out G_i in full as:

$$G_i = (1 - p_B)\left((1 - t_P^*)\frac{\gamma}{\beta} + V_{Ei}(t_P^* \bar{y}) - \frac{\gamma + t_A^*(1 - \gamma + k)}{\beta}\right) + c_{Ei} \quad (4.22)$$

$$= (1 - p_B)\left(V_{Ei}(t_P^* \bar{y}) - \frac{t_P^* \gamma + t_A^*(1 - \gamma + k)}{\beta}\right) + c_{Ei} \qquad (4.23)$$

We now examine the effects of the three types of inequality on the incentives of the incumbent elite to grant partial democracy peacefully.

Effects of Land Inequality on Elite's Decision to Grant Partial Democracy

$$\frac{\partial G_i}{\partial \gamma} = -\frac{\partial p_B}{\partial \gamma}\left(V_{Ei}(t_P^* \bar{y}) - \frac{t_P^* \gamma + t_A^*(1 - \gamma + k)}{\beta}\right) - (1 - p_B)\left(\frac{t_P^* - t_A^*}{\beta}\right)$$

$$(4.24)$$

The first element of this expression is the *probability effect* and is negative – higher land inequality makes the incumbent elite more likely to prevail in struggle against the bourgeoisie. Since partial democracy means the elite have to pay taxes on their income at t_P^* and they lose the ability to tax the income of the bourgeoisie and masses at t_A^*, gaining only the value of the public goods $V_{Ei}(t_P^* \bar{y})$, the landed elite is much better off retaining autocracy.

There is a small positive effect (assuming $t_A^* - t_P^* > 0$) that comes from the fact that increased land inequality reduces the amount the autocratic elite can predate in terms of land from the masses and therefore has a negative effect on the benefits of expropriation under autocracy. However, presuming that this "positive" effect of land inequality is small (since, after all, the masses already own little land when land inequality is high), land inequality overall has the effect of reducing the probability that the landed elite will peacefully grant partial democracy.

Effects of Industrial Inequality on Elite's Decision to Grant Partial Democracy

$$\frac{\partial G_i}{\partial \phi} = -\frac{\partial p_B}{\partial \phi}\left(V_{Ei}(t_P^*\bar{y}) - \frac{t_P^*\gamma + t_A^*(1 - \gamma + k)}{\beta}\right)$$

$$+ (1 - p_B)\left(\frac{\partial t_P^*}{\partial \phi}(V'_{Ei}(t_P^*\bar{y})\bar{y} - y_{Ei})\right) \quad > 0 \tag{4.25}$$

In contrast, increased industrial inequality makes the incumbent autocratic elite more likely to grant partial democracy. The probability effect works in reverse to that for land inequality: increased industrial inequality makes the bourgeoisie more likely to prevail in a struggle and hence increases the benefits to the landed elite of granting partial democracy relative to fighting. A second *tax rate* effect follows from the fact that higher industrial inequality also reduces the bourgeoisie's preferred tax rate under partial democracy ($\partial t_P^*/\partial \phi < 0$). This means relatively lower taxes for the landed elite but also lower public goods provision, with the former effect outweighing the latter effect (because $V'_{Ei}(t_P^*\bar{y})\bar{y} - y_{Ei} < 0$).

Effects of Intersectoral Inequality on Elite's Decision to Grant Partial Democracy

$$\frac{\partial G_i}{\partial k} = -\frac{\partial p_B}{\partial k}\left(V_{Ei}(t_P^*\bar{y}) - \frac{t_P^*\gamma + t_A^*(1 - \gamma + k)}{\beta}\right)$$

$$+ (1 - p_B)\left(\frac{\partial t_P^*}{\partial k}(V'_{Ei}(t_P^*\bar{y})\bar{y} - y_{Ei}) + t_P^*V'_{Ei}(t_P^*\bar{y}) - \frac{t_A^*}{\beta}\right) \tag{4.26}$$

The effects for increased intersectoral inequality are similar to those for increased industrial inequality, albeit with two extra terms. The first is a further positive effect of intersectoral inequality on the benefits to granting partial democracy for the incumbent elite: this is the *public goods* effect $t_P^*V'_{Ei}(t_P^*\bar{y})$, whereby growth in the industrial sector produces higher average income that can be taxed to provide public goods. Even though the elite benefit less than the bourgeoisie from public goods, public goods still provide the elite with some positive utility.

The second term is negative and reflects *lost expropriation* – that is, higher industrial growth under autocracy generates more wealth for the incumbent elite, through expropriation. However, the elite lose the ability to predate on the bourgeoisie under partial democracy. These effects combine with the positive *probability* and *tax rate* effects from before. Accordingly, unless the lost expropriation effect is vast, greater intersectoral inequality makes the elite more likely to grant partial democracy. We can summarize these three results in the following proposition:

Proposition 2 (Granting Partial Democracy) *The impact of economic funda-mentals on the elite's likelihood of peacefully granting partial democracy are as follows:*

> (i) *land inequality γ makes the elite less likely to grant partial democracy, provided that the losses from expropriating the masses' land under autocracy does not outweigh the probability effect.*
> (ii) *industrial inequality ϕ makes the elite unconditionally more likely to grant partial democracy.*
> (iii) *intersectoral inequality k (i.e. an industrial sector growing vis-à-vis the agricultural sector) makes the elite more likely to grant partial democracy, provided that the probability effect, tax rate effect, and public goods effects collectively outweigh the lost expropriation effect.*

The extra qualifications in Proposition Two as compared to Proposition One make apparent that the conditions for satisfying the negative effect of land inequality and positive effect of intersectoral inequality are stricter for the elite granting partial democracy than they are for the bourgeoisie choosing to rebel and, if victorious, imposing partial democracy by force. That is, the effects of land and income inequality on the incentive of the bourgeoisie to rebel and impose partial democracy from below are stronger than those incentivizing the elites to relinquish control of the regime and grant partial democracy from above.

Table 4.1 summarizes the findings in this section about how various types of inequality affect (a) the bourgeoisie's incentives to rebel, and (b) the elite's incentives to grant partial democracy peacefully, and putting these together, the likelihood of autocracy surviving versus partial democracy emerging.

Given these effects of inequality on the probability of rebellion, one might ask why the elite do not try to co-opt the bourgeoisie in order to forestall

TABLE 4.1. *Expected Effects of Different Forms of Inequality on Choices of Bourgeoisie and Elites*

	Bourgeoisie Rebel	Elite Grant Partial Democracy	Regime Effects
$\gamma \uparrow$	$\downarrow$	$\downarrow$	Autocracy $\uparrow\uparrow$ Partial Democracy $\downarrow\downarrow$
$\phi \uparrow$	$\uparrow$	$\uparrow$	Autocracy $\downarrow\downarrow$ Partial Democracy $\uparrow\uparrow$
$k \uparrow$	$\uparrow$	$\uparrow\downarrow$	Autocracy $\downarrow\downarrow$ Partial Democracy $\uparrow$

rebellion when income inequality is rising or land inequality is falling. To do so, they would presumably need to "buy off" the bourgeoisie while still retaining control of the autocracy themselves (providing a numerically larger bourgeoisie with control of political decision-making would simply mean partial democratization). Even if promises by the bourgeoisie not to rebel once having received such a payoff were credible, we argue that the attractiveness of co-optation as a strategy is declining in rising income inequality for precisely the same reasons argued above. The size of the payoff necessary to make the bourgeoisie indifferent between rebellion and being co-opted (that is, the least costly payoff) would be rising in the attractiveness of rebellion for the bourgeoisie. Hence since rising income inequality or falling land inequality make rebellion more attractive they also increase the size of this payoff. What the elite gain in forestalled rebellion they lose in paying off the bourgeoisie. Hence there is an "infernal logic" to changes in inequality – because material resources convert into potential political power, they cannot be simply bought off. A powerful bourgeoisie can command such a price that for the elite, relinquishing control over policymaking might actually be preferable.

Political Action (b): From Autocracy to Full Democracy. Under what conditions might we see a transition from autocracy to full rather than partial democracy? Earlier we argued that in many cases the costs of rebellion to members of the masses c_{Mi} might be too high to bear, leaving only the bourgeoisie with incomes high enough to risk the costs of rebellion. This provided a simple case to analyze, in which only the bourgeoisie have an interest in rebelling and only partial democracy could emerge as an alternative to autocracy. If, however, the cost of rebelling is low enough for members of the masses, or if the costs of rebelling are lower when both the bourgeoisie and masses rebel, then a more complicated picture emerges.

Figure 4.2 demonstrates the range of possibilities: the masses can decide to rebel on their own should the bourgeoisie refrain from rebelling, and they can decide to join the bourgeoisie, should the latter choose to rebel.[20] That is, transitions from autocracy to full democracy occur in our model after either a successful joint rebellion by the bourgeoisie and the masses or a successful solo rebellion by the masses. In either case, the resulting regime provides the masses, a numerical majority, with the right to set their preferred tax rate t_D^*.

A joint bourgeois-mass rebellion has greater probability of success than a solo bourgeois rebellion, which in turn is more likely to succeed than a solo mass rebellion: hence, we assume $p_J > p_B > p_M$. Since the probability of

---

[20] To simplify matters, since we focus only on the choices of the bourgeoisie and the masses whether to rebel in this section, we give the elite the same choice as before – whether to grant partial democracy or to retain autocracy. We thus bypass the possibility of the elite deciding to grant full democracy.

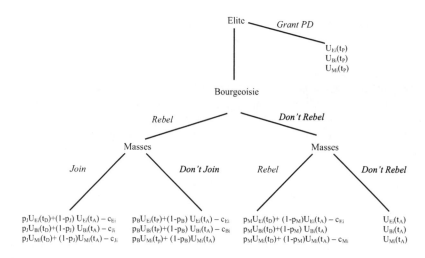

FIGURE 4.2. The Joint Democracy Game

joint rebellion succeeding is a function of the relative incomes of the two con-
flicting sides, in this case the autocratic elite versus the bourgeoisie and the
masses $(p_J = p_J(y_B + y_M, y_E))$, joint rebellion is most likely to succeed because,
although the masses are poor, they add some resources to the anti-regime
forces. Likewise, solo mass rebellion is least likely to succeed because the
bourgeoisie do not contribute to the rebellion's resources: $p_M = p_M(y_M, y_E)$.[21]

Of course, rebellion entails costs for all groups involved: the elite in every
case, and the masses and the bourgeoisie depending on whether they choose
to rebel. We assume that rebellion is least costly to members of bourgeoisie
and the masses when they rebel jointly. The individual cost of solo rebellion
for members of the bourgeoisie c_{Bi} is higher than for joint rebellion c_{Ji} but
is lower than the cost paid by individual member of the masses for solo rebellion c_{Mi} (this reflects the bourgeoisie's relatively greater organizational capacity
vis-á-vis the masses). Hence, $c_{Ji} < c_{Bi} < c_{Mi}$.

In our analysis of partial democratization, we assumed that the cost to individual members of the masses was too high to consider rebelling on their own:
$c_{Mi} > y_{Mi}$. However, it is worth examining both the case when this does not
hold and the case where of joint rebellion with the bourgeoisie. The gains to
regime change could be sufficiently large and costs sufficiently low, in which
case the masses might either rebel on their own or join the bourgeoisie in revolt.

The game tree in Figure 4.2 is more complex than that in Figure 4.1,
since to know whether the bourgeoisie wish to rebel, we need to know

---

[21] These relationships can be parameterized in a number of ways, including as direct ratios
of income, as ratios of individual income for fixed population shares, or as adjusted ratios
reflecting the greater organizational capacity of wealthier groups.

the strategy choices of the masses. In what follows we explore this question by asking how land, industrial and intersectoral inequality affect (a) the decisions of the masses to rebel or not should the bourgeoisie refrain from rebelling: $\{Rebel_M, \sim Rebel_M\}$, and (b) the decision of the masses whether to join a bourgeois rebellion $\{Join_M, \sim Join_M\}$. Once we have examined these effects we return to how land, income, and intersectoral inequality affect the decision of the bourgeoisie to rebel or not, given what they expect the masses to do.

Mass Rebellion. We begin by considering the masses' choice to rebel on their own should the bourgeoisie refrain from rebelling. We call R_{Mi} the individual expected benefit for a member of the masses from solo rebellion: $R_{Mi} = p_M(U_{Mi}^D - U_{Mi}^A) - c_{Mi}$, where the masses will rebel if $R_{Mi} > 0$. A few things are worth noting here: first, the cost of rebelling is higher than under joint rebellion (and indeed, higher than the bourgeoisie face if they choose to rebel). Second, incentives to rebel also depend on p_M – the probability of victory – which we know is lower than the probabilities of successful joint rebellion or of solo bourgeois rebellion. Finally, the choice to rebel or not will depend on the gap between the masses' utility under democracy, U_{Mi}^D, and under autocracy, U_{Mi}^A. Given the higher costs of rebelling and the lower likelihood of success, these benefits need to be fairly large for the masses to rebel on their own. Nonetheless, it is worth considering how changes in land, income, and intersectoral inequality affect those incentives.

The effects of rural inequality on the masses' incentives to engage in solo rebellion can be written as $\partial R_{Mi}/\partial \gamma = (\partial p_M/\partial \gamma)(U_{Mi}^D - U_{Mi}^A) - p_M/\sigma_M(t_A^* - t_D^*)$. This effect is negative unless the taxes under autocracy are far lower than under democracy, which is highly improbable. This negative effect comes from a *probability effect* due to a richer elite and poorer masses and a reduced *expropriation effect*.

The effect of industrial inequality is also negative and can be written as $\partial R_{Mi}/\partial \gamma = (\partial p_M/\partial \phi)(U_{Mi}^D - U_{Mi}^A) - p_M k/\sigma_M(t_A^* - t_D^*)$. This time the negative probability effect comes from the masses earning less from industry.

Finally, the effect of increased intersectoral inequality on the masses' incentive to engage in solo rebellion is positive: $\partial R_{Mi}/\partial k = (\partial p_M/\partial k)(U_{Mi}^D - U_{Mi}^A) + p_M((1-\phi)/\sigma_M(t_A^* - t_D^*) + t_D^* V_{Mi}'(t_D^* \bar{y}))$. Here a growing industrial sector vis-à-vis the agricultural sector makes the masses richer and, thus, more likely to prevail in struggle (a positive probability effect), makes them more threatened by expropriation under autocracy, and also provides a larger tax base for public goods provision under democracy.

Pulling this together, land inequality retards transitions to full democracy. However, industrial and intersectoral inequality push in different directions: Where income inequality is rising because the industrial sector is growing vis-à-vis agriculture, a mass-led rebellion becomes more likely. But where it is increasing because the bourgeoisie are taking a larger share of industrial production, mass rebellion becomes less likely.

Joint Rebellion.   We now turn to the other branch of the game tree, where the bourgeoisie rebel and the masses have to choose whether to join them or not. In this case, we examine the function $J_{Mi} = p_J[U_{Mi}^D - U_{Mi}^A] - p_B[U_{Mi}^P - U_{Mi}^A] - c_{Ji}$ – that is, the masses are choosing whether to join the bourgeoisie and attain full democracy with probability p_J while paying cost c_{Ji}, or opting out and receiving partial democracy with probability $p_B < p_J$ but paying no cost.

$$
\begin{aligned}
\frac{\partial J_{Mi}}{\partial \gamma} =& \frac{\partial p_J}{\partial \gamma}(U_{Mi}^D - U_{Mi}^A) - \frac{\partial p_B}{\partial \gamma}(U_{Mi}^P - U_{Mi}^A) \\
& - \left(\frac{p_J}{\sigma_M}(t_A^* - t_D^*) - \frac{p_B}{\sigma_M}(t_A^* - t_P^*)\right) < 0
\end{aligned}
\tag{4.27}
$$

The effects of different forms of inequality on the masses' choice to join the bourgeoisie are more complex than the choice over solo rebellion. First, land inequality continues to have a negative effect, because it makes the masses less helpful in winning a rebellion (the probability effect) and reduces the relative benefits of rebellion in terms of avoiding autocratic expropriation.[22]

$$
\begin{aligned}
\frac{\partial J_{Mi}}{\partial \phi} =& -\frac{\partial p_B}{\partial \phi}(U_{Mi}^P - U_{Mi}^A) - k\left(\frac{p_J}{\sigma_M}(t_A^* - t_D^*) - \frac{p_B}{\sigma_M}(t_A^* - t_P^*)\right) \\
& + p_B\left(\frac{\partial t_P^*}{\partial \phi}(y_{Mi} - \bar{y}V_{Mi}'(t_P^*\bar{y}))\right)
\end{aligned}
\tag{4.28}
$$

However, both industrial and intersectoral inequality have more ambiguous effects. Industrial inequality has no effect on the probability of joint rebellion succeeding (since making the bourgeoisie richer necessarily makes the masses poorer). However, it does make bourgeois solo rebellion more likely, raising the potential benefits to the masses of opting out and letting the bourgeoisie rebel on their own. When industrial inequality is higher the masses also face relatively low losses from expropriation, making joint rebellion additionally unattractive due to its costs.[23] Yet on the other hand, industrial inequality may also make joining a rebellion more attractive because the bourgeoisie set taxes in partial democracy at a level lower than what the masses prefer, providing

----

[22] Because the negative probability effect of land inequality on joint rebellion is greater than that on bourgeois rebellion, the second term is smaller than the first. The third term will also be negative, and hence $\partial J_{Mi}/\partial \gamma < 0$, if $\frac{p_J}{p_B} > \frac{t_A^* - t_P^*}{t_A^* - t_D^*}$.

[23] As with the case of rural inequality, the expropriation effect is negative if $\frac{p_J}{p_B} > \frac{t_A^* - t_P^*}{t_A^* - t_D^*}$.

lower public goods than what the latter want. Thus, rising industrial inequality has ambiguous effects on whether the masses will join a bourgeois rebellion.

$$
\begin{aligned}
\frac{\partial J_{Mi}}{\partial k} &= \frac{\partial p_J}{\partial k}(U_{Mi}^D - U_{Mi}^A) - \frac{\partial p_B}{\partial k}(U_{Mi}^P - U_{Mi}^A) \\
&+ \left(\frac{p_J}{\sigma_M}(t_A^* - t_D^*) - \frac{p_B}{\sigma_M}(t_A^* - t_P^*) \right) \\
&+ p_J t_D^* V'(t_D^* \bar{y}) - p_B t_P^* V'(t_P^* \bar{y}) + p_B \left(\frac{\partial t_P^*}{\partial k}(y_{Mi} - \bar{y} V_{Mi}'(t_P^* \bar{y})) \right)
\end{aligned}
$$

$$(4.29)$$

Finally, rising intersectoral inequality tends to encourage the masses to join a bourgeoisie revolt rather than opt out. The probability effects are positive since growing intersectoral inequality has a larger effect on the probability of joint victory than bourgeois victory. The expropriation effects are also positive, provided $\frac{p_J}{p_B} > \frac{t_A^* - t_P^*}{t_A^* - t_D^*}$, and the effects on public goods provision will be positive, provided $p_J t_D^* V'(t_D^* \bar{y}) > p_B t_P^* V'(t_P^* \bar{y})$. These latter effects come from the masses being able to take advantage of the larger tax base provided by a growing industrial sector in order to implement their preferred tax rate. Overall, when the bourgeois chose to rebel, land inequality lowers but intersectoral inequality increases the likelihood that the masses will join. Meanwhile, industrial inequality has an ambiguous effect.

Reconsidering the Bourgeoisie's Incentives to Rebel.

Reconsidering the Bourgeoisie's Incentives to Rebel. Returning to Figure 4.2, we can use these results to think about the bourgeoisie's decision whether to rebel in the first place. First, we know that rural inequality makes both solo mass and joint mass-bourgeois rebellion less likely. That being the case, the bourgeoisie know that if they rebel they will be on their own and if they refrain from rebelling autocracy is maintained. Since land inequality also makes partial democratization less likely, the effects of land inequality are similar no matter the situation, reducing the likelihood of a regime transition to either partial or full democracy.

Since rising industrial inequality makes the masses unlikely to rebel on their own, it increases the likelihood that, if the bourgeoisie choose not to rebel, they will be stuck with autocracy. Yet, if the bourgeoisie do rebel, rising industrial inequality has ambiguous effects on whether the masses will join. If the masses do not join, we return to the partial democratization case, where rising industrial inequality makes partial democracy more attractive to the bourgeoisie vis-à-vis autocracy. But what if, because of low costs or high probability of victory, it is in the masses' interest to join a bourgeois rebellion and institute full democracy? In this case, the bourgeoisie will need to compare the expected utility from joint rebellion to that of autocracy: $R_{Ji} = p_J(U_{Bi}^D - U_{Bi}^A) - c_{Ji}$. Compared to the bourgeoisie's expected utility of rebelling alone, there is a higher probability of winning and lower costs of rebelling, but the bourgeoisie must agree to be taxed by the masses under democracy. How do changes in industrial inequality affect this calculus?

$$\frac{\partial R_{Ji}}{\partial \phi} = p_J\left((t_A^* - t_D^*)k - \frac{\partial t_D^*}{\partial \phi}(y_{Bi} - \bar{y}V'_{Bi}(t_D^*\bar{y}))\right) \tag{4.30}$$

On the one hand, rising industrial inequality increases the bourgeoisie's income at risk of expropriation under autocracy, intensifying their demand for some type of regime change. Yet it also increases the masses' preferred level of taxation under full democracy (i.e., $\partial t_D^*/\partial \phi > 0$). While the bourgeoisie benefit from increased public goods provision under full democracy, this would not make up for their losses due to higher taxes. Thus, full democracy is a double-edged sword for the bourgeoisie if industrial inequality is rising, and it is clearly less preferable to them than partial democracy.

Putting this together, rising industrial inequality makes partial democracy more attractive to the bourgeoisie, but not full democracy. For the masses, rising industrial inequality makes solo rebellion less attractive, cutting off one path to full democracy, and it has ambiguous effects on whether the masses and the bourgeoisie are engage in joint rebellion, the other path to full democracy. This means that overall, rising industrial inequality should be positively associated with partial democratization but have weaker effects on full democratization.

Finally, let us turn to intersectoral inequality. We saw above that rising intersectoral inequality makes it more likely that the masses will revolt on their own and that they will join a bourgeois rebellion: that is, the masses are more likely to choose {*Join, Rebel*}. In terms of the bourgeoisie, rising intersectoral inequality makes partial democratization more likely if the masses do not participate. But if the masses revolt on their own and are likely to succeed, then they are also likely to join any bourgeois rebellion. Thus, the bourgeoisie know that full democracy is equally likely, either way. In this case, the choice of the bourgeoisie is not hugely important; rising intersectoral inequality produces a greater likelihood of full democratization. However, if the costs to the masses of solo rebellion are too high and their probability of victory too low, but joint rebellion is possible,[24] then the bourgeoisie must again compare the expected utility from joint rebellion to autocracy. That is, they must decide whether to rebel and accept the masses joining them or to not rebel, in order to prevent full democracy. How does increased intersectoral inequality effect this decision?

$$\begin{aligned}\frac{\partial R_{Ji}}{\partial k} =& \frac{\partial p_J}{\partial k}\left((t_A^* - t_D^*)y_{Bi} + V_{Bi}(t_D^*\bar{y})\right) \\ &+ p_J\left((t_A^* - t_D^*)\phi + t_D^*V'_{Bi}(t_D^*\bar{y}) - \frac{\partial t_D^*}{\partial k}(y_{Bi} - \bar{y}V'_{Bi}(t_D^*\bar{y}))\right)\end{aligned} \tag{4.31}$$

[24] That is if increased intersectoral inequality pushes J_{Mi} but not R_{Mi} above zero.

Growing intersectoral inequality makes joint rebellion more likely to succeed, increases the cost of autocratic expropriation, and provides a larger tax base for the potential provision of public goods. However, it also has a negative effect in that it raises taxes under democracy to a level higher than would be optimal for the bourgeoisie.[25] Unless the effect of inequality on democratic taxation is very high or autocratic expropriation is relatively low compared to democratic taxation, rising intersectoral inequality will still make the bourgeoisie more inclined to engage in joint rebellion. However, this is less attractive to them than solo rebellion and partial democracy.

Summarizing Inequality and Full Democratization. Table 4.2 sums up our expectations, showing the expected qualitative effects of the three types of inequality on the choices open to the masses and the bourgeoisie, and the implied impact on the probability of various regime transitions occurring.[26] Rising land inequality retards full democratization just as it did partial democratization. Industrial inequality generates incentives for the bourgeoisie to rebel, but reduces the attractiveness of rebellion (whether solo or joint) for the masses. Given this, it should have a strong positive impact on partial democratization, but a weaker impact on full democratization. By contrast, intersectoral inequality raises the potential gains of rebellion for the masses but weakens the attractiveness of rebellion for the bourgeoisie if they cannot keep the masses from joining them. We, therefore, expect intersectoral inequality to

TABLE 4.2. *Expected Effects of Different Forms of Inequality on Choices of Bourgeoisie and Masses*

	Masses Rebel	Masses Join	Bourgeoisie Rebel	Regime Effects
$\gamma \uparrow$	$\downarrow$	$\downarrow$	$\downarrow$	Autocracy $\uparrow\uparrow$ Partial Democracy $\downarrow\downarrow$ Full Democracy $\downarrow\downarrow$
$\phi \uparrow$	$\downarrow$	$\uparrow\downarrow$	$\uparrow$	Autocracy $\downarrow\downarrow$ Partial Democracy $\uparrow\uparrow$ Full Democracy $\uparrow$
$k \uparrow$	$\uparrow$	$\uparrow\downarrow$	$\uparrow$	Autocracy $\downarrow\downarrow$ Partial Democracy $\uparrow$ Full Democracy $\uparrow\uparrow$

[25] That is, $y_{Bi}/\bar{y} > V'_{Bi}(T^*_D \bar{y})$ – the marginal cost of taxes under democracy is higher than the marginal benefit of public goods for the bourgeoisie.

[26] This table applies to only the situation where the costs to rebellion are low enough that the masses may choose either to rebel alone or jointly with the bourgeoisie.

increase the probability of partial democratization where the masses are weak and the probability of full democratization where they are strong.

4.5 CONCLUSION

Our model formalizes the ways structural economic conditions – not per capita income, but the relative distribution of assets and income – shape different actors' incentives. Specifically, we suggest that transitions from autocracy are more likely as what we call "industrial" or "intersectoral" inequality increase, and less likely as under high land inequality. These conditions are also more likely to lead to partial rather than full democracy.

Redistributivist models see conflict over regime change as occurring largely between the wealthy minority and the poor majority. In contrast, our approach suggests that the key political struggle occurs between relatively wealthy competing economic elites and that only under narrow conditions will the poor masses play a relevant role.

In addition, while redistributivist models conceive of inequality as the distribution of goods along a single dimension, we examine the distribution of resources both within and between two sectors – a stagnant agricultural sector and a rising industrial sector. Accordingly, whereas redistributivist arguments associate rising inequality either with a uniformly declining likelihood of democratization (Boix 2003) or with an inverse U effect on democratization in which transitions are most likely at intermediate levels (Acemoglu and Robinson 2006), we argue that the probability of regime change depends on which *type* of inequality one considers. For land inequality, higher values tend to retard regime change. Yet for inequality produced either within the industrial sector or by the industrial sector's relative growth (intersectoral inequality), higher inequality tends to *promote* democratization. As we saw, these effects are at their strongest in terms of predicting transitions to partial democratization but they still hold, albeit more weakly, for transitions from autocracy to full democracy.

Our model permits a clearer understanding of why democracy emerged in rapidly industrializing countries with rising income inequality. Its main hypotheses follow Moore's (1966) famous aphorism of "no bourgeoisie, no democracy," which in truth requires both a rising bourgeoisie and a waning landed elite. However, the logic of our model extends beyond early industrializers, as the heuristic can be applied to any economy with competing political elites – insiders and outsiders – who tend to derive their income from sectors with differential growth rates.

In any economy, outsider economic elites who lack political representation have good reason to fear the taxing and expropriative power of the state. Accordingly, this model can be extended to tensions within Communist states with emergent capitalist classes (such as contemporary China or Vietnam) or to authoritarian import-substituting states with a stagnating elite-dominated sector and repressed commercial classes (such as Argentina or Brazil in the 1970s, or contemporary Egypt). In the next chapter, we test our theoretical argument's empirical implications in cases of regime change from the 19th to the 21st century.

4.6 APPENDIX: THINKING ABOUT ASSET MOBILITY

Boix (2003) emphasizes the relative mobility of elite assets as a key parameter in determining the likelihood of regime change. He suggests that because some resources are highly specific and easy to tax, whereas others are mobile and can be sheltered from taxation, inequality of resources only explains part of the reason why the rich fear the poor. A highly unequal society may still be one in which the rich do not fear the poor if the former are able to hide their wealth. Accordingly, if the rich hold mobile assets, democracy is more likely even when inequality is high. This insight has been further developed by Freeman and Quinn (2010) and Ahlquist and Wibbels (2012).

Despite this apparent consensus in the field, asset specificity has ambiguous theoretical implications in our model of partial democratization. Assume that the bourgeoisie – but not the elite nor the masses – can shield $(1 - v)$ of their income from taxes (this simply implies that capital is harder to tax than land or labor). We now explore the effects of asset specificity (which is increasing in $v \in [0, 1]$) on regime change by examining its effects on the incentives of the bourgeoisie to rebel and impose partial democracy (denoted as R_v) and on the incentives of the elite to grant partial democracy peacefully.

For notational purposes, we use $\bar{y}_v = \bar{y} - (1 - v)y_B$ to denote total taxable income, where it is clear that $\partial \bar{y}_v / \partial v > 0$. Asset specificity enters the analysis in three ways: by altering the bourgeoisie's net income for any given tax rate; by altering the amount of total revenues that can be taxed (through $\bar{y}_v$), and finally by potentially altering the preferred tax rate of the elite under dictatorship and of the bourgeoisie under partial democracy (i.e., $t_A^* = t_A^*(v)$ and $t_P^* = t_P^*(v)$).[27] We assume, however, that asset specificity does not, affect p_B – the probability the bourgeoisie will prevail in rebellion – since the bourgeoisie can access *all* of their income when engaged in struggle.

$$R_v = p_B[y_{Bi}v[t_A^*(v) - t_P^*(v)] + V_{Bi}(t_P^*(v)\bar{y}_v)]$$

$$\frac{\partial R_v}{\partial v} = p_B\left[y_{Bi}[t_A^* - t_P^*(v)] + \frac{\partial t_A^*}{\partial v}vy_{Bi} - \frac{\partial t_P^*}{\partial v}\left(vy_{Bi} - V_{Bi}'(t_P^*\bar{y}_v)\bar{y}_v\right) + V_{Bi}'(t_P^*)y_{Bi}\right]$$

$$= p_B\left[y_{Bi}[t_A^* - t_P^*(v)] + \frac{\partial t_A^*}{\partial v}vy_{Bi} + V_{Bi}'(t_P^*)y_{Bi}\right] > 0$$

---

[27] Implicit differentiation of group utility functions shows that $\partial t_A^*/\partial v \geq 0$ and $\partial t_P^*/\partial v < 0$.

Contra Boix, the impact of asset specificity is unambiguously *positive* on the bourgeoisie's incentive to revolt and impose partial democracy. This arises for two reasons. First, the more specific the bourgeoisie's assets, the harder it is to evade expropriation under autocracy. If assets were more mobile, the autocratic elite might expropriate less to avoid creating incentives for the bourgeoisie to send its assets abroad. Second, the more specific the bourgeoisie's assets, the larger the overall tax base that can provide public goods under partial democracy, increasing the relative attractiveness of partial democracy.

This result contrasts with Boix's argument that asset specificity makes democracy less likely. Our prediction regarding the bourgeoisie's incentives diverges so sharply because our model allows autocracies to tax, which completely reverses the bourgeoisie's incentives under different levels of asset specificity. To the extent that under autocracy the bourgeoisie have assets that are more easily expropriated, they will demand democracy more vehemently.[28]

Initially, we noted that the overall effects of asset specificity are ambiguous. This becomes clear when we examine the expression for the effects of asset specificity on the elite's incentive to grant democracy peacefully, G_v.

$$G_v = (1 - p_B) \left[V_{Ei}(t_P^*(v)\bar{y}_v) - \frac{1}{\beta} [t_P^*(v)\gamma + t_A^*(v)(1 - \gamma + \phi v k + (1-\phi)k)] \right] + c_{Ei}$$

$$\frac{\partial G_v}{\partial v} = (1 - p_B) \left[V'_{Ei}(t_P^*(v)\bar{y}_v) \left(\frac{\partial t_P^*}{\partial v} \bar{y}_v + \frac{\partial \bar{y}_v}{\partial v} t_P^* \right) \right.$$
$$\left. - \frac{1}{\beta} \left(\frac{\partial t_P^*}{\partial v} \gamma + \frac{\partial t_A^*}{\partial v} (1 - \gamma + \phi v k + (1 - \phi)k) + t_A^* \phi k \right) \right] (t_P^*(v)\bar{y}_v) \gtrless 0$$

Asset specificity does have some positive effects on the elites' incentives to grant partial democracy, since it reduces the preferred tax rate of the bourgeoisie under partial democracy and hence lowers the level of likely redistribution (it also increases the tax base and hence public goods provision). However, asset specificity also works to reduce the elite's incentive to grant partial democracy, since it increases the attractiveness of expropriation under autocracy. Hence higher asset specificity could retard democratization through this channel.

In summary, where the literature expects asset specificity to have a negative effect on the probability of democratization, our findings suggest the reverse pattern may occur in many cases. Where the bourgeoisie are hard to tax, expropriation loses its value and intra-elite conflict may actually be minimized.

---

[28] Indeed, it is also the case that $\partial^2 R_i / \partial v \partial k > 0$ and $\partial^2 R_i / \partial v \partial \phi > 0$: in other words, the positive effects of higher income inequality on the incentive to rebel and impose partial democracy are *increasing* in asset specificity.

5

Assessing the Relationship between Inequality and Democratization

5.1 INTRODUCTION

This chapter tests our elite-competition argument connecting inequality to regime change. We find strong support for our conjecture that income inequality is positively, while land inequality is negatively, associated with transitions from autocracy. We develop these findings using two sources of data on income inequality – one covering 1820–1992 and another, with broader country-coverage, covering 1955–2004 – as well as a variety of measures of democracy. The countervailing effects of land and income inequality on regime transitions show up across historical periods and differing measures of democracy and inequality, and are robust to a range of estimation techniques and sensitivity tests.

This chapter is organized as follows. Section 5.2 briefly summarizes existing empirical research. Since our datasets have different country- and time-period coverage, Section 5.3 then operationalizes our independent and dependent variables and discusses estimation techniques. Section 5.4 contains our empirical tests, and Section 5.5 the conclusion.

5.2 QUANTITATIVE RESEARCH ON INEQUALITY AND REGIME CHANGE

An enormous literature has explored the relationship between per capita income, inequality and democracy. One might say that quantitative analysis began with Lipset, given his hypothesis that democratization was only likely where a sizable middle class had emerged. As Rueschemeyer, Stephens, and Stephens (1992) noted, this hypothesis is not precisely about the *level* of wealth, but about the *distributional consequences* of economic growth. Most quantitative research, however, has focused on the link between democracy and development per se, partly because of ambiguity in Lipset's argument and partly because no cross-national income inequality data existed until relatively recently.

Early efforts to examine the impact of inequality were, thus, hampered by fragmentary data.[1] All the while, scholars continued to explore the impact of growth per se. Przeworski et al. (2000) prominently suggested that no relationship existed between development and democratization – and also dismissed the idea that inequality and democratization were causally related. Their claim that regime change is exogenous to underlying social forces raised a number of methodological and theoretical questions, and sparked renewed interest in the debate.[2]

Boix's and Acemoglu and Robinson's books directed attention to the potential political impact of the distributional consequences of economic development.[3] We have already discussed the differences between these two books: the former argues that inequality has a uniformly negative effect on transitions to democracy, while the latter posits an inverse U shaped effect.

Although Acemoglu and Robinson did not empirically test their claims, Boix did conduct a series of statistical tests, exploring two datasets: one covering 1850–1980 and another 1950–1990. In both cases he measured democracy as a dummy variable, à la Przeworski et al. (2000).

In his research with Stokes (Boix and Stokes 2003), Boix implied that a different dynamic may have characterized the relationship between democracy and development prior to 1950. Przeworski et al. (2000) did not consider this question because their data only cover 1950–1990, which limits one's willingness to accept their sweeping generalizations about the impact of modernization. However, Boix (2003) did not include a direct measure of income inequality in his analysis of the 1850–1980 period. He included a standard measure of economic development – the log of per capita income, and a measure of *land* inequality, Vanhanen's "Family Farms" measure (Vanhanen 2000), which is operationalized as a country's "area of family farms as a percentage of the total area of holdings" (Boix 2003, 89). A family farm employs no more than four people, including family members, and the family owns and cultivates the land. Higher proportions equals lower land inequality.

Boix hypothesized that both per capita wealth and a higher proportion of family farms would be positively related to regime change. He confirmed the former, but discovered that the Family Farms variable had a small but *negative* effect on the probability of democratization (p. 91). Given his reliance only on a measure of the relative distribution of land as a measure of inequality in his

---

[1] See, e.g., Bollen and Jackman (1985, 1989, 1995) on one side of this debate, and Muller (1988, 1995a,b) on the other.

[2] See, e.g., Boix (2011); Epstein et al. (2006); Geddes (2007); Acemoglu, Johnson, Robinson, and Yared (2008, 2005).

[3] See also Ahlquist and Wibbels (2012); Dunning (2008a); Freeman and Quinn (2010); Herb (2005); Houle (2009a,b); Ziblatt (2008).

historical analysis, this result casts doubt on the redistributivist aspect of his argument.

Instead of a measure of income inequality, Boix included in his historical analysis an indicator of educational attainment, also from Vanhanen: the average of the percentage of literate adults and the number of students per 100,000 population. Boix suggested that a more educated population proxies for greater income *equality*, and found that it positively predicted democratic transitions. However, there is considerable theoretical ambiguity in this measure. First, educational attainment is highly correlated with GDP per capita (.85). More importantly increased educational attainment in an autocracy might reflect the emergence and aspirations of a rising middle class à la the Kuznets effect or as our theoretical model predicts, implying that it might be correlated with income *inequality*.[4]

Finally, Boix included a proxy for asset-specificity in his historical analysis, Vanhanen's index of Occupational Diversity, which is the average of the percentage of nonagricultural population and the percentage of urban population. He found this variable to be positively associated with democratization. However, this measure is also theoretically ambiguous. It might be correlated with asset-specificity to some degree, but mostly it measures urbanization – and not surprisingly, it is highly correlated with variables associated with economic development such education (.83) and GDP per capita (.85) – levels too high to include all three in the same regression, as Boix did.

For his analysis of the 1950–1990 period, Boix used an array of independent variables similar to Przeworski et al. (2000), adding a measure of income inequality drawn from Deininger and Squire (1996). He found that inequality was negatively correlated with democratic transitions.

We have two concerns here. The first is the fragmentary nature of Boix's data, which include a maximum of only 1,042 observations (Boix 2003, 79–81) – compare against the 4,404 cases in our Table 5.7, which covers a similar period – and only a limited number of countries – just over 50 in the 1980s and as few as 12 in the 1950s (p. 75). This suggests that representativeness – and thus bias – is a potential concern, since the income inequality dataset Boix relied upon contained proportionally far more observations from wealthy democracies than from less-wealthy democracies and autocracies, relative to their actual proportions in the universe of cases.

Our second concern with the analysis of the 1950–1990 period is the absence of a test for the impact of land inequality. Land and income inequality are not substitutes, for they are likely to have different political consequences. There is also no reason to assume that they are perfectly correlated. Indeed, our

---

[4] Controlling for country and year effects, education is positively related to inequality, lending support to our skepticism. The exact relationship between inequality and educational attainment remains unclear, and likely depends on the type of education spending and its targeted recipients (Ansell 2010).

two measures of income inequality (the BM and BAR indices – see later sections) are correlated with our measure of land inequality at 0.58 and 0.26, respectively. Accordingly, we do not know whether the effects of income inequality Boix discovers for the 1950–1990 period are robust to the inclusion of land inequality.

In the next section, we discuss operationalization of our own independent and dependent variables. Subsequently, we test our elite-competition argument, finding strong support.

5.3 DEPENDENT AND INDEPENDENT VARIABLES

5.3.1 Conceptualizing Democracy

Democracy is an inherently contested concept and devilishly difficult to measure. For some, political regimes can be thought of as lying on a continuum from "most autocratic" to "most democratic." For others, a country either is a democracy or not – the concept is binary. Methodological choices are important, because concept measurement decisions may shape the answers we derive about theoretical propositions.[5]

We see no gain to picking sides in this debate and opt to demonstrate the robustness of our argument to different measures. We employ two sources of data on regime types: Boix and Rosato's (2001) dichotomous indicator, and the 21-point Polity Index of regime type developed by Marshall, Jaggers, and Gurr (2003). The Boix and Rosato measure equals zero for autocracies and one for democracies, has global coverage, and extends from 1820 to 1999. To qualify as a democracy, the following conditions must be met:

(1) the legislature is elected in free multiparty elections; (2) the executive is directly or indirectly elected in popular elections and is responsible directly to voters or a legislature elected according to the first condition; (3) a majority of the population (more precisely, at least 50 percent of adult men) has the right to vote. (Boix 2003, 66)

An important question is whether this measure operationalizes "full" or "partial" democracy as in our model from Chapter 4. From our perspective as citizens of imperfect twenty-century democracies, setting the bar below universal suffrage implies that the definition includes both partial *and* full democracies. From our perspective as social scientists, however, the important question is whether this matters for assessing our argument.

Given that we assume that the masses have a population share of more than 50%, this measure likely includes at least some members of the poor. However, when only 50% of men possess the vote, a member of the bourgeoisie or middle classes would likely be the "median voter," and it is unlikely

---

[5] See, e.g., Collier and Levitsky (1997); Collier and Adcock (1999); Przeworski et al. (2000); Elkins (2000); Munck and Verkuilen (2002); Epstein et al. (2006); Treier and Jackman (2008); Coppedge (2012).

that the poor have sufficient numbers and resources to gain control of government. Still, as the franchise widens further, we would approach full democracy.

This presents two problems. First, a 50% threshold is arbitrary, meaning that some countries that have partly liberalized are nonetheless coded as autocracies in the dataset. This is not a question of whether one accepts or rejects the notion of coding regimes as "either/or," it is simply a question of where to draw the line between them. Second, it is possible that some transitions from autocracy pass directly from none to universal suffrage, skipping partial democracy entirely. In this case, income and land inequality might still have their predicted effects, albeit much weaker.

The first problem could occlude transitions from autocracy to partial democracy, inducing measurement error. Insofar as this only increases standard errors in our statistical tests, using the dichotomous measure simply sets the bar higher for confirming our argument. However, measurement error can also cause bias as well as inefficiency, if there exists correlation across mismeasured variables. This suggests exploring our hypotheses with other measures of democracy.

To do so we use the 21-point Polity index. Although scholars have criticized this measure, we follow countless existing studies (see, for example Acemoglu et al. 2008) and take it at face value. This presents several advantages. First, as we do in this chapter, it provides a quasi-continuous scale that mimics the "interval" concept of democracy and thereby allows testing of the effects of inequality on incremental changes across a continuum from "full autocracy" to "full democracy." Second, we can break the index into ranges of autocracy, partial democracy, and full democracy – or even into a series of twenty thresholds across which regimes might transition, permitting tests of the impact of inequality (or other variables) on transitions between various "states" of regime type, including partial democracy. The Polity score can also be broken down into its subcomponents, allowing us to explore whether structural variables impact one or more of these components. We explore the second and third of these possibilities in Chapter 6.

5.3.2 Conceptualizing Inequality

Inequality is also difficult to measure. The central issue is, to paraphrase Sen (1980), "Inequality of what?" What sorts of inequality drive political behavior? We acknowledge that any empirical analysis will necessarily employ imperfect proxy measures. Nevertheless, having problematic data is no excuse for not testing theoretical propositions; it simply demands self-consciousness about what the data can and cannot tell us.

In this respect, consider a key issue: the potential difference between pre- and post-fiscal income.[6] If governments engage in extensive progressive

---

[6] See Atkinson and Brandolini (2001); Gottschalk and Smeeding (1997); Kenworthy and Pontusson (2005); Milanovic (2000); Pontusson (2005).

redistribution, many individuals' income from labor (pre-fiscal income) will be significantly lower than their total income after the government has taxed and transferred (post-fiscal income). Most formal theories of political economy (including Meltzer & Richard and our own) depend on distinguishing between pre- and post-tax income, since individuals' political behavior is driven by the gap between the two. Unfortunately, no broad cross-national dataset on individual income fully controls for income transfers.[7]

Our concerns about the gap between pre- and post-tax income inequality are mitigated in two complementary ways. First, much government social spending (e.g., on pensions) is actually not redistributive in nature, from rich to poor, but involves intergenerational transfers. Second, even if all social spending were redistributive, before 1930 (even in Western Europe) social-welfare spending was very low. Accordingly, for early eras the problem of the pre-tax/post-tax gap is minimal. The same situation holds in less developed countries in general, even in the current era: their governments spend relatively little on the poor. In any case, we use data that attempted to adjust for this problem (Babones and Álvarez-Rivadulla 2007).

In terms of operationalizing the key terms from our formal models in Chapter 4, recall that we considered three forms of inequality: rural, industrial, and intersectoral inequality. We do not have distinct measures for the last two concepts, which means that we acknowledge that we cannot empirically identify a causal distinction between them. Fortunately, this is not a grave problem, as we predict that both push in the same direction. In all of our empirical analyses we proxy for the impact of industrial and intersectoral inequality with a single measure of income inequality. We are confident that a measure of income inequality captures both forces, and not other factors, by controlling for rural inequality. We also control for income per capita, which removes the growth aspect from intersectoral inequality.

We have two sources of data for income inequality. The first is Bourguignon and Morrisson's (2002) estimates of the income distribution in fifty countries taken at twenty-year intervals from 1820 to 1992. Bourguignon and Morrisson – henceforth BM – estimated the share of income taken by each decile of the income distribution; we constructed a Gini coefficient from these data for each country at each relevant time-point, using the standard formula. Following Boix (2003), we then interpolated the data to produce country–year estimates of income inequality.

To our knowledge, the BM data represent the only cross-national estimates of income inequality for the pre-1945 period. While they were published in economists' flagship journal and cited more than 800 times within ten years of publication, we recognize that they have shortcomings. First, the estimates are taken at only twenty-year intervals. Second, many country estimates are

---

[7] The Luxembourg Income Study, available at http://www.lisdatacenter.org/, comes closest, but country-coverage remains limited.

based on evidence from another neighboring country with similar industrial structure. For example, at certain points Ireland's data derive from Britain's; the Scandinavian countries share the same inequality data, and so on. Consequently, though measures exist for fifteen countries, the rest share data with at least one other country. This is likely to increase measurement error for at least some countries in the dataset. However, the effect of this in regression analysis should be to inflate the size of standard errors rather than to bias coefficients, on the assumption that, if countries sharing income distribution data experience different regime transitions, estimates should be imprecise.

The Gini coefficients derived from the BM data do correlate highly (.84) with Deininger and Squire's (1996) "high quality" estimates for more recent decades. Moreover, to demonstrate that our results hold up when a different source of data is used, we also employ Gini estimates from Babones and Álvarez-Rivadulla (2007) – henceforth BAR – which builds on the Deininger and Squire (1996) database and which covers 126 countries from 1955 to 2004. In this way, we are able to include income inequality in a long-term historical analysis and also in tests on a broader sample for more recent decades.

We also include a measure of *Rural Inequality*. This improves upon Vanhanen's *Family Farms* variable, which leaves open the possibility that, even in countries where families own most of the cultivable land, most of the rural population might not live on a "family farm." That is, Vanhanen's measure does not control for the relative density of the rural population, which may contain a high proportion of tenants, seasonal or migrant workers, or landless peasants. For any given level of Family Farms, higher rural population density will be positively associated with greater rural inequality, because proportionally more individuals will not own any land. To properly measure overall inequality of agricultural landholding, we adjust the Family Farms measure by the size of the rural population, calculating *Rural Inequality* as *(1-Family Farms)(1-Urbanization)*, where *Urbanization*, also taken from Vanhanen (2000), is the percentage of urban inhabitants. As Rural Inequality increases, we expect the probability of democratization to decline.

5.3.3 Control Variables

Since we have two different sources of income inequality data, we conduct two sets of analyses, relying on slightly different control variables. Two are common across our analyses. The first is a standard measure of economic development, the log of per capita income in 1990 U.S. dollars, from Maddison (1997). We use Maddison's figures from Bourguignon and Morrisson (2002) or Babones and Álvarez-Rivadulla (2007), depending on whether we are examining the historical or modern dataset. This variable tests the narrow but conventional version of Modernization Theory, that economic development paves the way toward democratization.

The second control variable used across our analyses is Vanhanen's measure of "Educational Attainment," as described above, which we call simply Education. Boix used this as a proxy for income equality, but we suggested that its theoretical status is ambiguous, as it might well be correlated with income inequality in a developing autocracy. To compare our results with Boix's, we therefore use this variable as a control rather than as a proxy for inequality.

In the analysis using the BAR data we also include additional controls, again following Boix (2003) and other recent research (e.g., Dunning 2008a; Houle 2009a,b). In particular, we include a set of variables commonly thought to retard democratization: being an oil exporter, having a Muslim majority population, and having experienced a civil war in the previous decade. We take these variables from Przeworski et al. (2000) and Boix (2003). Finally, in all our analyses, we employ a set of dummy variables for country, region, year, and Bourguignon-Morrisson "group," depending on the specification.

5.4 EMPIRICAL ANALYSIS

Our empirical analysis in this section proceeds in five steps. The first two test our hypotheses on the dichotomous measure of democracy, using the BM data and then the BAR data. The second two steps undertake the same analyses but use the continuous measure of democracy. Given the differences in dependent variables, we employ different statistical techniques in each section, to probe the robustness of our findings. The last step subjects our results to a battery of tests that account for the potential endogeneity of inequality with regard to regime type. We find strong evidence supporting our main theoretical contentions.

5.4.1 Democracy as a Dichotomous Measure, 1820 to 1992

As in Przeworski et al. (2000) and Boix (2003), when measuring democracy dichotomously we employ a dynamic probit model with robust standard errors. This works by interacting each independent variable with the lag of the dependent variable, producing different estimations for the effects of income inequality, land inequality, GDP per capita, and so forth, for countries that were (a) autocracies in the previous period and (b) democracies in the previous period. Since an autocracy is coded as zero, the interacted variable also equals zero if a country was an autocracy in the previous period. Consequently, to interpret the impact of an independent variable on the probability of a transition from autocracy to democracy one need only examine the *un*interacted independent variables. To simplify presentation, we omit the interactions since they pertain solely to democratic consolidation rather than transition – the core focus of this book.

Table 5.1 provides initial results. Model 1 is the simplest specification, including just two independent variables – BM Gini and GDP per capita – as

TABLE 5.1. *Democracy as a Dichotomous Variable, 1820–1992*

	(1)	(2)	(3)	(4)	(5)	(6)
Lagged Democracy	5.734***	5.734***	6.162***	6.162***	5.736***	5.736***
	(0.928)	(0.791)	(1.070)	(1.031)	(1.093)	(1.102)
BM Gini	1.665**	1.665	2.280***	2.280*	2.730***	2.730**
	(0.814)	(1.146)	(0.867)	(1.227)	(0.891)	(1.235)
GDP Per Capita	0.214***	0.214***	0.144***	0.144***	0.178***	0.178***
	(0.042)	(0.042)	(0.052)	(0.045)	(0.055)	(0.055)
Education			0.867*	0.867**	0.060	0.060
			(0.463)	(0.415)	(0.568)	(0.597)
Rural Inequality					−1.406***	−1.406***
					(0.346)	(0.386)
Constant	−49.395	−49.395	91.474	91.474	−15.046	−15.046
	(81.847)	(120.973)	(134.206)	(192.432)	(136.292)	(253.014)
Observations	5687	5687	4769	4769	4769	4769
Clustered SEs	N	Y	N	Y	N	Y

Standard errors in parentheses. * $p < 0.10$, ** $p < 0.05$, *** $p < 0.01$

well as a time trend to control for temporal dependence (not reported).[8] We start off this way to reveal that in this simplest model, income inequality and GDP per capita are both robustly and positively related to the probability of democratization. In Model 2, when we cluster standard errors by BM "region," income inequality loses statistical significance. However, once additional variables are added in Models 3 through 6, income inequality regains robustness – and its effect even increases substantially in magnitude.

These effects reflect the importance of including omitted variables, especially *Rural Inequality*. Note that when Education variable is added (in Models 3 and 4), both it and income inequality are significant. However, Education loses significance once Rural Inequality is added in (Models 5 and 6), suggesting the latter is relatively more robustly related to the difference between autocracy and democracy. Note as well that in Model 6, which clusters standard errors by BM region just as in Model 2, income inequality remains statistically significant, as does rural inequality – in the directions our argument predicts.

Table 5.2 displays the annual probability of a transition to democracy at varying levels of income and rural inequality, using the coefficient estimates from Model 6. The effects are substantial for both. For example, holding land inequality constant at .58 (the 41st percentile of all observations, that is, just under the median level), moving from an income inequality Gini of 0.30 (the 3rd percentile, very equal) to 0.55 (the 97th percentile, very unequal) would quintuple the probability of a democratic transition, from 0.93% to 4.65%.

These are per-period probabilities. To interpret an autocracy's expected lifespan at different levels of inequality we can calculate its "half-life," the number of years it would take for it to have had a 50% chance of collapsing.[9] At a per-period probability of transition of 0.93% an autocracy would

TABLE 5.2. *Predicted Yearly Probability of a Democratic Transition, 1820–1992*

Rural Ineq.	Income Inequality: BM Gini						
	.30 (3rd)	.35 (8th)	.40 (14th)	.45 (41st)	.50 (66th)	.55 (97th)	X
.21 (3rd)	3.36	4.44	5.82	7.57	9.74	12.37	3.68
.33 (8th)	2.26	3.03	4.06	5.39	7.08	9.20	4.07
.58 (41st)	0.93	1.29	1.80	2.49	3.42	4.65	5.00
.71 (66th)	0.57	0.81	1.15	1.62	2.28	3.16	5.54
.92 (97th)	0.26	0.37	0.54	0.79	1.15	1.65	6.35
X	12.92	12.00	10.77	9.58	8.47	7.50	

---

[8] The time trend is modeled as a variable for year and its square.

[9] This is calculated as $0.5 = (1 - p)^n$, where p is the per period probability and n is the number of years elapsed before a 50% cumulative probability of collapse, presuming all independent variables are fixed across those periods.

last 74 years before cumulatively there was a 50% chance of it having collapsed. Conversely, at a 4.65% per-period probability of transition, the same autocracy with higher income inequality would only last fifteen years before reaching the same cumulative probability. These results imply that even a small increase in income inequality might shorten an autocracy's expected lifespan. For example, holding land inequality constant, an increase in income inequality from .45 to .50 decreases an autocracy's half-life from 27.5 to just under twenty years.

The impact of land inequality is even more dramatic. Holding income inequality constant at 0.45 and moving from a highly equal (.21, the 3rd percentile) to a highly unequal distribution of land (.92, the 97th percentile) reduces the per-period probability of a democratic transition from 7.57% (an autocratic half-life of nine years) to 0.79% (a half-life of 87 years). Even a small move in rural inequality, from .58 to .71 (equivalent to a .45 to .50 shift on the Gini coefficient) increases this autocracy's half-life from 27 to 42 years.

As our argument predicts, the corner elements of Table 5.2 reveal that the probability of democratization is maximized under high income inequality and low rural inequality – generating a 12.37% per period probability of transition (a half-life of just five years) and minimized under low income inequality and high rural inequality, which produced a 0.26% per period probability (a half-life of 266 years). The table also illustrates that these two variables can cancel each other out: there is very little difference in predicted probability of a transition when rural and income inequality are both low or both high. Both variables clearly exert substantively important yet distinct effects on the chances of regime change.

Let us now turn to Table 5.3, which assesses the robustness of the findings in Table 5.1 by incorporating spatial and temporal controls. For example, if waves of democratization (Huntington 1991) are common, regardless of the level of land and/or income inequality, then some of their effects should be picked up by employing year dummies. Similarly, since the BM data often share estimates of income inequality within groups of countries, and since countries in these groups might share other characteristics that might also be associated with regime change, we include dummy variables for each of the 27 BM groups.[10]

Finally, countries may have idiosyncratic but omitted characteristics that affect their chances of democratization, recommending the use of country dummies ("fixed effects"). This last specification, however, poses problems for the dynamic probit technique used in Table 5.1, related to the "incidental parameters" problem (Greene 2004; Heckman 1987). Accordingly,

---

[10] Table 5.1 uses standard errors clustered by BM group, which reduces, but does not eliminate, the problem of bias induced by omitted group-specific variables.

TABLE 5.3. *Conditional Logit Specifications, 1820–1992*

	(1)	(2)	(3)	(4)	(5)	(6)
Lagged Democracy	8.138***	10.028***	7.819***	10.217***	8.130***	9.870***
	(1.391)	(1.573)	(1.563)	(1.896)	(1.780)	(2.410)
BM Gini	5.417**	5.692***	7.195***	7.817***	6.372*	4.343
	(2.106)	(2.119)	(2.494)	(2.851)	(3.258)	(4.591)
GDP Per Capita	0.385***	0.403***	0.429***	0.526***	0.471***	0.433**
	(0.103)	(0.121)	(0.117)	(0.159)	(0.118)	(0.196)
Rural Inequality	−3.055***	−2.718***	−3.277***	−2.647**	−2.947**	−1.476
	(0.942)	(1.034)	(1.001)	(1.101)	(1.242)	(1.566)
Education	0.317	0.673	−1.666	−0.975	−1.088	−1.950
	(1.345)	(1.467)	(1.499)	(1.747)	(1.545)	(2.427)
Constant	158.466	−7.122***	279.111	−9.103***	248.282	−1.472
	(194.241)	(2.126)	(265.802)	(2.585)	(275.251)	(3.474)
Observations	4769	4769	3881	3881	3652	3332
Year Dummies	N	Y	N	Y	N	Y
BM Region Dummies	N	N	Y	Y	N	N
Country Dummies	N	N	N	N	Y	Y

Standard errors in parentheses. * $p < 0.10$, ** $p < 0.05$, *** $p < 0.01$

in Table 5.3 we use a dynamic conditional logit model, which can both incorporate country dummies and is appropriate in the case of rare events.[11]

Model 1 in Table 5.3 corresponds to Model 5 of Table 5.1. The estimated effects for the main independent variables are all similar, though different in magnitude because this is a conditional logit rather than probit analysis. Model 2 adds 134 year dummies. Rather than weakening the effect of inequality, this actually increases the magnitude of the coefficients on income inequality, rural inequality, and GDP per capita, thereby increasing the robustness of these estimates.

Models 3 and 4 add dummies for BM region, using a time trend (Model 3) and year dummies (Model 4), respectively. The size of the estimated coefficients for income inequality and GDP per capita grow yet again, while those for rural inequality remain similar. However, we lose about 15% of our observations when we add the BM group dummies, as groups with no countries experiencing a transition to democracy drop out. This problem grows worse once country-dummies are added in Models 5 and 6, when we lose an additional 10% of our observations. Accordingly, the standard errors for the effects of income inequality grow dramatically and in Model 6 this variable loses significance. (Again, in this analysis all countries with no change in regime type drop out – a problem due to combining fixed effects models and binary estimation techniques. We address this issue below, when we explore linear models.)

The analyses conducted thus far reveal a powerful positive effect of income inequality on regime change, and a similarly powerful negative effect of rural inequality. The finding on income inequality, which is always positive and statistically significant in most models, stands in sharp contrast to Boix's (2003) expectations. But what of the hypothesis of Acemoglu and Robinson (2006) that an inverse U relationship exists between inequality and the probability of democratization? To test this notion, we include squared terms for both income and rural inequality.

Let us first compare estimated coefficients for the linear and quadratic models. Model 1 in Table 5.4 replicates of Model 6 from Table 5.1 and, like the other models in Table 5.4, incorporates a time trend and has standard errors clustered by BM group. Model 2 adds the squared terms for income inequality.[12] Model 3 replaces the squared term for income inequality with the squared term for rural inequality, while Model 4 adds squared terms for both types of inequality.

These models offer scant support for Acemoglu and Robinson's conjecture. The signs of the coefficients on income inequality and its square in Models 2 and 4 do correspond to their predictions, in that the linear term on income inequality is positive and the squared term is negative (implying an inverse U shape), but the coefficients do not reach conventional significance levels.

[11] This is sometimes referred to as the "gompit" model (Zellner and Lee 1965)).
[12] The model also includes its interaction with the lag of democracy, not shown.

TABLE 5.4. *Testing Functional Forms, 1820–1992: Democracy as a Dichotomous Variable*

	(1)	(2)	(3)	(4)
Lagged Democracy	5.736***	7.178*	6.098***	7.030*
	(1.102)	(3.856)	(1.128)	(3.871)
BM Gini	2.730**	17.843**	2.704**	16.607*
	(1.235)	(9.016)	(1.259)	(9.201)
GDP Per Capita	0.178***	0.190***	0.181***	0.192***
	(0.055)	(0.050)	(0.054)	(0.050)
Education	0.060	0.096	−0.011	0.030
	(0.597)	(0.534)	(0.598)	(0.542)
Rural Inequality	−1.406***	−1.179***	0.027	0.032
	(0.386)	(0.371)	(0.951)	(0.914)
BM Gini Squared		−17.211		−15.848
		(10.593)		(10.776)
Rural Inequality Sq.			−1.474*	−1.254
			(0.847)	(0.801)
Constant	−15.046	9.521	4.698	30.690
	(253.014)	(255.411)	(252.093)	(253.256)
Observations	4769	4769	4769	4769
AIC	742.526	743.735	745.265	746.778
BIC	820.164	834.313	835.843	850.296

Standard errors in parentheses. * $p < 0.10$, ** $p < 0.05$, *** $p < 0.01$

The squared term on Rural Inequality returns a borderline significant negative effect in Model 3, but the linear term loses robustness and switches sign, as it also does in Model 4.

The relative size of the coefficients on the two squared terms raises additional questions. Using the coefficients from Model 2, we find that the point at which the probability of democratization is maximized in the quadratic model – the "peak" of the inverted U – comes at a Gini of .52.[13] This does not jibe with A&R's hypothesis that democratization is most likely at "middling" levels of inequality, as 0.52 lies just below the 75th percentile for all autocracies. Even if the coefficients were significant, this would suggest that income inequality is positively related to democratization in at least 75% of all autocracies (the upward part of the inverted U), and only in the most-unequal

[13] This is accomplished by dividing the coefficient on the linear term by twice that of the quadratic term, and multiplying by minus one. This is simple calculus: if the form of the effects of inequality on democratization is quadratic, it can be stated as $Pr(Democracy) = \beta_0 + \beta_1 Gini - \beta_2 Gini^2$, ignoring the effects of other variables and the error term. The level of income inequality where the probability of democratization reaches its maximum is simply the point at which the first derivative of $Pr(Dem)$ with respect to $Gini$ equals zero. This is calculated as $Gini^* = \beta_1/2\beta_2$.

autocracies might the effects of inequality turn negative (the downward part of the inverted U).

Support for A&R's hypothesis is even weaker using Rural Inequality. The reversal of the sign on the linear coefficient immediately suggests that no such relationship exists. And, following the same procedure as above, we discover that in either Model 2 or 4 the probability of democratization is maximized in a quadratic model at a Rural Inequality value of essentially zero. This means that – as our argument predicts – Rural Inequality exerts a straightforwardly negative effect on democratization across its entire range.

Goodness of fit statistics also support our approach. We explore the Akaike and Bayesian Information Criteria (AIC and BIC), comparing the log-likelihood ratios of the relevant models, adjusting for the number of variables employed. (The latter is more sensitive to the addition of extra parameters.) Lower levels imply a better fit. For each model in Table 5.4, the linear estimation returns the lower value on both criteria.

Graphs further illustrate the strength of the linear model. Because the results show no inverse U relationship for Rural Inequality at all, we will show results for income inequality only. Figures 5.1 and 5.2 use estimates from Models 1 and 2 of Table 5.4, respectively. We use the simulation techniques developed by King, Tomz, and Wittenberg (2000) to estimate the predicted probability of democratization in a given year for autocracies with different levels of income inequality, holding other variables at their mean.

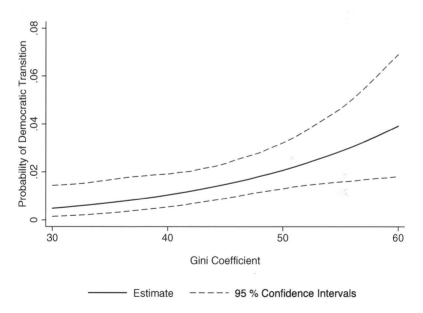

FIGURE 5.1. Linear Estimates of Probability of Democratic Transition 1820–1992 (BM Gini) Using Model 1 of Table 5.4

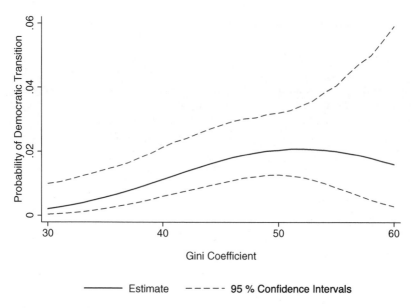

FIGURE 5.2. Quadratic Estimates of Probability of Democratic Transition 1820–1992 (BM Gini) Using Model 2 of Table 5.4

Figure 5.1 shows the predictions for the linear model. At a very low level of income inequality, the per-period predicted probability of regime change is less than 1%. This rises with income inequality, reaching almost 4%. Throughout the range of inequality the confidence interval is fairly tight, although it widens noticeably above a Gini of 0.55.

By comparison, Figure 5.2 shows the predictions for the quadratic model. Here we see A&R's inverse U hypothesis emerge. Yet as noted, the peak of the hump comes at a high level of inequality, and even at a Gini of 0.60 (the 99th percentile in the sample distribution) the predicted impact of income inequality is the same as at the median of 0.45. In other words, there is no evidence of a peak at "middling" levels of inequality, since the probability never really declines below its level at the actual "middling" level. What is more, from a Gini of 0.50 upwards, the confidence interval widens like the mouth of a funnel, suggesting that the chances of democratization are as likely to be rising as falling at high levels of inequality.

Our initial findings provide strong support for our hypotheses. Using a historical dataset spanning over 150 years and a dichotomous measure of democracy, we confirm our theoretical model's expectations that democratization is most likely under certain social-structural conditions – the combination of low land inequality and high income inequality. Both factors have substantively large effects on the per-period probability of democratization, and on the half-lives of autocracies.

5.4.2 Democracy as a Dichotomous Measure, 1955 to 1999

In this section, we continue to examine the determinants of regime change with a binary measure of democracy, but using estimates of the Gini coefficient developed by Babones and Álvarez-Rivadulla (2007) (BAR). Whereas the BM dataset contained information on 50 countries, the BAR dataset contains up to 126. With these data, we are also able to include additional controls, as discussed earlier. We find somewhat weaker evidence for the countervailing effects of income and land inequality, but this effect is limited to the Cold War period. Once the effects of the Cold War began to wane during the "Third Wave," the weight of international forces dissipated in relative terms, allowing endogenous factors to regain substantive importance.[14]

Since data for all our variables are not always available, we run a series of models. We begin Table 5.5 with an analog to Model 1 in Table 5.1, including only the BAR income inequality variable and GDP per capita. Once again, we obtain a positive estimate for the effect of income inequality, robust at the 5% level, on the probability of democratization. GDP per capita also has a positive effect.

Let us illustrate the marginal impact of income inequality on the probability of democratization from this model. Holding GDP per capita at its mean level for autocracies ($2,400 PPP), the per period probability more than triples from 1.1% at a low Gini of 0.25 (the 3rd percentile) to 3.7% at a high Gini of 0.62 (the 97th percentile). Moving from one standard deviation below the median to one standard deviation above it increases the per-period probability by 1.3%.[15]

Model 2 of Table 5.5 adds Rural Inequality and Education. Unlike our earlier analysis using the BM data, here we see no effect of Rural Inequality on the probability of a regime change. The magnitude of the impact of income inequality also declines while the standard errors on the estimate increase, making it robust at only the 10% level. Model 3 removes the Rural Inequality and Education variables and adds dummies for oil-exporting country, Muslim majority and recent civil wars, and measures of trade openness and (logged) population. Here, the income inequality variable increases somewhat in magnitude and is statistically significant at the 5% level again.

Finally, in Model 4 we add all the variables together and again find a positive coefficient estimate of income inequality, albeit at reduced levels of statistical significance. Rural inequality becomes significant at the 5% level once population and trade openness are controlled for. It is noteworthy that Model 4 has substantially fewer observations (reduced by 25%) and countries (reduced

---

[14] Our analysis ends in 1999 because that is when the time series for our dichotomous dependent variable ends.

[15] These results hold even in relatively wealthy autocracies. For example, in an autocracy with a per capita income of $5,300 (the 90th percentile), a two standard deviation increase in inequality increases the per-period probability of a regime transition by 1.7%.

TABLE 5.5. Democracy as a Dichotomous Variable, 1955–2004 (BAR Data)

	(1)	(2)	(3)	(4)	(5)	(6)
Lagged Democracy	3.384***	4.385***	5.176***	5.341***	6.464***	7.225
	(0.546)	(0.769)	(1.185)	(1.603)	(2.207)	(5.228)
BAR Gini	1.385**	1.306*	2.109**	1.746*	1.200	3.493***
	(0.647)	(0.719)	(0.897)	(0.947)	(1.285)	(1.237)
GDP per capita	0.048**	0.057**	0.056	0.046	0.169**	-0.097
	(0.020)	(0.028)	(0.035)	(0.045)	(0.079)	(0.096)
Rural Inequality		-0.100		-0.811**	-0.626	-2.010***
		(0.383)		(0.406)	(0.653)	(0.738)
Education		-0.026		-0.412	-0.439	-0.158
		(0.462)		(0.499)	(0.817)	(0.983)
Oil Exporter			-0.243	-0.194	-0.194	-3.688***
			(0.305)	(0.321)	(0.502)	(0.312)
Muslim Majority			-0.266	-0.258	-0.762*	-0.010
			(0.204)	(0.222)	(0.461)	(0.294)
Civil War within Decade			0.362**	0.385**	0.610**	0.022
			(0.173)	(0.176)	(0.248)	(0.290)
Openness			-0.001	0.000	0.004	-0.003
			(0.002)	(0.002)	(0.003)	(0.004)
Log Population			0.054	0.041	0.109	-0.048
			(0.056)	(0.064)	(0.076)	(0.110)
Constant	-2.649***	-2.837***	-25.195***	-14.616	36.923*	-77.574*
	(0.337)	(0.481)	(9.400)	(10.790)	(20.541)	(45.314)
Observations	4404	3828	3606	3157	1744	1391
Countries	126	124	122	101	90	100
Period	All	All	All	All	Pre 1980	Post 1980

Standard errors in parentheses. * $p < 0.10$, ** $p < 0.05$, *** $p < 0.01$

by 20%) compared to Model 1, due to data availability issues with the control variables. Of the remaining variables, only having had a recent civil war appears to make transition more likely.

These results are suggestive, but dividing the sample in Model 4 into two historical periods offers a crucial insight. Comparing Model 5 against Model 6 reveals that the weaker effects of income and land inequality are limited to the earlier part of this time period. After 1980, the predicted effects on our key variables reappear. As numerous scholars have suggested – most prominently perhaps Huntington (1991) – international factors tended to swamp factors related to endogenous democratization during the early part of the Cold War, as alliances with either the U.S. and/or the USSR strengthened dictatorships on both left and right. However, as the Soviet Union began to weaken and American foreign policy began shifting in the late 1970s – along with other important regional and global changes – the Third Wave of democratization began, after which domestic factors could again come to the fore. Any analysis limited to the Cold War period, as in Przeworski et al. (2000), is likely to be biased against finding effects of endogenous factors.

5.4.3 Democracy as a Continuous Measure, 1820 to 1992

To show that our argument holds regardless of the operational measure of the dependent variable, we now test for the impact of inequality using the Polity index, which requires using linear estimation techniques. We again begin with the BM data and then turn to the BAR data.

Table 5.6 examines both the within-country and pooled effects of income and rural inequality on the Polity index. Models 1 through 3 include country dummies and, therefore, only examine the effects of *within-country* changes in inequality on changes in the dependent variable. These models discard all cross-national variance on inequality, focusing solely on over-time differences within countries.

This is a fairly stringent estimation strategy, but has two advantages. First, including country dummies means that we are controlling for unobserved country-level idiosyncrasies that might make a country particularly likely (or not) to democratize, regardless of the country's level of inequality or per capita income. Moreover, if these idiosyncratic country "fixed effects" are correlated with the included independent variables but not included in the analysis, there may be bias in our estimates (Green, Kim, and Yoon 2001). Including fixed effects should reduce bias in our estimates.

Second, because including fixed effects means we are examining solely within-country changes, these models more closely correspond to the formal model in Chapter 4, which presumes that changes in inequality within countries increase or decrease the benefits to political action for various groups.

TABLE 5.6. *Examining the Polity Index, 1820–1992*

	Within (1)	Within (2)	Within (3)	Pooled (4)	Pooled (5)	Pooled (6)
Lag Polity 2	0.925***	0.924***		0.936***	0.916***	0.921***
	(0.006)	(0.006)		(0.008)	(0.009)	(0.006)
BM Gini	1.369*	0.105	11.828**	1.855**	2.874***	1.615**
	(0.798)	(0.892)	(5.654)	(0.744)	(1.108)	(0.782)
GDP Per Capita	−0.015	−0.026	0.217**	0.056***	0.001	−0.008
	(0.015)	(0.017)	(0.106)	(0.020)	(0.021)	(0.019)
Rural Inequality	−0.556**	−0.613**	−9.700***	−0.670**	−0.531	−0.522**
	(0.256)	(0.263)	(1.900)	(0.271)	(0.341)	(0.234)
Education	−0.883**	−0.733*	0.267	0.258	−0.766	−0.379
	(0.397)	(0.413)	(2.436)	(0.330)	(0.580)	(0.415)
Constant	253.864***	0.180	−0.040	110.298		
	(86.891)	(0.605)	(0.203)	(120.260)		
Observations	4797	4797	4761	4797	4797	4797
Countries	53	53	53	53	53	53
Time	Trend	Years	AR1	Trend+AR1	Trend+AR1	Years+AR1
Dummies	Country	Country	Country	None	BM Group	BM Group

Standard errors in parentheses. * $p < 0.10$, ** $p < 0.05$, *** $p < 0.01$

Model 1 also includes a time trend, and a lagged dependent variable. Here we find a positive estimated effect of income inequality on the Polity index, not quite significant at the 5% level, and a more robust negative estimated coefficient of rural inequality. In Model 2, which includes year dummies, income inequality loses statistical significance (although its sign remains positive) and the effect of rural inequality remains robust.

Model 3 provides a somewhat different specification, removing the lagged dependent variable – as recommended by Nickell (1981) – and instead employing an autoregressive error term of order one to capture time dependence. Here, we see a robust and much larger positive effect of income inequality and a similarly large and robust negative effect of rural inequality. In Model 1, for example, a *within*-country increase of 0.10 in the Gini index is associated with a long-run increase of 1.8 points in the Polity index.[16] An increase in rural inequality of 0.10 is associated with a decrease in the Polity score of 0.7 points in Model 1, and of one point in Model 3. An increase in rural inequality of 0.10 is associated with a decrease in the Polity score of 0.7 points in Model 1, and of one point in Model 3.

Models 4 through 6 are pooled models, which estimate effects of both within- and between-country differences in inequality by removing the country dummies. Model 4 contains no spatial dummies at all, while Models 5 and 6 add dummies for the BM groups. Models 4 and 5 include a time trend and an AR1 error term, while Model 6 replaces the time trend with year dummies. Broadly, we find results consistent with those obtained in Model 1, albeit with greater statistical robustness and somewhat larger magnitude. For example, the estimated long-run effect of a 0.10 increase in the BM Gini is almost three points on the Polity score in Model 4. Rural inequality is robust in Models 4 and 6 (though not in Model 5), with a coefficient very similar to that found in Model 1. These results strongly suggest that both within-country as well as cross-sectional variation in income and rural inequality make democracy more or less likely.

Using the BM data with the Polity index, we again find evidence that income and rural inequality have the effects our elite-competition model predicts.[17] It is worth noting that support for a positive effect of GDP per capita on the Polity Index is far less consistent than those for either income or land inequality. In Table 5.6, the effect is positive and robust in two models but negative and insignificant in three. This inconsistency echoes findings in Acemoglu, Johnson, Robinson, and Yared (2008). However, this result should not lead to the conclusion that "development" has no effect on regime change.

[16] The long-run effect is calculated by dividing the effect of the coefficient by $1 - \gamma$, where γ is the coefficient on the lagged dependent variable. Although this calculation is over the infinite horizon, most of this effect will be accrued within a decade.

[17] We tested for an inverse U shaped effect on democratization using the Polity index and the BM data (results not shown), but again found no evidence of a "quadratic" effect of either type of inequality.

Results on the inequality variables suggest that distributional consequences of economic development, rather than growth per se, have important political consequences.

5.4.4 Democracy as a Continuous Measure, 1955 to 2004

We now examine the estimated effects of income and rural inequality during the 1955 to 2004 period, using the BAR data and the Polity index as the dependent variable.[18] Models 1 through 3 in Table 5.7 are fixed effects models. As in Table 5.5, we begin by examining the effect of income inequality and GDP per capita, holding off on adding Rural Inequality and Education. Model 1 shows a robust and substantively sizable effect of income inequality: a 0.10 increase in income inequality increases the Polity score by 1.5 points over the long run.

Models 2 and 3 add Rural Inequality, trade openness and population, with Model 3 also employing an AR1 error term. Income inequality's estimated effect increases substantially in these models – an increase of 0.10 in the BAR Gini is associated with an increase in Polity scores in over the long run by 1.7 (Model 2) and 1.9 points (Model 3). Moreover, across both models we find that rural inequality is robustly negatively related to changes in the Polity index, with a 0.10 increase in rural inequality having estimated long-run effects of decreasing the Polity index by between 1.1 (Model 2) and 1.5 points. Openness and population appear to have a positive relationship to the Polity index, but only in Model 3.

Models 4 through 6 present pooled estimations, all including AR1 error terms and region dummies. Across these models, we again observe robust and sizable effects of income and rural inequality: A 0.10 increase in the Gini coefficient generates a long-run increase in the Polity index of between 1.2–1.3 points, while a 0.1 increase in rural inequality tends to lower the Polity score by about 1.5 points. Model 6 adds the oil exporter, Muslim majority, and recent civil war variables, but none have any impact.[19]

Note that in Models 1 through 3, GDP per capita has a robustly *negative* impact. In contrast, the pooled analyses reveal a positive relationship. Other scholars who have encountered the latter finding (Acemoglu et al. 2008; Przeworski et al. 2000) attribute it to the joint effects of long-run institutional or cultural conditions that predispose countries to both wealth and democracy, rather than to a causal connection between growth and regime change. The negative fixed effects relationship between per capita income and the Polity score in Models 1–3 supports this interpretation.

However, even if one accepts this view, one cannot draw the same inference about the effect of economic inequality, given the results in these same models.

---

[18] Our sample now ends in 2004 rather than 1999 because Polity has longer coverage than our binary dependent variable.

[19] We again found no evidence of a quadratic pattern using the BAR data and the Polity score.

TABLE 5.7. *Examining the Polity Index, 1955–2004*

	Within (1)	Within (2)	Within (3)	Pooled (4)	Pooled (5)	Pooled (6)
Lag Polity 2	0.884***	0.864***	0.831***	0.872***	0.831***	0.835***
	(0.011)	(0.015)	(0.009)	(0.013)	(0.017)	(0.019)
BAR Gini	1.703**	2.279**	3.188**	1.534***	2.168***	1.788***
	(0.822)	(0.989)	(1.445)	(0.509)	(0.684)	(0.692)
GDP Per Capita	-0.039***	-0.056***	-0.011	0.033***	0.025**	0.033**
	(0.012)	(0.018)	(0.014)	(0.008)	(0.012)	(0.015)
Rural Inequality		-1.561***	-2.487***		-2.616***	-2.402***
		(0.576)	(0.546)		(0.576)	(0.597)
Openness		0.005	0.007***		0.000	0.000
		(0.003)	(0.002)		(0.002)	(0.002)
Log Population		-0.373	0.613**		-0.024	-0.013
		(0.346)	(0.255)		(0.045)	(0.048)
Oil Exporter						-0.198
						(0.252)
Muslim Majority						-0.367**
						(0.178)
Civil War within Decade						-0.000
						(0.168)
Constant	-59.907***	-57.876***	-6.166***	-31.048***	-8.261	-6.541
	(7.650)	(17.840)	(2.278)	(7.696)	(10.923)	(13.496)
Observations	4907	3728	3600	4907	3728	3269
Countries	131	128	107	131	128	106
Time	Trend	Trend	AR1	AR1	AR1	AR1
Dummies	Country	Country	Country	Region	Region	Region

Standard errors in parentheses. * $p < 0.10$, ** $p < 0.05$, *** $p < 0.01$

Neither land not income inequality appear compromised by particularities of model specification: the estimated effects of inequality in the fixed-effects and pooled models are extremely similar, suggesting that cross-country and within-country differences in income and rural inequality similarly impact the Polity score.

5.4.5 Instrumental Variables and Checks on Exogeneity

We now examine how well our findings hold up to a series of stringent robustness checks that question the exogeneity of income inequality. There are many reasons to believe that inequality may be endogenous, in both democracies and autocracies. For example, democracies typically allow collective labor negotiations permitting unions to negotiate for higher wages, which presumably has the effect of reducing income inequality (Rodrik 1999). Likewise, some autocracies may endogenize inequality by imposing restrictions on the entrance to certain professions, the trading of various goods, or the buying and selling of property. This might limit economic opportunities of rising economic groups such as merchants or entrepreneurs, but it also might reduce or at least limit increases in income inequality.

The standard method for dealing with concerns about endogeneity is to use instrumental variables (IV) estimation. This involves finding an instrument that predicts the potentially endogenous variable but that is substantively and statistically itself exogenous.[20] As Dunning (2008b) notes, such instruments are very rare in social science data, particularly in historical observational data, and when they are available they are likely to be *weak instruments* – that is, they are likely to be correlated with the suspect variable at only low levels.

An additional concern about using instruments in historical time-series cross-sectional regressions is that an effective instrument for a suspect key variable such as inequality, which varies both across and within countries, must have a similar range of variation. One cannot use countries' time-invariant characteristics as instruments in fixed-effects regressions, nor can one use an instrument based on one-time variation caused by a "natural experiment" (Acemoglu, Johnson, and Robinson 2000; Angrist and Krueger 2001; Diamond and Robinson 2010), because such approaches would not produce an instrument that tracks changes in inequality over time.

In short, finding an exogenous instrument that varies both over time and across countries and that is correlated strongly enough with our measure of inequality is extremely difficult. We employ two instruments, each with its own strengths and weaknesses. The first is a lag of income inequality – lagged by twenty years in the case of the BM data and by five years in the case of the BAR data. Lagged levels of income inequality are substantively exogenous,

---

[20] Technically, the IV should be correlated with the suspect key variable, not itself endogenous with regard to the dependent variable, and should affect the dependent variable *only* through its effect on the suspect key variable.

but they may remain statistically problematic since there is a high level of autocorrelation in our measures.

For this reason, we employ a second instrument, the *regional* lagged level of inequality. We assume that this regional inequality variable (1) predicts an individual country's level of inequality, (2) is not itself endogenous (nor subject to the autocorrelation problem of using lags as instruments), and (3) affects a country's level of democracy only through its effect on *that country's* level of inequality. This third condition may be hardest to justify since it assumes away interdependencies caused by diffusion (for example a country democratizing because there were inequality-provoked democratic transitions in neighboring countries).

Table 5.8 analyzes the two instruments for income inequality, using the BM data. Models 1 and 2 employ a probit analysis corresponding to Model 5 of Table 5.1, that is, with democracy as a dichotomous variable. Model 1 uses the twenty-year lag as an instrument, and Model 2 uses the regional lagged level of inequality.[21] Both reveal highly robust and sizable effects of income inequality. For example, using Model 2, at an instrumented BM Gini level of 0.30, there is only a 0.75% per-period chance of democratization. In contrast, at a Gini of 0.55 the probability rises to 6.60%.

The other models use the Polity index as a dependent variable and, hence, use linear methods. Models 3 and 4 include country fixed effects, while Models 5 and 6 are pooled models using regional dummies. In Models 4 and 6 (with the regional instrument), income inequality is significant at the 5% level, but the twenty-year lag as an instrument is insignificant in Model 3 and only weakly significant in Model 5. Overall, particularly with the less problematic regional instrument, these findings suggest that our findings about the impact of income inequality using the BM data are robust to concerns about endogeneity.

These results generally hold up in Table 5.9, where we use the BAR Gini estimate, this time employing a five-year lag as our first instrument. In Models 1 and 2 the coefficients are larger than in their equivalent noninstrumented regressions in Table 5.5. Similarly substantively large effects are seen in the linear models using the Polity index in Models 3, 5, and 6, with only Model 4 not returning a significant result on income inequality at conventional levels.[22]

---

[21] We use two-stage least squares, predicting the level of income inequality using the instrument and the other independent variables, excluding *LagDemXBMGini* and then employ the predicted level of inequality and its interaction with the lag of democracy in place of the *BMGini* and *LagDemXBMGini* variables. This adjusts the 2SLS process for use in a dynamic probit model.

[22] The regional instrument might be a rather weak instrument in the fixed effects models since it relies on *changes* in inequality in the region rather than levels acting as an instrument for changes in inequality in the country under analysis. Changes are unlikely to be as closely correlated as levels of inequality within a region – particularly changes lagged one year. Using the ten-year change in regional inequality as an instrument does produce results robust at the 5% level.

TABLE 5.8. *Instrumental Variables Tests: BM Gini, 1820–1992*

	Dummy Probit (1)	Dummy Probit (2)	Polity Fixed FX (3)	Polity Fixed FX (4)	Polity Pooled (5)	Polity Pooled (6)
BM Gini	4.205***	3.906***	1.336	2.246**	2.523*	5.308**
	(0.943)	(1.417)	(1.225)	(0.996)	(1.527)	(2.146)
GDP Per Capita	0.234***	0.166***	-0.025	-0.001	-0.017	0.017
	(0.059)	(0.055)	(0.016)	(0.017)	(0.021)	(0.024)
Education	0.778	0.113	-0.940**	-0.935**	-1.086	-0.959
	(0.593)	(0.631)	(0.420)	(0.411)	(0.773)	(0.758)
Rural Inequality	-1.166***	-1.446***	-0.570**	-0.471*	-0.674*	-0.799**
	(0.402)	(0.356)	(0.263)	(0.264)	(0.373)	(0.403)
Lagged Democracy	7.154***	7.213***				
	(1.273)	(1.611)				
Lag Polity 2			0.932***	0.925***	0.918***	0.906***
			(0.006)	(0.006)	(0.010)	(0.010)
Constant	-205.782	18.284	278.729***	220.653**	378.006***	
	(157.295)	(135.704)	(90.789)	(91.795)	(137.049)	
Observations	4268	4552	4311	4617	4074	4238
Instrument	Lag	Region	Lag	Region	Lag	Region

Standard errors in parentheses. * $p < 0.10$, ** $p < 0.05$, *** $p < 0.01$

TABLE 5.9. *Instrumental Variables Tests: BAR Gini, 1950–2000*

	Dummy Probit (1)	Dummy Probit (2)	Polity Fixed FX (3)	Polity Fixed FX (4)	Polity Pooled (5)	Polity Pooled (6)
Lagged Democracy	3.896***	6.939***				
	(0.908)	(1.835)				
BAR Gini	1.740*	6.648*	5.494**	2.749	2.792***	4.613**
	(0.934)	(3.424)	(2.227)	(4.775)	(0.767)	(1.896)
GDP Per Capita	0.034	0.089**	-0.080***	-0.075***	0.061**	0.063***
	(0.037)	(0.038)	(0.025)	(0.022)	(0.025)	(0.022)
Rural Inequality	-0.653*	-0.617*	-1.207**	-0.920**	-1.713***	-1.517***
	(0.390)	(0.372)	(0.484)	(0.448)	(0.589)	(0.515)
Education	-0.322	-0.532	-2.624***	-2.538***	0.659	0.760
	(0.500)	(0.520)	(0.740)	(0.711)	(0.523)	(0.488)
Oil Exporter	-0.434	-0.076			-0.249	-0.204
	(0.417)	(0.339)			(0.252)	(0.258)
Muslim Majority	-0.184	-0.235			-0.161	-0.177
	(0.206)	(0.207)			(0.177)	(0.185)
Civil War within Decade	0.370*	0.540***			0.116	0.168
	(0.193)	(0.177)			(0.171)	(0.163)
Lag Polity 2			0.865***	0.868***	0.834***	0.846***
			(0.009)	(0.008)	(0.020)	(0.018)
Constant	-37.816***	-30.393***	-96.600***	-88.697***	-27.900**	-16.385
	(12.207)	(10.670)	(14.658)	(13.191)	(13.137)	(10.897)
Observations	3057	3378	3501	3823	3089	3413
Instrument	Lag	Region	Lag	Region	Lag	Region

Standard errors in parentheses. * $p < 0.10$, ** $p < 0.05$, *** $p < 0.01$

In all, Tables 5.8 and 5.9 tend to support our claim that income inequality has a positive impact on regime change.

5.5 CONCLUSION

Existing research on the relationship between inequality and regime change has posited either no relationship, as in Przeworski et al. (2000) or Houle (2009a), a negative relationship, as in Muller (1988) or Boix (2003), or an inverted U shaped relationship, with transitions most likely at middling levels of inequality, as in Acemoglu and Robinson (2006).

Our analysis of the relationship between income and land inequality and regime change offers strong empirical support for our elite-competition argument. Using a far broader sample both temporally and spatially, different measures of inequality and democracy, multiple estimation techniques and a set of increasingly stringent model specifications, we find that regime change is most likely under the combination of low land inequality paired with high income inequality.

These results draw attention to the notion that scholars have misinterpreted what Gini coefficients look like in the real world. In a developing autocracy, low Gini coefficients of income inequality do not indicate a large middle class, but rather that nearly everyone is equally poor. A growing Gini coefficient, by contrast, suggests the growth of the middle classes, which have strong interests in reining in the expropriative authority of the state.

Our tests generated fairly consistently robust results on economic inequality measures – far more so than for per capita income. This suggests that the search for a connection between economic and political change should focus not on the direct impact of growth, but rather on the distributional consequences of different paths of economic development.

To be clear, we are hardly claiming that our results suggest an inevitable relationship between development, income inequality, and democratization. What we can affirm is that, historically, as autocracies have developed, the size of the bourgeois, middle, and working classes has grown. In most cases, this has meant an increase in income inequality. To the extent this is so, democratization is more likely. By implication, autocracies – such as the USSR or Singapore – that find ways to "endogenize" equality should last relatively longer. Our results offer good evidence that a relationship between income inequality and regime change exists, in broad strokes, across history and across cases, but we can also affirm that this relationship is stronger at some times (after 1980, for example) and weaker at others (during the peak of the Cold War), when international forces swamp the effects of domestic factors.

However, it should not be forgotten that the impact of income inequality depends partly on the effect of land inequality. A powerful landed elite may offset the growing influence of the bourgeois and middle classes, postponing democratization. On the other hand, relatively weak bourgeois and middle classes may successfully force regime change, if landed elites are also weak.

In the next chapter, we consider some questions our results raise, exploring additional measures of democracy and inequality as well as testing for a relationship between inequality and regime change at different levels of economic development.

6

Inequality and Democratization: Empirical Extensions

6.1 INTRODUCTION

In this chapter, we explore additional empirical implications of our theoretical model. Our model suggests that income inequality should be a better predictor of bourgeois-led transitions to "partial" rather than "full" democracy, whereas land inequality should retard both types of regime transitions. We examine this question empirically by considering additional ways to operationalize democracy using the Polity index, and a variety of new empirical techniques to address this question.

We then consider how different paths of economic development might shape which forms of inequality matter most politically. Our formal model predicts that income inequality should hasten transitions to democracy where an emerging (industrial) sector is growing rapidly compared to a stagnant (agricultural) sector. Conversely, rural inequality should matter more when the agricultural sector is relatively larger than the industrial sector. Using the level of economic development to indicate the relative size of the industrial sector, we find support for this conjecture.

Finally, we consider the impact of asset mobility. Our model suggested that asset mobility has an ambiguous theoretical impact on regime change, because although it decreases the bourgeoisie's incentives to rebel it also increases the elite's incentives to grant democracy. Using a country's capital share of income to measure asset-mobility, we find weak support for the latter hypothesis. However, introducing this variable does not change the predicted impact of income or land inequality.

6.2 VARIETIES OF REGIMES

Here we explore our model's implication that inequality better predicts transitions to partial rather than full democracy. We do so in three steps. First, we examine the extent to which our argument can empirically distinguish transitions from autocracy to partial and/or full democracy by splitting political regimes into these three types and using Markov switching models. Second, we examine the effects of inequality across all possible thresholds along the Polity index, expecting weaker results as one approaches transitions across "most democratic" scores. Results using both approaches confirm our hypothesis that land and income inequality better predict transitions to partial democracy. Finally, we examine the impact of different forms of inequality on changes in different institutional elements of democracy, by breaking the Polity index into its components of executive recruitment, constraints on the executive, and political competition. Our argument suggests that rising land and income inequality should be more likely to generate contestation over the last two components, and we find support for this conjecture.

6.2.1 Autocracy, Partial Democracy, and Full Democracy

In Chapter 4, we suggested that in a society with three economic groups, each of which could potentially control political decision making, three ideal-type regimes could emerge, depending on the configuration of land and income inequality: an elite-controlled autocracy, a bourgeois-controlled partial democracy, and a full democracy controlled by the masses. We also hypothesized that both land and income inequality should better predict transitions to partial democracy than to full democracy.

We now test this proposition on the historical dataset using Markov transition models, as in Epstein et al. (2006). This technique lets us weigh the determinants of transitions from any one of these three states of the world to each of the others.[1] We define the regime types, per Epstein et al. (2006), as follows: full autocracies have Polity scores of zero or lower, partial democracies have Polity scores between 1 and 7, and full democracies have Polity scores of 8 or higher.

For ease of interpretation, in Table 6.1 we present only the predicted change in the per-period probability of transitioning among these regime types given large changes in income and rural inequality (from the 5th to the 95th percentile of each). Rows in the tables represent the regime type at time t, while columns represent the regime at time t + 1. Standard errors for the predicted probabilities are in parentheses.

It is immediately apparent that the only robust results from these sorts of changes in land and income inequality involve transitions from autocracy, and that the magnitude of the predicted changes are much greater for

---

[1] The dataset for these models codes a country's regime type at each year. The Markov model assesses the probability of being in any one of the three states at time t+1, given the regime type at time t. As such, the technique also generates probabilities of staying in the same regime type from one period to the next.

TABLE 6.1A. *Regime Change Probabilities: BM Gini, .30 to .55*

| Transition From | Transition to | | |
	Autocracy	Partial Democracy	Democracy
Autocracy	−0.13	0.13	0.002
	(0.06)	(0.06)	(0.001)
Partial Democracy	0.01	0.02	−0.03
	(−0.01)	(−0.05)	(−0.06)
Democracy	0.00	−0.04	0.04
	(0.00)	(−0.04)	(−0.04)

TABLE 6.1B. *Regime Change Probabilities: Rural Inequality,*
0 to .95

| Transition From | Transition to | | |
	Autocracy	Partial Democracy	Democracy
Autocracy	0.20	−0.20	−0.002
	(0.08)	(0.08)	(0.001)
Partial Democracy	0.002	−0.02	−0.02
	(−0.01)	(−0.09)	(−0.10)
Democracy	0.00	0.06	−0.05
	(0.00)	(−0.06)	(−0.06)

transitions to partial democracy than to full democracy. Therefore, the conjecture in our formal model that income inequality should matter most for
transitions to regimes led by the bourgeoisie and/or middle classes finds clear
support here.

6.2.2 Polity Thresholds

We know from Treier and Jackman (2008) that the Polity index does not
consistently measure the underlying latent variable of "democracy" and that
jumps between points along the index do not distinguish equally among types
of political regimes. Given this, results using a trichotomous operationalization
of our dependent variable could be artifacts of the arbitrary choice along the
index of where to separate one regime from another. Therefore, we reassess
our hypotheses by analyzing transitions across *all* potential threshold points
on the Polity scale.

This approach mimics the dummy-variable approach used in Chapter 5.
However, instead of using a dichotomous coding of democracy, here we create a series of 20 dummy variable "thresholds" along the Polity index, from

−9 to +10. For each threshold, we examine a dynamic probit model in which the dependent variable is a dummy signifying whether the Polity score in the previous period was either below or equal/above that threshold, given the country's Polity score in the current period. For example, for a threshold of −5, the dummy dependent variable codes countries as having either Polity scores of between −10 and −6 (0, no transition across the threshold) or having Polity scores ranging between −5 and +10 (1, transition across the threshold).

By reconceiving of the Polity index as an ordered but not linear variable, where each point marks a transition to a somewhat more democratic regime, we address concerns about what Polity scores actually measure, to some extent. The use of these Polity thresholds also has the useful payoff of helping us identify the sorts of regimes in which our key variables have the substantively largest effects. For example, using a threshold of −5 means we are exploring whether particular values of land and income inequality shape transitions from "total autocracies" to a set of regimes that run the range from fairly autocratic all the way to "full democracies" (from −5 all the way to +10). In contrast, using a threshold of +5 means we are exploring whether land and income inequality shape transitions in both total and partial autocracies (−10 to +4) to mostly full democracies (+5 to +10).

To analyze the determinants of movements across these Polity thresholds, we explored each of the twenty thresholds, for both the historical and modern datasets. Figures 6.1 though 6.4 show the predicted change in the per period

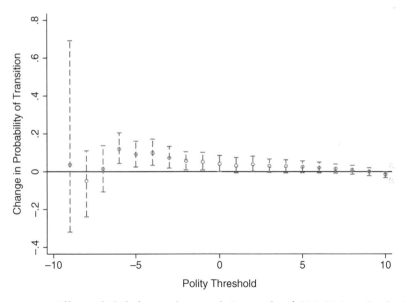

FIGURE 6.1. Effects of Shift from 5th to 95th Percentile of BM Gini on Per-Period Probability of Transition for Polity Thresholds

probability of transition – along with 95% confidence intervals – following a shift from the 5th to the 95th percentile in income inequality (the BM or BAR measure depending on the dataset) or rural inequality. Each figure thus has twenty predicted intervals, one for each threshold along the Polity index, for the predicted impact of a change in inequality on transition.

Our argument implies that the bourgeoisie have stronger incentives to seek partial democracy than ally with the masses to push for full democracy. We find further empirical support for this notion in Figure 6.1, which uses the BM Gini data. For the first three thresholds, the standard errors are very large and there is no robust effect of income inequality on a transition from below to equal or above the threshold.[2] However, by the Polity threshold of −6 (transitioning from −7 or below to −6 or above), we see sizable positive and robust estimates for the effect of income inequality on the probability of a transition. For Polity thresholds of between −6 and −3 the per period probability of a transition increases by 10% if inequality moves from very low to very high levels.[3] As the Polity thresholds increase further the magnitude of the inequality effect attenuates to around 5% for much of the range between −2 and +4, becoming less robust as the threshold rises until it becomes insignificant by a threshold of +5, and even negatively significant (albeit with a tiny coefficient in substantive terms) at a threshold of +10.

These results indicate that income inequality only promotes a shift toward further democracy in regimes that are between highly authoritarian and weakly democratic. Once countries reach a moderately democratic level – a Polity score of around +5, income inequality no longer has a robust effect on the probability of further democratization. This finding jibes with the implications of our formal model in Chapter 4, as well as the analysis above using the trichotomous operationalization – the democratizing effects of income inequality are stronger in transitions from autocracy to partial than those from with autocracy or partial democracy to full democracy.

Figure 6.2 shows results of a similar simulation, using rural inequality. Here we are testing a different hypothesis, the relative incentives of the landed elite to *resist* regime change. Recall that our model implied that elites have incentives to resist democracy, whether partial or full. The threshold tests here offer a more precise test of this hypothesis than the trichotomous approach above.

---

[2] This imprecision partly results from the relatively small number of cases with Polity scores under −7. This also suggests that where the dictatorship is extremely repressive, successful bourgeois rebellion may be more difficult, perhaps because of higher organizational costs.

[3] Obviously no country actually experiences this degree of shock to its level of income inequality, at least within the medium term. Thus, it is most helpful to think of this change in income inequality as cross-national comparison between states with similar levels of rural inequality and per capita income but very different income inequality levels. The size of the shift in income inequality affects only the magnitude of predicted changes in these figures, not their statistical robustness.

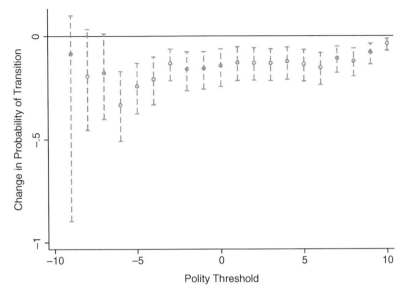

FIGURE 6.2. Effects of Shift from 5th to 95th Percentile of Rural Inequality on Per-Period Probability of Transition for Polity Thresholds: Historical Dataset

The negative effect of rural inequality on transitions toward democracy is substantial and robust across almost all thresholds, except the very lowest (a function of the limited sample at very low Polity scores). The effect is also substantively large, with a move from the 5th to the 95th percentile on the rural inequality variable associated with a reduction in the probability of transition of around 20% between Polity thresholds of −6 to −4, and 10–15% across the remainder of the thresholds. As with the trichotomous results this implies that the effect of moving across (nearly) the full range of land inequality is between 50% and 100% larger than the effect of moving across (nearly) the full range of income inequality.

A further contrast to the effects of income inequality is striking: rural inequality consistently retards increases in the level of democracy, regardless of a country's starting position. Considering the comparative statics of the formal model in Chapter 4, this should not be surprising: Rural inequality is associated with the relative wealth of the autocratic landed elite, not with rising but politically unrepresented economic groups. As qualitative research has also concluded, our results suggest that a wealthy landed elite will always resist further liberalization, regardless of whatever concessions to democracy have already been made.

Figures 6.3 and 6.4 repeat this exercise using the BAR income inequality data from 1955 to 2004. The patterns are very similar. From a Polity threshold of −6 upwards, the BAR Gini variable has substantial and positive effects

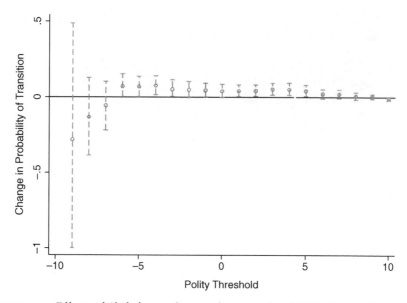

FIGURE 6.3. Effects of Shift from 5th to 95th Percentile of BAR Gini on Per-Period Probability of Transition for Polity Thresholds

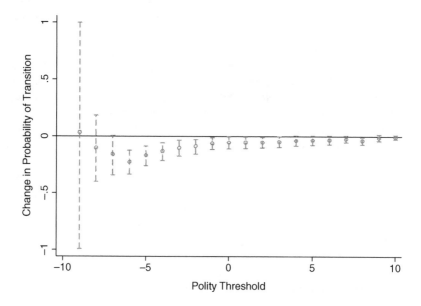

FIGURE 6.4. Effects of Shift from 5th to 95th Percentile of Rural Inequality on Per-Period Probability of Transition for Polity Thresholds: Modern Dataset

on the probability of transitioning across that threshold, up to a Polity score of around +5, after which the effect becomes less robust and eventually slightly negative at a threshold of +10. Similarly, just as we found in Chapter 5, rural inequality always has a negative effect, albeit slightly weaker than in the historical dataset.

An important difference with the findings using the BM versus the BAR datasets is that the range of thresholds over which both income and rural inequality are robust predictors of transition is wider when we use the latter, suggesting that the effects of income inequality may not be limited to partial democratization in the more recent era, but apply to a wider array of regime types – including transitions from partial to full democracy.

6.2.3 Decomposing the Elements of Democracy

In this section, we explore whether land and income inequality have stronger or weaker effects on particular components of the Polity index – that is, whether socioeconomic structural variables play more or less important roles in bringing about particular institutional changes associated with democracy.

Our theoretical model ignores such questions, defining political regimes by whichever group or groups control taxing and spending. However, our discussion of the elite-competition dynamic of regime change implied that a number of institutional solutions to the problem of expropriation exist, including parliamentary sovereignty, limitations on executive authority, and mechanisms for channeling popular representation.

Polity scores are generated by aggregating scores from six dimensions of political authority. These are then further aggregated into three 'concept variables': (1) Executive Recruitment (EXREC), which considers the relative openness and competitiveness of executive recruitment; (2) Executive Constraints (EXCONST), which considers the relative limits on executive authority; and (3) Political Competition (POLCOMP), which assesses the extent of restrictions on political participation and contestation Marshall, Jaggers, and Gurr (2003).

A key problem with using the components of Polity scores is that, as Goertz (2006) explains, they are measured using different scales. For example, the executive constraints variable has seven points, the executive recruitment variable has eight, and the political competition variable has ten. Moreover, gaps between points on each scale do not appear to reflect equal underlying distinctions on the unmeasured index of democracy (Treier and Jackman 2008). Following Goertz (2006, p.97), we adjust these measures to all fit a 0–5 scale, with intervals to better reflect differences among regimes.[4]

---

[4] Goertz does not code regulation of political participation (PARREG in the Polity dataset, a subcomponent of the political competition component) on a five-point scale. Accordingly, we use only his measure of the competitiveness of political participation (PARCOMP) as our proxy

Table 6.2 examines factors associated with changes on each of these three components of the Polity score, using both the BM (Models 1 to 6) and BAR data (Models 7 to 12). For each component of democracy we run two models: a linear regression with a lagged dependent variable and clustered standard errors, and an ordered probit model without lags.[5] We omit the lagged dependent variable in the ordered probit models, as this is problematic where we do not know the lagged level of the unobserved scale that we are trying to measure (see Wooldridge 2002, 2005).

Although the results across all three component of the Polity score generally tend to support our argument, we find the largest coefficients and most consistently robust results on the political competition and executive constraints components. This finding lends additional support to our elite competition argument, as demands for expanded suffrage and greater constraints on executive authority tend to quickly follow from the growth of a rising economic elite, with opposition coming from an entrenched landed elite.

For example, as in the UK, in many countries expansions of the franchise (an increase in PARCOMP) preceded final elimination of an unelected monarch's ability to influence elections (an increase in EXREC). A similar pattern can be seen in the July monarchy in France (1830–1848), during which political competition was robust (although the franchise was very limited) and substantial constraints existed on the monarch – yet power over executive selection and deselection remained with the king. Constitutional monarchy gradually evolved toward democracy in both countries (more fitfully in France, of course) – but importantly, coincided with a considerable expansion of income inequality as the process of industrialization accelerated.

6.3 INEQUALITY AND REGIME CHANGE AT DIFFERENT LEVELS OF DEVELOPMENT

Income and rural inequality appear to be relatively more important for transitions to partial rather than full democracy. Given this, let us turn to a second implication of our elite-competition approach. Rooting our argument in Kuznets' hypothesis that (income) inequality rises as countries grow, we suggested that income inequality matters politically in an autocracy because it signifies the rise of new economic groups that want to rein in expropriative state power – an emergent bourgeoisie or middle class, for example. Likewise,

---

for POLCOMP. For EXREC, Goertz codes separate five-point scales for the competitiveness of executive recruitment (XRCOMP) and the openness of executive recruitment (XROPEN), but does not recode the regulation of executive recruitment (XRREG). We average the first two to produce a zero to five EXREC executive recruitment scale.

[5] The reason for using an ordered model is that the Polity component indices summarize ordered categorical differences in political institutions, which may not correspond to an underlying but unobserved interval scale. See Marshall, Jaggers, and Gurr (2003) or Treier and Jackman (2008) for discussion.

TABLE 6.2. *Goertz Components of Polity Index*

Polity Component	XCONST (1)	EXREC (2)	PARCOMP (3)	XCONST (4)	EXREC (5)	PARCOMP (6)
Lagged DV	0.960***	0.987***	0.966***			
	(0.008)	(0.004)	(0.006)			
BM Gini	0.240*	0.080*	0.234**	1.972***	4.619***	4.418***
	(0.125)	(0.048)	(0.097)	(0.321)	(0.321)	(0.336)
GDP Per Capita	0.007**	0.002	0.010***	0.159***	0.284***	0.369***
	(0.003)	(0.001)	(0.003)	(0.011)	(0.014)	(0.013)
Rural Inequality	−0.107**	−0.013	−0.143***	−1.982***	−1.136***	−3.145***
	(0.047)	(0.021)	(0.039)	(0.111)	(0.112)	(0.125)
Education	0.092	−0.002	0.006	1.349***	0.232	−1.281***
	(0.059)	(0.026)	(0.034)	(0.159)	(0.170)	(0.166)
Constant	9.227	−0.317	−2.065			
	(21.879)	(10.980)	(21.736)			
Observations	4547	4295	4484	4631	4382	4569

TABLE 6.2. (Continued)

	XCONST (1)	EXREC (2)	PARCOMP (3)	XCONST (4)	EXREC (5)	PARCOMP (6)
Lagged DV	0.928***	0.967***	0.942***			
	(0.009)	(0.007)	(0.008)			
BAR Gini	0.450***	0.013	0.360***	1.811***	0.805**	3.107***
	(0.133)	(0.064)	(0.101)	(0.284)	(0.347)	(0.283)
GDP Per Capita	0.004	-0.001	0.001	0.142***	0.097***	0.169***
	(0.002)	(0.002)	(0.002)	(0.012)	(0.013)	(0.014)
Rural Inequality	-0.175***	-0.095**	-0.246***	-0.842***	-1.593***	-2.147***
	(0.063)	(0.041)	(0.064)	(0.137)	(0.147)	(0.168)
Education	0.157*	0.015	0.097	1.635***	2.081***	0.865***
	(0.089)	(0.055)	(0.078)	(0.231)	(0.286)	(0.251)
Oil Exporter	-0.025	0.003	0.007	-0.519***	-0.369***	-0.023
	(0.044)	(0.020)	(0.043)	(0.082)	(0.103)	(0.083)
Muslim Majority	-0.017	0.009	0.023	-0.030	0.002	0.029
	(0.036)	(0.018)	(0.030)	(0.064)	(0.075)	(0.071)
Constant	-4.296***	-1.362*	-4.404***			
	(1.463)	(0.695)	(1.363)			
Observations	3707	3184	3679	3758	3246	3732

rural inequality reflects the strength of the incumbent landed elites. By implication, rural inequality should matter relatively more than income inequality
in relatively poorer autocracies, where landed elites are dominant and rising
groups weak or even nonexistent, while income inequality should matter relatively more in wealthier autocracies, where rising urban groups will be stronger
and landed elites weakened as the importance of agriculture declines.

This hypothesis suggests testing for the impact of rural and income inequality conditional on level of development, comparing countries with incomes
equal to or below the international median for a given year against those with
incomes above that level. We use this dividing line since our theory focuses on
the relative strength of land versus industry in a given country as opposed
to the simpler version of Modernization Theory that considers a country's
per capita income. Examining countries by their relationship to the global
median for a given year also eases comparability across time periods, which
is especially important in our analysis of the historical dataset.

Table 6.3 presents results from four models. The first two use the BM data
and the latter two the BAR measure. As in Tables 5.1 and 5.5, all models
employ dynamic probit estimations and the democracy dummy dependent

TABLE 6.3. *High- and Low-Income Countries*

	Historical Low (1)	Historical High (2)	Modern Low (3)	Modern High (4)
Lagged Democracy	4.981***	11.563***	3.395***	6.980***
	(1.152)	(1.697)	(1.169)	(1.865)
BM Gini	1.609	5.718***		
	(1.535)	(1.766)		
GDP Per Capita	0.119	0.482***	0.097	0.154**
	(0.094)	(0.121)	(0.212)	(0.062)
Education	−0.001	−0.290	−1.031	0.348
	(0.782)	(0.952)	(0.812)	(0.958)
Rural Inequality	−0.933**	−0.060	−1.153**	0.334
	(0.466)	(1.164)	(0.541)	(0.571)
BAR Gini			1.032	3.449**
			(1.064)	(1.399)
Muslim Majority			−0.219	−3.277***
			(0.227)	(0.521)
Civil War within Decade			0.374*	0.543
			(0.198)	(0.349)
Constant	283.447	−549.244	−34.207**	−19.640
	(332.823)	(399.997)	(16.614)	(13.831)
Observations	2363	2406	1471	1907

Standard errors in parentheses. * $p < 0.10$, ** $p < 0.05$, *** $p < 0.01$

variable but split each dataset into two groups of below and above median income countries.

The results confirm the logical extension of our argument that rural inequality should matter more in less developed autocracies, but income inequality should matter more in relatively wealthier dictatorships. Comparing Models 1 and 2, we see that although income inequality is positively signed in both subsamples, only in the higher income group is it robust. Its effect in that latter estimation is also extremely large in magnitude – double the size of its equivalent in the full sample (Table 5.1, Model 6).

In contrast, rural inequality – though always signed in the negative direction – is only robust in Model 1, the poorer countries. It is also worth noting that GDP per capita is only a robust positive predictor of democratization in the relatively wealthier countries. To the degree that this result is partly picking up intersectoral inequality – a growing industrial sector vis-à-vis agriculture – this also tends to support our argument.

Strikingly, precisely the same pattern can be seen in Models 3 and 4. Income inequality is only robust in the high-income countries (and the coefficient is again twice the magnitude of its equivalent in the full sample, in Table 5.5), as is GDP per capita, while rural inequality is only robust in the low-income countries (and is substantially larger and more robust than its equivalent in the full sample).[6]

Results here clearly follow our model's implication: income inequality matters most when a rising economic group is acquiring wealth through economic development, but landed elites are stronger in poorer countries where agriculture tends to dominate.

6.4 THE IMPACT OF ASSET MOBILITY

Given our model, we have weak priors regarding the impact of asset mobility on regime change. This is because, as we showed in the Appendix to Chapter 4, although asset mobility decreases the bourgeoisie's incentives to demand democracy, it also increases the elite's incentives to concede it. As we noted, a reliable measure of asset mobility has proven elusive. Here, we use a measure of the share of national income accruing to capital (versus labor) as a measure of asset-mobility.[7]

Both Houle (2009a,b) and Dunning (2008a) use estimates of capital share created by Rodriguez and Ortega (2006), but as a proxy for income inequality. Rodriguez and Ortega define the capital share of a given industry as one

[6] This result is not a function of time period, since the high and low income groups are judged relative to the median income for that year. Breaking income relative to the median income into quintiles and interacting this with income and rural inequality generates similar effects: income inequality has its strongest positive effects in the third and fourth quintiles, whereas rural inequality has its strongest effects in the first and second quintiles.

[7] In Chapter 4, we used the term asset-specificity, which is simply the inverse of asset mobility.

minus the ratio of wages and salaries to total value added. Houle and Dunning adopt different approaches to aggregating the industry-level capital shares into a national-level score. Houle aggregates across all industries.[8] Dunning (2008a) uses the same data, but since his book is primarily concerned with the interactive effect of oil rents and inequality, he strips all extractive industries out of his measure of capital share. Not surprisingly, since extractive industries are highly capital-intensive, Dunning's average capital share measure across countries is substantially lower (.57) than Houle's (.65).

In our view, Dunning's capital-share measure assesses asset mobility, rather than inequality. Extractive industries are the least mobile form of capital, since they depend entirely on extraction of resources from the ground. Although not all of the remaining capital is fully mobile, if we strip out the fixed assets from the share of national income attaining to capital rather than to labor, we are left with a measure of the share of national income attaining to relatively more mobile assets.

More theoretically pertinent, just like any resource, capital can be more or less equally distributed – meaning that the share of capital in an economy tells us nothing about how equally or unequally it is distributed. As its share in an economy increases, capital could be relatively more *or* less equally distributed – to the top 0.1%, 1%, or 10% perhaps.

Moreover, intuitively one would expect capital share and a country's Gini coefficient to be correlated if the variables were measuring the same underlying concept, income inequality. However, the correlation between both Dunning's and Houle's measures of capital share and the BAR Gini variable is below 0.1, suggesting that neither's measure of capital share is a valid proxy for income inequality – although Dunning's capital share indicator might be a useful measure of capital mobility, independently of whether capital is more or less equally distributed.[9]

Using capital share as a measure of asset mobility, Table 6.4 replicates our baseline probit analysis of democratization using the BAR data from the previous chapter, replacing income inequality with Dunning's version of the capital share measure.[10]

Models 1 and 2 exclude a measure of income inequality, but Model 2 introduces Rural Inequality and several controls. Capital Share has a positive effect on the probability of democratic transition in both models, although it is robust only at the 10% level. Models 3 and 4 both include the BAR Gini data.

---

[8] His findings are ambiguous: in Houle (2009a) he finds no effect of capital share on transitions to democracy, but in Houle (2009b) he finds a positive effect on transitions to democracy, but only for middle-income countries.

[9] For this reason, we question how much Houle's findings tell us about the relationship between inequality and regime change.

[10] We exclude the oil exporter dummy we had previously included, given that the difference between Dunning's measures centers on the role of extractive industries. Results are similar if this measure is retained.

TABLE 6.4. *Capital Shares*

	(1)	(2)	(3)	(4)
Lagged Democracy	4.546***	3.007**	4.811***	3.269
	(0.634)	(1.531)	(1.048)	(2.015)
Capital Share	1.358*	1.368*	1.395*	1.620**
	(0.715)	(0.749)	(0.753)	(0.779)
GDP Per Capita	−0.026	−0.065	−0.022	−0.067
	(0.025)	(0.063)	(0.032)	(0.065)
BAR Gini			2.041**	1.961*
			(1.003)	(1.183)
Rural Inequality		−1.242**		−1.309**
		(0.559)		(0.581)
Civil War within Decade		0.007		0.036
		(0.230)		(0.244)
Muslim Majority		−0.400		−0.446
		(0.253)		(0.287)
Log Population		0.012		0.058
		(0.082)		(0.096)
Openness		−0.001		−0.001
		(0.003)		(0.003)
Constant	−48.234***	−1.605*	−45.375***	−3.165***
	(14.499)	(0.965)	(14.942)	(1.125)
Observations	2858	2122	2612	1997

Standard errors in parentheses. * $p < 0.10$, ** $p < 0.05$, *** $p < 0.01$

Income inequality has a positive effect on the probability of regime change, *distinct from capital share*, although it is only robust at the 10% level in Model 4. In that same model, we see that Rural Inequality retains its strongly negative effect, again independently of Capital Share.

To the extent that Dunning's measure reflects mobile capital's share in the economy, at first glance this result would appear to (weakly) support Boix's hypothesis that democracy is more likely where assets are more mobile. However, the theoretical mechanism driving this result remains obscure. Boix hypothesized that mobile asset holders fear neither the poor nor the redistributive consequences of democracy, because they can hide their wealth more easily. In contrast, our argument in Chapter 4 suggests that mobile asset holders face different incentives: because the an incumbent autocratic elite has a harder time targeting those who hold mobile assets for expropriation, members of a bourgeoisie have stronger incentives to demand democracy to the extent that their assets are relatively *less* mobile.

Given this, the results on Capital Share appear to support Boix's hypothesis—but only if the incentives of the bourgeoisie were all that matters when thinking about the political consequences of asset mobility. Because our model allows for taxation under autocracy, it implies that asset mobility also affects the incentives of the autocratic elite, who have greater reason to *concede* partial democracy where assets are more mobile. This is because when the bourgeoisie's assets are more mobile the total possible amount obtainable via expropriation declines. The statistical results on Capital Share in Table 6.4 cannot distinguish between Boix's hypothesis and ours; both are equally plausible mechanisms. Further research on this question is required. In any case, the addition of Capital Share does not substantially change the empirical results on land and income inequality, which followed our elite-competition model's predictions.

6.5 CONCLUSION

This chapter explored several empirical implications of our theoretical model, bolstering our argument linking socioeconomic structure to regime change. We first considered several measures of our dependent variable, democratization. These results matter if one finds dichotomous measures of democracy wanting for one reason or another. Our model predicted land and income inequality would have stronger effects on transitions from autocracy to partial democracy. We found support for this hypothesis when we analyzed both a trichotomous measure of political regimes and a series of twenty thresholds across the range of the Polity score. And when we broke the Polity score into its component parts, we discovered that income and rural inequality have particularly strong effects on increasing constraints on the executive and improving political competition, but weaker results on changing the actual composition of the executive. These results all follow from our theoretical argument in that what appears to matter from the perspective of rising classes is the ability to secure political representation and constrain the state, rather than actually taking on the tasks of ruling.

We then considered our model's implication that land inequality should have a relatively stronger effect in poor autocracies, while income inequality should matter more as autocracies grow wealthier. The empirical results again supported this proposition, distinguishing between a narrow version of Modernization Theory and our approach, which incorporates the distinct political consequences of land and income inequality as economies develop.

Finally, we explored the potential consequences of asset mobility. Although our theoretical model generated ambiguous predictions, empirical tests revealed a positive effect on the probability of regime change. The theoretical mechanism driving this result remains unclear, however. Moreover, our empirical analysis confirmed that adding asset mobility to empirical analysis does not undermine our elite-competition model's primary predictions, that democratization is most likely when land inequality is low but income inequality high.

The findings in this chapter offer further confirmation of our argument about the relationship between development, class formation and regime change in Chapters 2 and 3, as well as the comparative statics generated by our formal model in Chapter 4. Here we are able to better isolate how development shapes which socioeconomic classes matter, and when.

7

Democracy, Inequality, and Public Spending: Reassessing the Evidence

7.1 INTRODUCTION

The utility of any theory of democratization depends on the descriptive and predictive accuracy of its core assumptions. In this chapter, we illustrate the fruitfulness of our elite-competition approach by turning to the question of the relationship between political regimes, inequality, and social-welfare spending.

The Meltzer-Richard model assumes that, under democracy, inequality increases the median voter's demand for redistribution, which takes the form of pure public goods distributed equally to everyone. Our argument, by contrast, holds that groups demand democracy because they want to rein in autocratic elites' ability to tax and expropriate their wealth and income. Building on the model in Chapter 4, here we also assume that government social-welfare programs can be targeted, so that they do not necessarily benefit everyone equally. This is a more realistic approach, as much social spending in the real world actually benefits relatively wealthier citizens (Lizzeri and Persico 2004; Moene and Wallerstein 2001; Ross 2006).

We expect elite competition to continue to matter after regime change. The former autocratic elites should oppose any form of redistribution, and to the extent that they remain important political players even under universal suffrage, redistributive spending should be lower. Likewise, we would not expect a newly empowered bourgeoisie to dramatically increase social-welfare spending, but to use tax revenue to fund infrastructure investment designed to help grow the economy, in particular the urban industrial sectors. To the extent that the bourgeoisie implement social-welfare programs, they should seek to target benefits to members of their own group rather than implement universalistic redistribution that primarily benefits those further down the income scale.

As for the masses, although under full democracy their electoral weight should increase purely redistributive social-welfare spending, their influence will be mitigated to the extent that wealthy citizens – both the former incumbent elite and the arriviste bourgeoisie and middle classes – dominate politics. Since land and income inequality proxy for the relative political strength of such groups, our elite-competition approach predicts that although democracy might have a positive effect on social-welfare spending, redistribution should *decline* as both forms of inequality increase. Moreover, inequality should have the strongest impact on purely redistributive social-welfare programs rather than those that target relatively wealthier citizens.

We reexamine these hypotheses using new data on government social-welfare spending from around the world, from an earlier historical period than most scholars consider – 1880–1930 – and for more contemporary decades as well. For both eras, using spending levels under autocracy as the basis for comparison, we find that although democracy has a small positive effect, redistributive spending does decline as both forms of inequality increase. Moreover, spending targeted on the poor does tend to decline faster as inequality increases.

These findings present a stark challenge to redistributivist theories of democratization that build off the Meltzer-Richard model. If redistribution does not follow from inequality under democracy, elites should have little to fear where inequality is high. By contrast, these findings flow directly from our understanding of how inequality reflects different levels of political power across groups: as rising elites grow richer, they become more powerful in both autocracies *and* democracies. This illustrates the dual-edged effects of income inequality: powerful outsider groups may help liberalize autocratic regimes, but once ensconced in power these same groups have little incentive to increase taxation and government spending in ways that would primarily benefit less-powerful members of society. Hence the 'redistributive threat' of the poor, such as it is, is likely to be *lower* where income inequality is relatively higher.

In the next section, we articulate our expectations about the interplay between political regimes, inequality, and redistribution and extend the formal model of Chapter 4 to account for impact of inequality on the provision of more or less purely redistributive social-welfare spending. The remainder of the chapter empirically tests our hypotheses.

7.2 DEMOCRACY AND REDISTRIBUTION: THEORETICAL EXPECTATIONS

Theories grounded in the median-voter logic presume that inequality retards democratization because elites fear increased social-welfare spending. But what if the elites' fears are groundless? What if higher inequality actually decreases redistributive social-welfare spending? Such a finding would demand a different explanation for real-world redistribution we do observe – and for regime change.

Acemoglu and Robinson (2006) do not empirically test the implications of their model on levels or type of redistributive spending under autocracy and democracy, but Boix (2003) does. However, he actually finds that the interaction of inequality and democracy tends to reduce redistributive spending, a result at odds with his (and Meltzer and Richard's) theoretical model (see his Table 5.5). Boix claims that this result follows from his theory, since he expects democracy to emerge only where inequality is low – and in such countries, demand for redistribution will also be low (p. 171).

This argument is problematic. Boix's theory of regime change necessarily assumes that autocratic elites believe democracy causes undesired levels of redistribution. Yet if democracy only emerges at low levels of inequality and levels of redistributive spending are concomitantly low, elites are expected to assess the danger of potential future regimes based on outcomes that never occur. In other words, what happens off the equilibrium path becomes crucial for Boix's argument about elite motivations.

However, if democratization is at least partly exogenous rather than endogenous (Przeworski et al. 2000), then regime change might sometimes occur under conditions of moderate or high inequality. And were this to occur – and if the Meltzer-Richard model's assumptions were true – then we would expect to see some confirmation of the model's expectations that redistributive spending under democracy should increase with inequality.

Our results in Chapters 5 and 6 suggest that democracies often *do* emerge under conditions of relatively high income inequality, even though such an effect might be offset by relatively high land inequality. In cases of regime change where income inequality is high but land inequality average, the Meltzer-Richard model would certainly expect relatively high levels of redistribution to follow. Yet as we shall demonstrate below, there is no evidence for this hypothesis.

Even more importantly, our argument predicts the opposite should occur. In Chapters 2 through 4 we provided reasons to suspect that the poor do not represent a redistributive threat – primarily because they are fragmented, disorganized and have few resources. In contrast, relatively wealthy groups by definition have more resources, and are more likely to mobilize on their own behalf. Under democracy, such groups may be able to target public spending away from the poor and toward themselves. Hence higher inequality may produce lower social-welfare spending, or less progressive spending, or both.

To show how this dynamic works, we extend our elite-competition model from Chapter 4 to examine how inequality affects the size and composition of redistribution under democracy. The most relevant consideration is the link between income inequality and the political influence of bourgeois and middle class groups relative to landed elites and the masses. As political influence follows economic influence, a natural extension of our model assumes that economic elites should have considerable influence not only during but also *after* regime change, leveraging resources to influence the nature and extent of government spending.

Our model reflects the dominant dynamic of policy making in democracies the world over: As noted in Chapter 1, critics have long decried the disconnect between formal equality and informal inequality under democracy, where policy never closely embodies the preferences of the median voter. Instead, organized, well-financed groups tend to have influence disproportionate to their numbers. To the extent this is true, we have little reason to expect that democracy and redistribution go hand in hand – or that the greater the inequality, the greater the redistribution to the poor.

In fact, the opposite should be true: if inequality reflects the rise of moneyed interest groups, then the greater the inequality, the *lower* the redistributive spending to the poor, precisely because those with material resources to invest in politics also have a strong desire to shape policy to fit their preferences. Moreover, by implication, wealthier citizens have strong incentives to lobby for the creation of "club goods," targeted government benefits that are unequally distributed, but weaker incentives to push for spending on universalistic "public goods," which are distributed to all citizens more or less equally (Olson 1982). The more unequal the society, the stronger these incentives.

This argument echoes Moene and Wallerstein (2001), who suggest that to the extent that government spending programs can be targeted at specific groups, support for spending on the poor will decline as inequality increases. Similarly, Lizzeri and Persico (2004) suggest that some elements of the economic elite may demand an increase in investment in government spending on infrastructure, healthcare, and education, the benefits of which disproportionately accrue to the better-off – a hypothesis bolstered by Ross (2006), who found that public spending in democracies does not particularly benefit the poor.

In Chapter 4, for sake of parsimony and to illustrate that our results do not depend on departing from this assumption, we followed the MR model and presumed that under democracy all citizens are taxed at the same flat rate and all receive a lump sum in return. Depending on the tax rate and the level of inequality, such a system can be highly progressive.[1]

We now examine the case of full democracy, where the masses set taxes-but we allow social welfare spending to be targeted to greater or lesser degrees by splitting spending between universal goods that all citizens receive and club goods received only by relatively wealthy citizens. Access to club goods can be

---

[1] How does the possibility of targeting public social-welfare spending alter our model of partial democratization as developed in Chapter 4? The existence of club goods actually increases the positive effects of industrial inequality on the bourgeoisie's incentive to rebel, both on their own and with the masses, because it increases the bourgeoisie's *de facto* control over public spending under democracy. Higher inequality means the bourgeoisie know they are likely to pay less in taxation, since they can limit the distribution of club goods to their own members and decline to pay for universalistic public goods.

an either/or proposition, or based on some probability. For example, all members of the bourgeoisie and elite might receive a club good with probability of one, but only a proportion of the masses. This mirrors the slow expansion of access to public goods such as health and education in developing democracies (Ansell 2010). Since we assume all members of the masses have the same income, we model unequal access probabilistically, such that each individual member of the poor only receives the good with a probability $q \in [0, 1]$. (In Chapter 4, we assumed $q = 1$.)

Excluding the former autocratic elite for simplicity, we model the relative "clubness" of social-welfare spending as a function of the ratio of the income of the bourgeoisie to that of the masses. The larger this ratio, the more that social-welfare spending will resemble club goods. Accordingly, $q = q(y_B/y_M)$, where $\partial q/\partial (y_B/y_M) < 0$.[2] Note, that even though the masses nominally control policymaking, we presume that wealthy elites are able to divert resources toward themselves. Because all types of inequality make the masses relatively less wealthy and, therefore, less politically powerful, the share of social welfare spending going to the masses *decreases* with all types of inequality: $\partial q/\partial \gamma < 0$, $\partial q/\partial \phi < 0$, and $\partial q/\partial k < 0$.[3] This reverses the Meltzer-Richard formulation.

With club goods, we alter the budget constraint under full democracy to $t\bar{y} = g(1 - (1 - q)\sigma_M)$, where the last term reflects the fact that everybody save a share $(1 - q)$ of the poor population σ_M receives the club good. We assume that q is determined by relative *gross* income; even though the masses control government they cannot change q directly because existing elites can influence the distribution of public goods.

Accordingly the utility function for a representative member of the masses can now be written as:

$$U_{Mi} = (1 - t_{DC})Y_{Mi} + qV_{Mi}\left(\frac{t_{DC}^* \bar{y}}{1 - (1 - q)\sigma_M}\right) \tag{7.1}$$

In short, the masses must consider that they only receive the public good with probability q when setting their preferred tax rate – t_{DC} – producing the following first order condition:

$$V_{Mi}'\left(\frac{t_{DC}^* \bar{y}}{1 - (1 - q)\sigma_M}\right) = \frac{y_{Mi}}{\bar{y}}\left(\frac{(1 - (1 - q)\sigma_M)}{q}\right) \tag{7.2}$$

The simplest way to analyze how changes in q affect the masses' preferred tax rate in democracy is to examine the two extreme conditions of $q = 1$ (pure public goods) and $q = 0$ (masses completely excluded). In the former case, the equation collapses to Equation 4.10 – the masses' preferred

---

[2] This can be extended to including the income of the former autocratic elite so that $q = q((y_B + y_E)/y_M)$ without loss of generality, because increased land, industrial, and intersectoral inequality all reduce q.

[3] It is simple to show that $\partial(y_B/y_M)/\partial \gamma > 0$, $\partial(y_B/y_M)/\partial \phi > 0$, and $\partial(y_B/y_M)/\partial k > 0$.

tax rate under full democracy without club goods: thus $t^*_{DC} = t^*_D$. By contrast, if $q = 0$, the right-hand side of Equation 7.2 explodes, meaning an 'infinite' marginal utility and, thus, a tax rate of $t^*_{DC} = 0$. This means that $\partial t^*_{DC}/\partial q > 0$. Accordingly, higher levels of q produce higher preferred tax rates and spending. Since q is *decreasing* in all types of inequality, this implies that rising inequality under democracy will produce lower levels of overall spending.

To put this intuitively, spending will rise when the masses can assure themselves greater access to social welfare spending. However, such assurance only comes when their political influence increases relative to elites' – and this only occurs when inequality is relatively low.[4] Note that since both land and income inequality reduce the income of the masses and thereby reduce their access to club goods, both are associated with reduced taxing and redistributive spending under democracy.

A further implication is that if different types of spending can be more or less universal, we should expect that rising inequality (by weakening mass control of policymaking) should have the most dramatic negative impact on universal public goods, for example, on general redistributive payouts. By contrast, the negative effect of inequality on spending should be dramatically weaker for public goods that can be targeted to wealthier citizens, for example healthcare in developing countries (as in Ross 2006).

We now test these hypotheses on original data on redistributive spending from 62 countries from 1880 to 1930, and then on more contemporary data on government consumption from 1950 to 1999.

7.3 REDISTRIBUTION 1880 TO 1930: REEXAMINING THE EVIDENCE

The theoretically relevant variables scholars have employed to explain variation in the extent of government redistributive spending fall into three categories: political, economic, and demographic. The most important political variable is regime-type: most broadly, the redistributivist logic suggests that democracy should have an independent effect on social-welfare spending, since all can vote yet the median voter earns less than average income. Similarly, this approach suggests that the degree of democracy should also directly increase redistributive spending.

Scholars have also suggested that the level of electoral participation should impact redistributive spending in democracies (Franzese 1998; Lindert 2004). This is because differences in turnout change the relative position of the median voter: In the Meltzer-Richard framework, when turnout is high as a proportion of the population, the median voter is relatively poorer. This should increase demand for redistribution.

---

4 Formally, through the club goods effect: $\frac{\partial t^*_{DC}}{\partial q}\frac{\partial q}{\partial \gamma} < 0$, $\frac{\partial t^*_{DC}}{\partial q}\frac{\partial q}{\partial \phi} < 0$, and $\frac{\partial t^*_{DC}}{\partial q}\frac{\partial q}{\partial k} < 0$.

Finally, some scholars suggest that because political parties have distinct redistributive policy preferences, spending outcomes may depend on which parties perform well at elections (Bradley et al. 2003; Iversen and Soskice 2006). In particular, turnout may matter less than the relative performance of leftist parties.

Turning to economic variables, we begin with the level of economic development, typically measured as per capita income. Wagner's Law suggests that demand for government intervention in the economy increases with economic development, regardless of the level of inequality. For example, industrialization creates an urban working class that experiences job turnover and job-related injuries relatively more frequently, generating increased demand for unemployment compensation, disability payments, public health care, and so forth.

Inequality is the second key economic variable, as per the Meltzer-Richard model. However, the hypothesized effect of inequality is only indirect. Boix (2003) suggests that, "The presence of sharp income differentials... should lead to very high taxes and transfers" (173), but notes that we should observe this effect *only in democracies*. That is, the key theoretical mechanism is the supposed *interactive* effects of inequality and democracy in determining spending outcomes.

In a dataset that includes both democracies and autocracies, the direct impact of both democracy and inequality are relatively unimportant for assessing competing theories of redistributive spending *under democracy*. Redistributive models of regime change do suggest that democracies should redistribute more than autocracies, independently of the level of inequality, but the crucial component is that the threat of such spending only increases with inequality under democracy. Likewise, independently of regime type, neither the elite-competition nor the redistributivist model has much to say about the direct effect of inequality on government spending. The redistributivist model does not predict that inequality tends to generate increased social welfare spending under autocracy; only under democracy does inequality matter for redistribution. The interaction of democracy and inequality does the theoretical heavy lifting in redistributivist models, as in ours. To reiterate the hypothesis developed in the previous section, we expect the combination of democracy and inequality to *reduce* government spending overall and especially on the most universalistic of public goods. By contrast, redistributivist models expect the combination of democracy and inequality to increase public spending, especially on universal goods.

A third economic variable often included in studies of redistributive spending is globalization, typically operationalized as openness to international trade. Much recent scholarship hypothesized that greater exposure to trade leads governments to construct a deeper and wider safety net for citizens harmed by international competition (e.g., Alesina and Rodrik 1994).

Finally, demographic variables are also important. Scholars interested in patterns of redistributive spending typically include population. The hypothesis here is that the larger the population, the smaller the proportion of GDP the government needs to spend, all else equal, because of economies of scale: in smaller countries, it takes a greater fiscal effort to provide social welfare and insurance than in a larger country, simply because it is expensive to set up a government redistribution program but relatively cheap to add additional people to the program (Alesina and Spolaore 2005).

Other demographic variables said to increase social-welfare spending include ethnic and/or religious diversity (e.g., Alesina and Glaeser 2005) and the average age of the population. Lindert (2004, 183) notes that the impact of this last variable has been seen ever since life expectancy began to accelerate in the late 19th century, and that the effect of an aging population appears across all types of social-welfare spending (i.e., not just old-age pensions).

7.3.1 Sample

The research in this chapter was inspired by the work of economic historian Peter Lindert (2004), who suggested that evidence for the Meltzer-Richard hypothesis is inconclusive for two reasons. The first is that while data on social-welfare spending are readily available for wealthy democracies, the incidence of per capita income and regime type is not random among other cases. Focusing on wealthy countries will bias results toward confirming that democracy and redistribution go hand in hand.

The second source of ambiguity is that empirical research has relied on data from after World War II. By this time, democracy was already well established in many high-spending countries, and other factors that might drive social-welfare spending were also at relatively high levels in these same countries, such as an aging population and the presence of bureaucratic machinery that permits high levels of both taxing and spending. This means that political, economic and demographic variables are all endogenous to each other in the postwar era, making identification of causal connections difficult if not impossible, and severely restricting the inferences scholars can derive about relationships between variables.

Lindert inferred that postwar data would not allow a reliable test of the Meltzer-Richard hypothesis, and suggested that data from the era when welfare-state policies first emerged – 1880 to 1930 – would offer advantages. Prior to 1880 too few countries were democracies, and too few spent anything on social welfare. Lindert reasoned that to the extent that the MR model can explain patterns of redistributive spending, it should be able to distinguish spending in countries that were among the first to expand the franchise from countries that delayed democratization until later. Moreover, during this period even within Europe considerable variation existed on both the dependent variable as well as on key independent variables such as democracy, inequality, demography, and per capita income.

Despite his efforts, Lindert's data are also biased in an important respect. The Polity dataset counts 53 independent countries in 1880, and 68 in 1930. Yet Lindert (2004, following Lindert 1994) gathered data for only 30 countries – and his statistical analysis is largely limited to 19 mostly Western European cases. This means that his sample covers only a fraction of the universe of cases, and is biased toward wealthier democracies.

We gathered government spending data for 62 countries, a far more representative sample. For example, in 1880 the countries in Lindert's dataset had an average Polity score of 0.90, while the same score for our cases was −0.88. The actual average for the 53 countries in the Polity dataset that year was −1.15. Similarly, in 1930 the average Polity score for the countries in Lindert's sample was 4.80, while the average for the 55 countries in our sample was 1.05 – and the overall Polity average was 0.00. In general, our sample more closely reflects the actual distribution of independent states during this period than Lindert's.[5]

7.3.2 Dependent Variables

Let us now operationalize "redistributive spending." Our efforts hewed as closely as possible to Lindert's measures, which in turn closely echo contemporary OECD definitions of social expenditures. Thus we gathered information on spending as a percentage of GDP for four types of government programs: (1) welfare and unemployment compensation, (2) pensions, (3) housing subsidies, and (4) healthcare. From this information we created an indicator of aggregate social-welfare spending, as well as disaggregated spending levels by type.

As suggested above, separating social-welfare spending into these four categories is crucial for testing competing models of politics because each has different redistributive implications. If the Meltzer-Richard model were correct, we should see a strongly positive relationship between inequality and universalistic redistributive social-welfare spending programs. In contrast, if our argument were correct, we should see the opposite: a strongly negative relationship between inequality and spending on the poor.

We list the four categories of spending programs from most to least progressive (Lindert 2004, 3): welfare/unemployment, pensions, housing, and health. This is because the first comes in the form of direct transfers from

---

5 Our sample includes Afghanistan, Albania, *Argentina, Australia, Austria, Belgium*, Bolivia, *Brazil, Bulgaria, Canada*, Chile, China, Colombia, Costa Rica, Cuba, *Czechoslovakia Denmark*, Dominican Republic, Ecuador, El Salvador, Estonia, Ethiopia, *Finland, France, Germany, Greece*, Guatemala, Haiti, Honduras, *Hungary*, Iran, *Ireland, Italy, Japan*, Latvia, Lithuania, *Mexico*, Morocco, Nepal, *Netherlands, New Zealand*, Nicaragua, *Norway*, Paraguay, Peru, *Poland, Portugal, Romania*, Russia (and the USSR), Saudi Arabia, South Africa, *Spain, Sweden, Switzerland*, Thailand, Turkey, *United Kingdom, United States*, Uruguay, Venezuela, and *Yugoslavia*. Lindert's 1994 sample is in italics.

richer citizens to the very poor and unemployed, whereas the other policies, particularly health spending, were typically limited during this time period in geographic scope and often targeted to middle/high income citizens The redistributivist model, thus, predicts that inequality and democracy should have the clearest positive impact on welfare and unemployment compensation, but the least on health spending, whereas our elite competition theory predicts that inequality and democracy should have a clear *negative* impact on welfare and unemployment spending, becoming weaker as we move toward healthcare.

To gather historical data on social-welfare spending as a percentage of GDP, we started with Lindert's data.[6] Lindert relied on detailed International Labour Office (later Organization) (ILO) surveys, *International Survey of Social Services* (ILO 1933, 1936). To add cases we used the same sources, different countries' official national statistical yearbooks, and a variety of additional primary and secondary sources.[7]

Like Lindert, we collected information for each country at decade intervals, for 1880, 1890, 1900, 1910, 1920, and 1930.[8] This reduces the time-dependence of consecutive observations. To further correct for time-dependence we use both year dummies and assume one-period autocorrelated error for all models.[9]

7.3.3 Independent Variables

We sought to stick closely to the key independent variables scholars have employed to test for relationships between democracy, inequality, and redistribution. We also sought to maximize sample size under the constraint of including theoretically relevant controls – hence our estimation model is relatively stripped down. For democracy, we use both the dichotomous and continuous measures employed in Chapters 5 and 6. As in previous chapters we run a variety of statistical specifications, some examining the impact of cross-sectional differences in the level of democracy across countries, others the impact of within-country changes in regime type.

We use measures for electoral turnout as a percentage of the population and the proportion of vote share pertaining to left-wing parties drawn from Lindert (2004), Nohlen (2005) and Caramani et al. (2000). In terms of economic variables, our measures of per capita income, income inequality, and land inequality are also all the same as employed in Chapter 5. We measure economic openness in the standard fashion, as the volume of trade as

---

[6] We thank Peter Lindert for providing the core databases for *Growing Public*.

[7] The authors' websites links to the database, codebook and list of sources.

[8] These are not decade averages but data for that particular year.

[9] Because we are examining ten-year intervals, autocorrelation is fairly low, rarely higher than 0.5. Using panel-specific autocorrelation produces similar results, although many panels are too short to estimate their autocorrelation parameters.

a percentage of GDP.[10] Finally, as controls we include population and a full set of regional or country dummies (depending on the specification), as well as year dummies.

7.3.4 Aggregate Public Spending

We begin by analyzing total public spending during the 1880–1930 period. Table 7.1 presents a series of estimations of the determinants of total public social spending, with democracy measured as a dummy variable. All models include decade dummies (not reported), have standard errors clustered by country, and assume a sample-wide one-period autocorrelation ρ. We alternate between two specifications: odd numbered models are pooled regressions (with regional dummies), whereas even-numbered models include country fixed effects. We maintain this pattern throughout this section.

Models 1 and 2 include only democracy, GDP per capita, and (logged) population. Note that the estimate for democracy's direct effect is positive, but either negligible (Model 1) or borderline significant and small (Model 2). To get a sense of the size of the predicted effect in Model 2, a transition to democracy tends to increase spending by 0.15% of GDP, which is only 1/4 of a standard deviation. This effect is not only weak substantively, it is weak statistically – barely significant at the ten percent level. It is implausible, in our view, that such a weak effect could constitute a clear and present danger to incumbent autocratic elites.

The result on democracy is usefully contrasted with the result on per capita income, the effect of which is independent of regime type. Higher-income countries have higher overall levels of social-welfare spending, as an increase of one standard deviation ($2,000) is associated with an increase of between 0.22% (Model 1) and 0.50% (Model 2) of GDP – up to three times larger than the effect of a transition from autocracy to democracy.

Models 3 and 4 introduce our Rural Inequality measure. Unsurprisingly, in these and all remaining models, its effect is always negative – and almost always statistically significant. The implication is that *regardless of regime type*, higher rural inequality is associated with lower social spending. Moreover, the effects are sizable – a one standard deviation increase in rural inequality reduces social spending by 0.40% of GDP, similar to the effect of per capita income and much larger than for democracy. Rural inequality also appears to absorb the effect of per capita income in Model 3, suggesting that cross-sectional differences in public spending appear to relate to differences in the distribution of land ownership rather than the level of national income (these are, indeed, negatively correlated with one another at −0.73).

---

[10] Further details on the construction of all these variables are contained in the authors' codebook.

TABLE 7.1. *1880–1930 Total Social Spending: Democracy Dummy*

	(1) OLS	(2) FE	(3) OLS	(4) FE	(5) OLS	(6) FE	(7) OLS	(8) FE	(9) OLS	(10) FE
Democracy	0.005	0.150*	0.038	0.154*	0.076	0.125	1.126***	1.475***	6.287***	2.494*
	(0.096)	(0.084)	(0.113)	(0.084)	(0.120)	(0.086)	(0.377)	(0.320)	(1.370)	(1.371)
GDP Per Capita	0.114**	0.254***	0.047	0.191***	0.071	0.126***	0.028	0.125***	0.056	0.114***
	(0.044)	(0.043)	(0.044)	(0.038)	(0.057)	(0.037)	(0.046)	(0.035)	(0.058)	(0.038)
Population	0.010	-0.271*	-0.051	-0.498***	-0.117*	-0.186	-0.036	-0.268**	-0.112*	-0.171
	(0.080)	(0.145)	(0.060)	(0.127)	(0.064)	(0.127)	(0.065)	(0.095)	(0.060)	(0.129)
Rural Ineq.			-1.230***	-1.823***	-1.188***	-0.877**	-0.393	-0.945**	-1.404***	-0.846**
			(0.327)	(0.460)	(0.430)	(0.378)	(0.413)	(0.373)	(0.382)	(0.368)
Openness					-0.004	0.023	0.020	0.014	-0.021	0.039
					(0.046)	(0.037)	(0.036)	(0.036)	(0.044)	(0.036)
BM Gini					0.191	-9.797***			4.867***	-6.126**
					(1.717)	(2.042)			(1.705)	(2.617)
Dem X RI.							-1.918***	-2.289***		
							(0.583)	(0.499)		
Dem X Gini									-13.195***	-4.958*
									(2.912)	(2.884)
Constant	-0.145	3.669	1.818**	8.757***	2.576*	7.980***	0.924	4.069**	0.302	6.056***
	(1.087)	(2.720)	(0.838)	(2.391)	(1.390)	(2.120)	(0.935)	(1.807)	(1.135)	(2.220)
Observations	243	243	224	224	160	160	216	216	160	160
Countries	62	62	57	57	39	39	55	55	39	39

Standard errors in parentheses

* $p < 0.10$, ** $p < 0.05$, *** $p < 0.01$

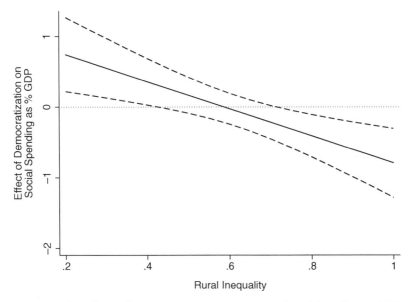

FIGURE 7.1. The Effects of Democratization (0 to 1) on Social Spending at Different Levels of Rural Inequality

Models 5 and 6 add in trade openness and income inequality. Openness has no effect on social spending, but all else equal, income inequality has either no effect (Model 5) or a strongly negative effect (Model 6). Even so, as noted above this result is not very interesting theoretically, since it holds *regardless of regime type.*

Models 7 through 10 explore the crucial theoretical hypotheses, testing for the joint effects of inequality and democracy. The Meltzer-Richard model implies that under democracy, inequality should be associated with higher public spending, but our approach suggests the opposite: a negative sign on the interaction term. Results are fully consistent with our expectations. Interacted coefficients are difficult to interpret on their own, so we present results graphically in Figures 7.1 and 7.2, which are estimated from Models 7 and 9 of Table 7.1. These show the predicted impact of democratization on social spending at various levels of rural and income inequality.

In both cases, as inequality increases the estimated effect of democratization on social spending is *negative.* These effects are both statistically significant and substantively large. For rural inequality, Figure 7.1 reveals that above a level of 0.7 (around the 55th percentile in the sample) we see a statistically significant negative effect of democratization on the level of social spending, which is worth 0.5% of national income at a rural inequality level of 0.9 (the 90th percentile). By contrast, at levels of rural inequality below 0.4 (the 15th percentile), there is evidence of a statistically significant *positive* effect of

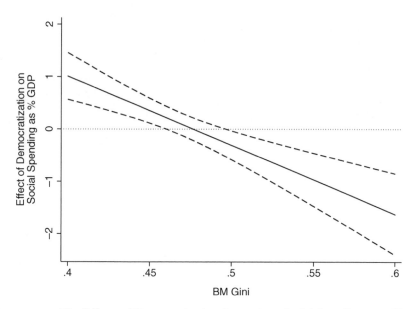

FIGURE 7.2. The Effects of Democratization (0 to 1) on Social Spending at Different Levels of Income Inequality

democratization on aggregate public spending. Only where land inequality is low do we see a positive relationship between democracy and redistribution.

We see similar effects for income inequality in Figure 7.2, even controlling for the effect of rural inequality. Democratization has a statistically significant negative effect on social spending starting at a Gini of 0.5 (around the 65th percentile). For example, regime change in a country with a Gini of 0.53 (the 90th percentile) is associated with a decline in spending of around 0.7% of GDP. Again, we only see a positive relationship between democracy and redistribution at low levels of income inequality (below a Gini of 0.45, around the 25th percentile).

We can also interpret the interaction by examining the effect of an increase in rural and income inequality in autocracies versus democracies. For rural inequality we find that a 0.1 increase has an insignificant estimated effect on public spending in autocracies of just −.04% of GDP (standard error of .04%), but in democracies this change in rural inequality is associated with a reduction in spending of 0.25% of GDP (standard error of 0.05%). For income inequality, we find that a 0.1 increase actually increases public spending by 0.5% (standard error of 0.17%) of GDP in autocracies, but decreases it by 0.83% (standard error of 0.27%) in democracies. The pattern, whereby inequality produces *negative* effects on spending under democracy is, thus, consistent across both measures of inequality.

Perhaps the dummy operationalization of democracy is too blunt an instrument to effectively proxy for the political determinants of public spending. To explore this possibility and confirm that our results stand up to alternative operationalizations of a key independent variable, in Table 7.2 we use the Polity index.

Doing so changes little. We note that in the fixed effects models with no interactions (2, 4 and 6), democracy on its own has a positive and significant effect on public spending. Regardless of the level of inequality, a one standard deviation shift in the Polity score increases public spending by about 0.15% of GDP averaging across these three models – tiny in absolute terms, less than a quarter of a standard deviation in public spending. Likewise, a one standard deviation shift in democracy produces less than a third of the direct effect of a similar shift in either income or rural inequality when those variables are included in Models 4 and 6. Again, this is hardly sufficient to credibly threaten the economic position of the rich under autocracy.

Now turn to the crucial interactive tests, in Models 7–10. Once again we find strong evidence of a negative interactive effect of inequality and democracy. At low levels of rural inequality (0.35, the 10th percentile), a ten-point shift in the Polity index is associated with an *increase* in social spending of 0.33% of GDP. But when rural inequality is high (0.90, the 90th percentile), the same shift on the Polity index is associated with a *decrease* in spending of about 0.20% of GDP. At median levels of rural inequality there is no discernible effect of any change along the Polity index.[11]

Similarly, where income inequality is low (0.43, the 10th percentile), a ten-point increase in the Polity index is associated with an increase in social-welfare spending of 0.4% of GDP, but at high levels (0.53, the 90th percentile), the same shift is associated with a decrease in spending of 0.3% of GDP.[12]

Putting the results in Tables 7.1 and 7.2 together, examination of aggregate levels of government social spending around the world from 1880 to 1930 reveals no evidence supporting the median-voter model, and strong support for our theoretical conjecture that the effect of inequality on aggregate levels of social spending under democracy is robustly negative. Thus far, we find no evidence that inequality, democracy and redistribution go hand in hand.

We now consider the effects of electoral turnout. Following Meltzer & Richard, assuming that poorer people are less likely to vote, higher turnout tends to lower voters' average income. All else equal, this should increase demands for redistributive spending. Moreover, this effect should be stronger

---

[11] These estimates use Model 7. Those for income inequality use Model 9.

[12] Symmetrically, increases in inequality have a significant negative effect on social spending for Polity scores of seven or above, and a positive effect for Polity scores of minus two or below. Thus, the purported positive effects of inequality on the size of government in democracy are nowhere to be found.

TABLE 7.2. *1880–1930 Total Social Spending: Polity Score*

	(1) OLS	(2) FE	(3) OLS	(4) FE	(5) OLS	(6) FE	(7) OLS	(8) FE	(9) OLS	(10) FE
Polity	0.006	0.022***	0.005	0.019***	0.010	0.023***	0.064**	0.123***	0.342***	0.179***
	(0.005)	(0.005)	(0.006)	(0.005)	(0.007)	(0.006)	(0.026)	(0.015)	(0.071)	(0.049)
GDP Per Capita	0.108**	0.249***	0.047	0.189***	0.068	0.136***	0.028	0.096***	0.045	0.124***
	(0.044)	(0.040)	(0.044)	(0.036)	(0.057)	(0.037)	(0.046)	(0.029)	(0.057)	(0.036)
Population	0.018	−0.147	−0.045	−0.371***	−0.109*	−0.080	−0.038	−0.244***	−0.102	−0.078
	(0.083)	(0.127)	(0.063)	(0.112)	(0.065)	(0.117)	(0.069)	(0.086)	(0.063)	(0.110)
Rural Ineq.			−1.210***	−1.824***	−1.122**	−0.750**	−0.904**	−1.500***	−1.380***	−0.794**
			(0.326)	(0.457)	(0.442)	(0.379)	(0.374)	(0.362)	(0.403)	(0.358)
Openness					0.001	0.036	0.009	0.049	−0.019	0.049
					(0.045)	(0.036)	(0.033)	(0.030)	(0.043)	(0.035)
BM Gini					0.322	−8.634***			1.535	−6.036***
					(1.728)	(1.981)			(1.573)	(1.939)
Pol. X RI.							−0.090***	−0.152***		
							(0.034)	(0.020)		
Pol. X Gini									−0.690***	−0.320***
									(0.146)	(0.099)
Constant	−0.268	1.354	1.715*	6.385***	2.374	5.259**	1.335	4.030**	1.745	4.074**
	(1.136)	(2.414)	(0.891)	(2.160)	(1.467)	(2.096)	(0.998)	(1.645)	(1.299)	(1.939)
Observations	248	248	228	228	161	161	220	220	161	161
Countries	62	62	57	57	39	39	55	55	39	39

Standard errors in parentheses

* $p < 0.10$, ** $p < 0.05$, *** $p < 0.01$

as inequality increases. Although turnout data is more fragmentary than regime-type data we are nonetheless able to examine a sample of up to fifty-one countries (190 observations).

Table 7.3 shows a series of estimations of the interactive effect of turnout and inequality. Models 1 through 4 control for regime type with the democracy dummy, whereas Models 5 through 8 employ the Polity index. We focus on the relationship between turnout and inequality, and find similar results to those in Tables 7.1 and 7.2: The impact of turnout on spending *declines* with both rural and income inequality.

As before, this relationship is easier to interpret graphically. Figures 7.3 and 7.4 build on Models 5 and 6 of Table 7.3, setting the Polity score to equal eight (i.e. a democratic country). The figures show the estimated impact on spending of a one percent increase in turnout. In both cases, turnout only has a positive effect on spending in countries with low rural or income inequality. When inequality rises, even if poorer citizens turn out to vote they appear unable to translate that political participation into redistribution. This jibes with our argument that under conditions of high inequality, weak economic strength translates into limited political efficacy, *even if* formal democratic institutions and participation are present.

One rejoinder might be that greater turnout might only produce more redistribution if it generates votes for parties that favor redistribution – that is, parties associated with the left. The redistributivist literature tends to neglect partisan politics, presuming that elected officials will converge in their policy platforms (and resulting policy outcomes) to the preferences of the median voter. However, we can extend the redistributivist approach to partisan politics: if left-wing parties represent poorer voters, their own median voter should be even more pro-redistributive than the democratic median voter, and this should be intensified under high levels of inequality.

Table 7.4 shows, however, that redistribution continues to be stymied by inequality even when leftist parties gain votes. As before, mass representation – this time through left-wing parties – only produces redistribution under conditions of very low rural and income inequality. In contrast, at higher levels of rural and income inequality there is no clear effect of left-wing vote on spending outcomes. Although this analysis is conducted on a truncated sample of 30 countries and 74 cases, the results are consistent with our earlier findings – inequality prevents political representation from translating into redistribution.

7.3.5 Disaggregating Public Spending

In this section, we test our corollary hypothesis that inequality has distinct effects on different types of social-welfare spending: welfare and unemployment, pensions, housing, and healthcare. Together with public

TABLE 7.3. *1880–1930 Total Social Spending and Turnout*

	(1) OLS	(2) OLS	(3) FE	(4) FE	(5) OLS	(6) OLS	(7) FE	(8) FE
Dem. Dummy	-0.091 (0.113)	-0.082 (0.127)	-0.012 (0.073)	-0.002 (0.077)				
Polity					-0.001 (0.006)	0.006 (0.008)	0.007 (0.004)	0.015*** (0.005)
GDP Per Capita	0.052 (0.044)	0.059 (0.058)	0.079** (0.036)	0.077** (0.036)	0.051 (0.045)	0.057 (0.056)	0.074** (0.034)	0.072** (0.033)
Openness	0.010 (0.035)	-0.003 (0.049)	0.046 (0.034)	0.046 (0.041)	0.005 (0.033)	-0.005 (0.048)	0.047 (0.032)	0.060 (0.038)
Population	-0.106** (0.042)	-0.134* (0.070)	-0.214** (0.093)	-0.163 (0.158)	-0.109** (0.043)	-0.126* (0.070)	-0.164* (0.087)	-0.053 (0.153)
Turnout	0.044*** (0.008)	0.148*** (0.044)	0.041*** (0.005)	0.089** (0.042)	0.043*** (0.008)	0.155*** (0.045)	0.038*** (0.005)	0.106*** (0.037)
Rural Ineq.	-0.140 (0.348)	-1.191*** (0.423)	-1.033*** (0.400)	-0.711* (0.393)	-0.084 (0.355)	-1.115*** (0.424)	-0.916** (0.365)	-0.552 (0.368)
Turnout X RI	-0.061*** (0.012)		-0.053*** (0.008)		-0.060*** (0.012)		-0.047*** (0.008)	
BM Gini		6.364*** (2.192)		-2.585 (3.465)		6.950*** (2.105)		-1.552 (3.100)
Turnout X Gini		-0.291*** (0.103)		-0.157* (0.093)		-0.311*** (0.106)		-0.202** (0.083)
Constant	1.611** (0.694)	-0.350 (1.692)	3.634** (1.732)	4.138* (2.157)	1.625** (0.715)	-0.785 (1.647)	2.666 (1.653)	1.586 (2.203)
Observations	188	136	188	136	190	137	190	137
Countries	51	37	51	37	51	37	51	37

Standard errors in parentheses

* $p < 0.10$, ** $p < 0.05$, *** $p < 0.01$

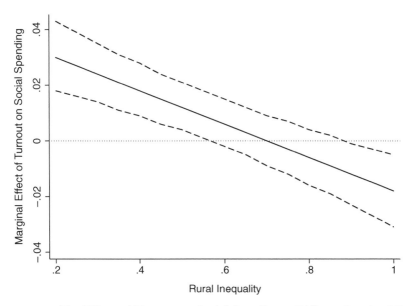

FIGURE 7.3. The Effects of Turnout on Social Spending at Different Levels of Rural Inequality

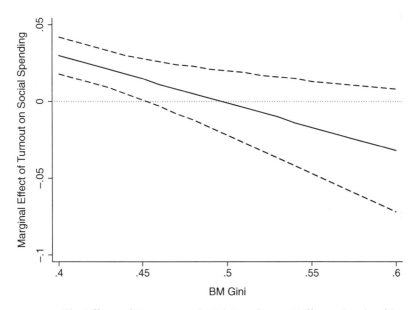

FIGURE 7.4. The Effects of Turnout on Social Spending at Different Levels of Income Inequality

TABLE 7.4. *1880–1930 Total Social Spending and Left Vote Share*

	(1) OLS	(2) OLS	(3) FE	(4) FE	(5) OLS	(6) OLS	(7) FE	(8) FE
Dem. Dummy	0.119 (0.256)	-0.138 (0.261)	0.231 (0.177)	0.070 (0.184)				
Polity					0.038** (0.016)	0.028 (0.020)	0.064*** (0.017)	0.084*** (0.014)
GDP Per Capita	0.028 (0.092)	-0.033 (0.084)	0.174*** (0.054)	-0.002 (0.064)	0.006 (0.090)	-0.051 (0.078)	0.141*** (0.053)	0.010 (0.060)
Openness	-0.002 (0.076)	-0.015 (0.079)	-0.021 (0.054)	-0.068 (0.053)	0.015 (0.065)	-0.007 (0.079)	0.097* (0.051)	0.082* (0.042)
Population	-0.063 (0.092)	-0.163 (0.122)	-0.117 (0.534)	0.419 (0.625)	-0.025 (0.090)	-0.112 (0.129)	-0.241 (0.425)	0.703* (0.407)
Left Vote	3.623** (1.583)	23.577*** (7.039)	5.231*** (1.816)	23.343*** (6.451)	3.541** (1.578)	19.889** (8.170)	4.151*** (1.581)	24.922*** (5.276)
Rural Ineq.	-0.773 (0.771)	-2.408*** (0.564)	-0.152 (2.042)	2.601 (1.918)	-0.330 (0.700)	-1.780*** (0.687)	2.217 (2.069)	6.174*** (1.666)
Left Vote X RI	-6.106* (3.185)		-10.875*** (3.396)		-5.752* (3.070)		-8.835*** (2.775)	
BM Gini		7.422** (3.430)		-3.273 (6.758)		7.073** (3.069)		0.396 (5.164)
Left Vote X Gini		-49.643*** (15.097)		-49.790*** (13.474)		-41.699** (17.901)		-52.585*** (10.624)
Constant	1.651 (1.471)	1.105 (2.274)	1.260 (10.276)	-6.024 (10.597)	0.785 (1.473)	-0.026 (2.279)	2.969 (8.034)	-14.753* (7.571)
Observations	73	67	73	67	74	67	74	67
Countries	29	26	29	26	30	26	30	26

Standard errors in parentheses
* $p < 0.10$, ** $p < 0.05$, *** $p < 0.01$

education, these four policy areas formed the core of what we now call welfare state spending.[13]

Each type of social spending entails distinct redistributive consequences. Historically, poorer citizens tended to benefit most from welfare (poor relief) and unemployment insurance. The initial growth of spending on public pensions and housing, by contrast, tended to benefit members of the upper working class, while spending on healthcare tended to primarily benefit higher-income citizens (Lindert 2004; Lizzeri and Persico 2004; Ross 2006).

If the Meltzer-Richard logic were sound, we should see the strongest positive relationship between inequality, democracy and social spending for welfare and unemployment, and the weakest for spending on healthcare. Our argument predicts the opposite: a strongly negative relationship between inequality, democracy and spending on welfare and unemployment, but only a weakly negative effect for healthcare spending, with the other spending types seeing more moderate effects.

Results support our conjecture. For illustrative purposes, Tables 7.5 and 7.6 present results with democracy coded, respectively, dichotomously and continuously, in both cases interacted with income inequality.[14] Models 1 through 4 are pooled regressions, whereas Models 5 through 8 include country fixed effects. We order the columns from the most to least universalistic policies (welfare, pensions, housing, health).

Of particular interest is the contrast in both tables between the consistently negative coefficients on the interaction between democracy and inequality for welfare spending in Models 1 and 5 (the conditional coefficients are both statistically significant at the 1% level) and the results for healthcare spending in Models 4 and 8. These conditional coefficients can be used to generate predicted differences of the impact of democracy at different levels of income inequality: at low levels (a Gini of 0.4) democracies are associated with welfare spending 0.54% of GDP *higher* than autocracies – but at high levels of inequality (a Gini of 0.6) democracies are associated with 0.83% of GDP *less* welfare spending. To be perfectly clear: under democracy, as inequality increases, universalistic redistributive spending *goes down*.

The effects for the intermediate categories of pensions and housing are similar in direction but lower in magnitude and statistical significance. For health

[13] Lindert (2004) devotes considerable attention to education in his work. However, for three reasons we did not collect data on resources devoted to education. First, during this period education involved substantially more variation in the public/private share of funding than the other programs, making direct comparisons difficult (Ansell and Lindvall 2013). Second, much education spending was conducted at the local level, exacerbating the already serious data collection challenges for this period. Third, education was more closely to connected to debates about the proper role of religion versus secular government and hence to conflicts between majority and minority religions than were other forms of spending (Kalyvas 1996).

[14] We obtain similar results using the interaction of rural inequality and democracy, omitted in the interest of brevity.

TABLE 7.5. *1880–1930 Types of Spending: Democracy Dummy*

	(1) Welfare OLS	(2) Pensions OLS	(3) Housing OLS	(4) Health OLS	(5) Welfare FE	(6) Pensions FE	(7) Housing FE	(8) Health FE
Democracy	3.285***	1.804***	0.398***	0.666	4.486***	-0.160	0.324	-1.478***
	(0.859)	(0.581)	(0.128)	(0.526)	(1.193)	(0.725)	(0.200)	(0.523)
GDP Per Capita	0.019	0.010	0.007	0.013	0.005	0.065***	0.001	0.043***
	(0.035)	(0.020)	(0.005)	(0.020)	(0.024)	(0.021)	(0.004)	(0.012)
Openness	-0.019	0.013	-0.003	-0.003	0.016	-0.009	-0.001	0.033*
	(0.031)	(0.026)	(0.004)	(0.016)	(0.024)	(0.023)	(0.006)	(0.017)
Population	-0.056	-0.013	0.001	-0.038	-0.215**	0.045	0.031**	-0.019
	(0.039)	(0.022)	(0.006)	(0.025)	(0.087)	(0.073)	(0.013)	(0.044)
Rural Ineq.	-0.831***	-0.334**	0.007	-0.251*	0.443	-0.551**	-0.007	-0.292*
	(0.283)	(0.163)	(0.032)	(0.148)	(0.318)	(0.238)	(0.072)	(0.167)
BM Gini	3.208***	0.766	0.190	0.304	5.474**	-4.161***	-1.094***	-4.750***
	(0.965)	(0.608)	(0.172)	(0.610)	(2.320)	(1.558)	(0.343)	(1.015)
Dem. X Gini	-6.854***	-3.864***	-0.844***	-1.394	-9.070***	0.318	-0.692	3.135***
	(1.793)	(1.221)	(0.281)	(1.106)	(2.413)	(1.507)	(0.440)	(1.122)
Constant	-0.128	0.016	-0.145	0.695	1.533	0.843	-0.029	2.589***
	(0.703)	(0.395)	(0.146)	(0.500)	(1.112)	(1.194)	(0.277)	(0.835)
Observations	156	158	162	156	156	158	162	156
Countries	39	39	39	39	39	39	39	39

Standard errors in parentheses

$* \ p < 0.10, \ ** \ p < 0.05, \ *** \ p < 0.01$

TABLE 7.6. *1880–1930 Types of Spending: Polity Score*

	(1) Welfare OLS	(2) Pensions OLS	(3) Housing OLS	(4) Health OLS	(5) Welfare FE	(6) Pensions FE	(7) Housing FE	(8) Health FE
Polity	0.154***	0.133***	0.025***	0.019	0.115***	0.076***	0.021***	-0.037
	(0.044)	(0.032)	(0.007)	(0.025)	(0.038)	(0.028)	(0.006)	(0.024)
GDP Per Capita	0.017	0.002	0.006	0.008	0.019	0.068***	0.002	0.032**
	(0.034)	(0.020)	(0.005)	(0.020)	(0.025)	(0.021)	(0.004)	(0.014)
Openness	-0.018	0.012	-0.004	-0.001	0.008	0.002	-0.001	0.026
	(0.030)	(0.025)	(0.004)	(0.016)	(0.028)	(0.021)	(0.005)	(0.017)
Population	-0.057	-0.007	0.003	-0.037	-0.206**	0.080	0.031**	0.002
	(0.037)	(0.022)	(0.007)	(0.028)	(0.087)	(0.063)	(0.012)	(0.048)
Rural Ineq.	-0.928***	-0.299*	0.013	-0.218	-0.096	-0.359	0.008	-0.212
	(0.293)	(0.166)	(0.033)	(0.154)	(0.307)	(0.228)	(0.076)	(0.158)
BM Gini	1.394	0.071	-0.027	-0.363	0.014	-2.054*	-1.177***	-3.030***
	(0.928)	(0.627)	(0.194)	(0.648)	(1.662)	(1.147)	(0.315)	(0.861)
Pol. X Gini	-0.318***	-0.268***	-0.051***	-0.035	-0.232***	-0.126**	-0.040***	0.084*
	(0.089)	(0.065)	(0.014)	(0.051)	(0.075)	(0.056)	(0.013)	(0.048)
Constant	0.853	0.218	-0.064	0.995	4.093***	-1.027	-0.027	1.444*
	(0.773)	(0.445)	(0.169)	(0.630)	(1.353)	(1.111)	(0.273)	(0.855)
Observations	157	159	163	157	157	159	163	157
Countries	39	39	39	39	39	39	39	39

Standard errors in parentheses

$* p < 0.10$, $** p < 0.05$, $*** p < 0.01$

spending, however, there are no statistically significant differences between democracies and autocracies in spending at any level of inequality.

7.3.6 Spending 1880–1930: Summary

Our analysis of the relationship between democracy and redistribution in the era when both were first emerging on a wide scale serves several useful purposes. Most fundamentally, we find no support for the redistributivist hypothesis: democracy on its own sometimes generates a small increase in spending, but much less than per capita income or inequality. More importantly, the interaction of democracy with inequality produces a consistently *negative* effect – under democracy, as inequality increases social spending declines, a finding completely at odds with the median-voter hypothesis, but in line with our own theoretical expectations. Finally, when we disaggregate spending, we find further support for our contention that as inequality increases we should see sharply reduced spending on truly redistributive social-welfare programs but more mixed results for club-goods type programs, which benefit individuals who were relatively well-off to being with. Let us now consider whether these results hold up when we examine data from the post–World War II era.

7.4 FINDINGS: 1950–1999

We now compare the effect of inequality and democracy on redistribution in more recent decades, examining 118 countries from 1950 to 1999. We agree with Lindert that any test on data from this era are suspect because public spending was generally much higher, meaning it is harder to separate out pre- and post-tax levels of inequality. The historical legacy of preexisting levels of government spending also plays a greater role in explaining cross-sectional differences than in the 1880–1930 era, making identification of causal effects of other key variables more difficult to establish confidently. Nonetheless, this is the era that Boix (2003) – along with nearly all other research – has explored, and it is important to establish whether our results in the previous section hold during this time period as well. We confirm the pattern: under democracy, public spending is higher at lower levels of inequality, but declines as inequality increases – the precise opposite of the redistributivist logic.

In this section, the dependent variable is aggregate government consumption (spending) as a percentage of GDP. This variable has been used in a number of studies, including Boix (2003), Rodrik (1998) and Shelton (2007) and has the advantage of permitting us the broadest cross-country sample coverage. For independent variables, in the interest of brevity we limit our analysis to the continuous measure of democracy.[15] In some models, we

---

[15] Using the binary measure produces similar results, though marginally weaker in magnitude and statistical significance.

also use turnout in legislative elections (drawn from the IDEA dataset, at http://www.idea.int/vt/viewdata.cfm), and its interaction with the Gini coefficient. We retain the same rural inequality variable as used above, but for income inequality we replace the BM inequality data with the BAR data, allowing broader coverage.

Since a wider variety of indicators are available for the postwar era, we also included a broader array of controls. In addition to GDP per capita and population (both logged), we include a measure of trade openness (imports plus exports over GDP, drawn from the Penn World Tables), the percentage of the population either under fifteen or over sixty-five (from the World Development Indicators), and three measures of social heterogeneity drawn from Alesina et al. (2003): ethnic heterogeneity, linguistic diversity, and religious diversity. We also included a measure of the proportion of the population identifying as Muslim, and a variable measuring agricultural value-added as a percentage of GDP. Finally, we employ a series of country or year dummies depending on the specification.[16]

Table 7.7 contains eight models, employing various statistical estimations, alternating between pooled and country fixed effects models and adding decade dummies in Models 5 through 8. Each model uses an AR1 error term specification to capture temporal dependency. Models 1 and 2 show no direct effect of democracy or either type of inequality on public spending.[17] Per capita income is positively related to government consumption – the Wagner's Law effect – and as expected population is negatively related to government consumption, due to economies of scale. Furthermore, as one would expect, the relative size of dependent populations (youth and elderly) tends to increase spending. Trade openness has no estimable effect on spending, nor do ethnic or linguistic fractionalization. However, both religious fractionalization and Muslim population are associated with higher spending.

Models 3 and 4 reintroduce the same interactive specification as in the historical analysis, by including the product term of the Polity and Gini indices. Here we again see powerful evidence of a negative interactive effect: as inequality increases under democracy, government consumption declines. That this pattern emerges consistently, across time periods and across different sets of data suggests that this conditional relationship is a powerful determinant of social spending.

Figure 7.5, derived from Model 3, illustrates the impact of inequality under democracy, showing that at the 10th percentile of income inequality

---

[16] An important distinction between our analyses and Boix's (in his Chapter 5) comes in terms of sample coverage: Boix's largest sample containing a Gini coefficient includes 763 cases, whereas we triple that figure in many of our models. We point to this fact because Boix's sample of Ginis is heavily weighted toward wealthy, relatively equal democracies.

[17] Rural inequality its estimated to have a positive effect in the fixed effects model but this is only significant at the ten percent level and the coefficient is negatively signed in the pooled model.

TABLE 7.7. 1950–1999 Total Government Consumption

	(1)	(2)	(3)	(4)	(5)	(6)	(7)	(8)
Polity	−0.023	−0.022	0.329***	0.311***	−0.015	−0.009	0.225*	0.240**
	(0.018)	(0.017)	(0.105)	(0.099)	(0.017)	(0.017)	(0.118)	(0.113)
Gini	−1.678	−4.584	−0.567	−1.693	−1.874	1.648	−2.007	−1.188
	(3.346)	(3.859)	(3.377)	(4.009)	(2.988)	(4.042)	(7.804)	(8.730)
Rural Inequality	−1.388	4.258*	−1.097	4.673*	−0.708	2.186	−4.891***	−2.863
	(1.951)	(2.444)	(1.967)	(2.441)	(1.660)	(2.254)	(1.761)	(2.242)
Population (log)	−0.770***	1.595	−0.710***	1.998*	−0.778***	−0.870	−0.738***	−2.110*
	(0.229)	(1.189)	(0.232)	(1.190)	(0.195)	(1.046)	(0.208)	(1.175)
GDP Per Capita (log)	1.894***	2.880***	1.808***	2.739***	1.106**	2.117***	0.473	1.985***
	(0.459)	(0.654)	(0.456)	(0.650)	(0.450)	(0.625)	(0.461)	(0.742)
Population > 65	0.793***	0.791***	0.757***	0.779***	0.835***	0.412***	0.924***	0.356***
	(0.121)	(0.127)	(0.121)	(0.127)	(0.106)	(0.123)	(0.100)	(0.123)
Population < 15	0.244***	0.178***	0.235***	0.183***	0.219***	0.092	0.295***	0.150**
	(0.065)	(0.060)	(0.064)	(0.060)	(0.061)	(0.057)	(0.059)	(0.059)
Openness	0.006	−0.001	0.006	−0.001	0.007	−0.003	0.008	0.005
	(0.006)	(0.007)	(0.006)	(0.007)	(0.006)	(0.007)	(0.006)	(0.008)
Ethnic Frac.	−0.363		−0.170		0.087		−0.513	
	(1.421)		(1.421)		(1.065)		(0.965)	
Linguistic Frac.	0.664		0.216		−0.159		1.371	
	(1.471)		(1.484)		(1.000)		(0.950)	

Religious Frac	2.999***		2.933**		3.685***		2.821***	-0.514**
	(1.157)		(1.148)		(0.898)		(0.902)	(0.242)
Muslim Pop.	0.044***		0.046***		0.044***		0.022***	-0.057**
	(0.012)		(0.012)		(0.009)		(0.008)	(0.026)
Polity X Gini			-0.734***	-0.692***			-0.458*	
			(0.229)	(0.217)			(0.252)	
Agriculture					-0.035	-0.032	-0.076***	-0.903
					(0.021)	(0.022)	(0.025)	(4.575)
Turnout							-0.984	1.678
							(4.515)	(9.758)
Turnout X Gini							0.590	17.192
							(9.792)	(13.938)
Constant	-8.797	-32.714**	-8.746	-36.732***	-1.305	1.734	2.790	
	(6.093)	(13.228)	(6.111)	(13.262)	(6.358)	(12.588)	(7.045)	
Fixed Effects	No	Yes	No	Yes	No	Yes	No	Yes
Decade Dummies	No	No	No	No	Yes	Yes	Yes	Yes
Observations	2888	2974	2888	2974	2450	2504	1920	1930
Countries	113	118	113	118	112	117	106	108

Standard errors in parentheses

* $p < 0.10$, ** $p < 0.05$, *** $p < 0.01$

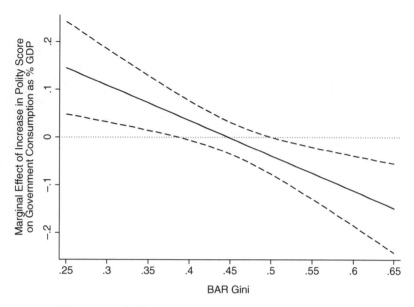

FIGURE 7.5. The Marginal Effect of the Polity Score on Government Consumption at Different Levels of Income Inequality

(0.36) the effect of a one-point increase in the Polity index tends to increase government consumption by about 0.1% of GDP. However, at the 90th percentile of inequality (0.58) the effect of a one-point increase in the Polity index is to *decrease* government consumption by the same amount. Similarly, an increase in income inequality has statistically significant negative effects on government consumption at Polity levels of seven or above. We find no conditional effect of turnout and inequality on government consumption.[18] However, the interactive effect of democracy and income inequality remains negative and statistically significant in these specifications, again confirming our expectations.[19]

---

[18] In models not reported, we also find no direct effect of turnout. All results are also robust to using year dummies rather than decade dummies.

[19] We hesitate to say that this result disconfirms Boix's results, because ironically Boix consistently finds this same negative interaction between democracy (and turnout) and inequality in his analyses of public spending (see Boix 2003, Tables 5.1, 5.2, 5.3, and 5.5), and he recognizes that this contradicts his model's expectations. He explains this result by suggesting that "the very high coefficient of [the direct effect of] democratic regime... compensates for the negative coefficient of the interactive term" (191), but this abandons the Meltzer-Richard logic and ignores the likelihood that although public spending in democracies may be greater, it may be minimally redistributive because it reflects the interests of relatively well-off groups who may seek club-goods "transfers to themselves" in the form of social security, public pensions, or healthcare spending.

The crucial theoretical issue at hand is not whether democracy has a direct effect on social-welfare spending, but whether the interaction of democracy and inequality has such an effect. If the effect is positive *and* the size of government and/or redistributive spending is larger in democracy than in autocracy, then our argument fails. Yet if democracies have larger governments but the size of government or of redistributive spending *shrinks* as inequality increases, then our argument gains credence. Our results support the notion that the political dynamic that shapes public spending – just like the political dynamic that drives regime change – is driven largely by groups at the upper end of the income scale, not by the median voter. The relatively well-off prefer government programs that enhance their own welfare, but do not support universalistic redistribution that favors the poor. This explains the negative coefficients on the interaction of democracy and inequality that appear across our statistical results.

7.5 CONCLUSION

In this chapter, we subjected our elite-competition model of democratization to an indirect test, exploring social-welfare spending data from two eras, including 1880 to 1930, for which we developed a novel dataset on public spending. We find no evidence that the interaction of democracy and inequality increases social-welfare spending, but rather that there is a robust negative conditional relationship between democracy, inequality of both land and income, and redistribution. This relationship holds at the aggregate level, and also when we disaggregate types of social-welfare spending. Not only do democracy and redistribution not go hand in hand, but as inequality increases, redistributive spending to the poor tends to decline.

These results do not merely represent a null finding for the Meltzer-Richard model; they directly contradict the theory's core premise. Our results do, however, follow logically from the formal model developed in Section 7.2, which suggested that fiscal policy in democracies should reflect the relative political power of different economic groups.

Overall, the findings in this chapter illustrate the theoretical fruitfulness of our elite-competition theory. We suggested that in a developing autocracy, land inequality reflects the historical strength of landed elites, who will oppose redistributive spending to the poor. Likewise, income inequality reflects the growing political strength of the bourgeoisie and middle classes. If regime change occurs under relatively high inequality, once in power, there is no reason to expect these same actors to demand highly redistributive social-welfare spending. Indeed, individuals with well above-median incomes have far stronger incentives to *limit* the size of government, particularly if autocracy had been associated with threats of expropriation of private property.

Even under universal suffrage, relatively well-off groups may be able to shift the balance of government spending away from purely redistributive social-welfare programs and toward club goods type spending. Only when democratization occurs under relatively low income inequality – a distinct possibility, depending on the level of rural inequality – would the relatively smaller gap between rich and poor facilitate adoption of social-welfare programs that benefit everyone.

8

Democracy, Redistribution, and Preferences

8.1 INTRODUCTION

What do citizens in autocracies want from government? What do they want *for* a government? Redistributive approaches presume that individuals' opposition to redistribution increases with their income and with national-level inequality. The poorer the voter and the greater the inequality, the stronger the preferences for democracy and redistribution.

Our elite-competition approach, by contrast, presumes that relatively wealthy citizens fear expropriation by those who control the state far more than they fear redistribution to the poor, and that they believe democracy provides improved protection of life, liberty, and property. Moreover, greater overall income inequality does not signify growing redistributive threats, but the growing strength of groups demanding democracy. Except among the members of the incumbent autocratic elite, opposition to democracy should *decline* as individual income increases.

As we saw in the previous chapter, the arrival of democracy in countries with high levels of inequality does not herald redistribution. Instead, high income inequality means that public spending in democracies becomes distorted away from the preferences of the masses and toward those of the elites. Accordingly, the poor's preferred level of spending should *decline* as inequality increases in democracies.

So far, we have tested these theories by examining aggregate data: How does inequality affect democratization; how does inequality condition the effect of democratization on redistribution? Our theoretical approach would gain additional credence if these macro-patterns were bolstered by empirical support at the individual level. This is especially crucial since our theoretical approach makes a series of assumptions about the individuals' preferences over democracy, redistribution, and expropriation.

In this chapter, we consider how individual-level income and societal-level inequality shape individual-level preferences for democracy and redistribution *in autocracies.* Our results lend further support to our elite-competition theory. If theories rooted in the Meltzer-Richard model were correct, we should see a positive relationship between national-level inequality and demand for redistribution across autocracies, especially among the poor. However, we find the opposite effects: a negative relationship between inequality and average demand for redistribution, and a negative relationship between inequality and the importance of income in terms of determining individual redistributive preferences. This result may explain why cross-national support for the Meltzer-Richard model is so weak: quite simply, the median voter does not demand more redistribution as inequality increases, and the effects of income on redistributive preferences actually *decline* in countries with high inequality.

Were the Meltzer-Richard model correct, we would also expect to see a negative relationship between individual income, *societal* inequality, and opinions about democracy itself. After all, the model implies that as inequality goes up, wealthier individuals in autocracies stand to lose more under democracy. In contrast, our argument presumes that democracy's leading advocates will be relatively well-off but politically disenfranchised, suggesting that the relationship between individual income and democracy should be positive. Moreover, as inequality rises, these high income individuals should be particularly concerned about an overbearing state interfering with the economy. As we argued in Chapter 4, rising inequality heightens fears about state expropriation.

In this chapter, we first elaborate our theoretical expectations about the connections between individual income, national level inequality and preferences over redistribution, expropriation, and democracy, and then test our propositions with data drawn from the World Values Survey for over 46,000 individuals across 26 autocracies.

8.2 PREFERENCES OVER REDISTRIBUTION AND DEMOCRACY: THEORY

Theories rooted in the Meltzer-Richard model assume that voters' income relative to the average defines their preferences for or against redistribution, and that these then define their preferences for or against democracy. The poorer you are, the more you favor democracy and redistribution. Cross-nationally, higher societal inequality should intensify these preferences – that is, that there is an interactive relationship between individual-level income and societal-level inequality.

By contrast, our elite-competition approach assumes that income drives individuals' demand for limits on government's expropriative power, and that the stronger such preferences are, the stronger are individual preferences for democracy. This means that relatively *wealthier* individuals – except for the very wealthiest elites, who are unlikely to be picked up in cross-national surveys – want democracy and protection. Moreover, presuming (as we did in

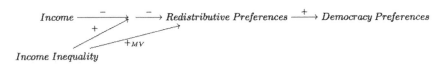

FIGURE 8.1A. Redistributivist Preference Formation Model

Chapter 7) that higher societal inequality reduces the likely universality of public goods provision, then higher societal inequality tends to reduce demand for universalistic redistribution but increase demand for democracy.

Which approach better describes citizens' preferences, in autocracies? Relatively little research has explored the implications of the Meltzer-Richard model using individual-level data, and none in autocracies. A few papers have explored this question in wealthy democracies. For example, Finseraas (2009) finds a positive relationship between inequality, income, and the median voter's preferences over redistribution, but others have found no support for the redistributivist thesis (Huber and Stanig 2009; Kenworthy and McCall 2008; Lübker 2007). Most research on this question instead uses aggregate-level data – for example, regressing societal-level inequality on aggregate government spending levels.

Figure 8.1a illustrates the logic of the redistributivist model. The path diagram shows four arrows. First, individual income is negatively related to demand for redistribution. Second, higher societal inequality has a direct and positive impact on the democratic median voter's (MV) demand for redistribution.[1] Third, societal inequality and individual income have an interactive effect. That is, poorer individuals' demand for redistribution should be greater in societies where inequality is also greater. Finally, the arrow furthest to the right suggests that preferences over democracy follow directly from preferences over redistribution.

Our elite-competition approach offers sharply contrasting hypotheses regarding preferences for both redistribution and democracy. Although redistribution is not the core concern of the formal model in Chapter 4 and extended in Chapter 7, our argument has clear implications regarding the connection between income, inequality, and redistributive preferences. We agree that wealthier individuals prefer less universalistic redistribution as per the Meltzer-Richard model, but argue that (a) the nature of such preferences depend on whether government spending comes in the form of universal (public) or club goods; (b) this balance of spending depends on the level of societal inequality, with demand for universal goods more likely under

---

[1] The "democratic median voter" is defined as the person with median income among all those who would be eligible to vote in democracy.

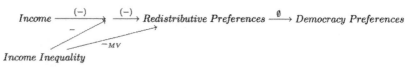

FIGURE 8.1B. Elite-Competition View of Redistributive Preferences

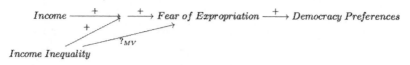

FIGURE 8.1C. Elite-Competition View of Democracy Preferences

low income inequality but demand for club goods increasing with inequality; and (c) that preferences over democracy are largely not determined by redistributive preferences.

These conjectures are spelled out in Figure 8.1b. First, the relationship between income and redistributive preferences is negative, but contingent. However, income inequality – by biasing demands for spending toward club goods that the wealthy prefer – tends to attenuate the negative relationship between income and redistributive preferences *and* tends to reduce the median voter's support for redistribution. Finally, redistributive preferences do not determine preferences over democracy.

Our model's core concern is with the fear of expropriation, not redistribution, which drives preference formation about democracy. Figure 8.1c sets out our expectations. Fear of expropriation increases with individual income, since richer citizens have more to lose from predatory autocrats. Income inequality intensifies this fear, because it signifies the emergence of greater numbers of individuals who have more to lose. Finally, our argument makes no clear prediction about whether income inequality has a direct effect on the median voter's preferences. On the one hand, since autocrats are unlikely to target the median voter for expropriation, a rise in societal inequality may have little impact on his or her preferences. On the other hand, greater predation on relatively wealthier citizens following rising inequality may unnerve the median voter, raising the potential likelihood of joint mass-bourgeois revolt.

Putting these causal paths together we can list a series of contrasting hypotheses about preferences over redistribution and democracy for the redistributivist and elite-competition approaches.

Redistributivist Hypotheses about Preferences over Redistribution and Democracy

- H1a: Holding societal inequality constant, as individual income goes up, demand for redistribution should go down.

- H1b: As societal inequality increases, the democratic median voter will desire more redistribution.
- H1c: As societal inequality increases, the negative relationship between individual income and demand for redistribution should intensify.

Link between Redistribution and Democracy

- H2a: Citizens desiring more redistribution should have stronger preferences for democracy.

Democracy Preferences

- H3a: Holding societal inequality constant, as individual income goes up, preferences for democracy should go down.
- H3b: As societal inequality increases, the democratic median voter will have stronger preferences for democracy.
- H3c: As societal inequality increases, the negative relationship between individual income and demand for democracy should intensify.

Hypothesis 1a is simply the core hypothesis of the Meltzer-Richard model – that demand for redistribution decreases with income. A test of this hypothesis can be done on individual-level data without reference to any national context.

Hypothesis 1b follows directly from the core hypothesis of the Meltzer-Richard model: across societies (or across a single society over time), as the gap between mean and median income widens, the person with median income will desire more redistribution.[2] Think of this as a test for changes in the baseline level of demand for redistribution, at different levels of societal inequality. To test this hypothesis we must examine the preferences of median-income citizens in societies with different levels of inequality.

Hypothesis 1c echoes Hypothesis 1b. Redistributivist models assume a continuous and monotonic relationship between personal income and the preferred rate of taxation/redistribution. That is, moving from the 10th down to the 5th percentile of income produces an incrementally higher preferred rate of redistribution, just as a similar move from the 90th to 95th percentile produces an incrementally lower rate. However, in a relatively unequal society, those at the 95th percentile would lose relatively more from government redistribution, while those at the 5th percentile would gain relatively more, relative to those two individuals in an equal society. Accordingly, wealthier individuals in the unequal society should have relatively stronger preferences against redistribution, while poorer individuals' should have relatively stronger preferences in the opposite direction.

---

[2] This can occur either through a mean-preserving spread of income (that is, because the median citizen is becoming relatively poorer) or through a median-preserving spread of income (that is, the rich are growing richer, and the poor are growing poorer, but the middle stays the same).

As for preferences over democracy – since the redistributivist theory argues preferences over democracy follow straightforwardly from preferences over redistribution (itself tested by Hypothesis 2a), Hypotheses 3a, 3b, 3c are simple extensions of Hypotheses 1a, 1b, and 1c.

Elite-Competition Hypotheses about Preferences over Redistribution and Democracy

Redistribution Preferences

- $H1a'$: Holding societal inequality constant, as individual income goes up, demand for redistribution should go down.
- $H1b'$: As societal inequality increases, the democratic median voter will desire less redistribution.
- $H1c'$: As societal inequality increases, the negative relationship between individual income and demand for redistribution should weaken.

Link between Redistribution / Expropriation and Democracy

- $H2a'$: There is no unambiguously positive connection between demand for redistribution and preferences for democracy. Instead,
- $H2b'$: Higher income people should be more concerned about expropriation by the state, and this fear will increase with national inequality.
- $H2c'$: There should be a positive connection between concerns about expropriation and preferences for democracy, increasing with income.

Democracy Preferences

- $H3a'$: Holding societal inequality constant, as individual income goes up, demand for democracy should increase – at least for all citizens not currently part of the autocratic elite.
- $H3b'$: As societal inequality increases, there is no clear effect on the 'median democratic voter's' preferences for democracy.
- $H3c'$: As societal inequality increases, the positive relationship between individual income and support for democracy should strengthen.

For the most part, our elite-competition hypotheses contrast sharply with redistributivist hypotheses. However, $H1a'$ is the same as $H1a$. Our argument, like the redistributive argument, assumes that all else equal, the rich are less likely to prefer *universalistic and progressive* redistribution than the poor. However, we part ways in thinking both about how inequality affects this relationship, and by arguing that this relationship does not affect preferences over democracy.

Hypotheses $H1b'$ and $H1c'$ spell out this distinction. As we have argued, higher-income voters favor government spending on club goods that benefit them, while poorer voters favor universalistic public spending. Moreover, higher societal income inequality tends to shift spending toward club goods and away from universalistic programs, because it signifies the political

TABLE 8.1. *Competing Hypotheses about Preferences*

Hypothesis	Redistributivist	Elite-Competition
H1a: Income → Redistribution	+	+
H1b: Inequality → MV Redistribution	+	-
H1c: Inequality → (Income → Redistribution)	+	-
H2a: Redistribution Pref → Democracy Pref	+	o
H2b: Income + Inequality → Fear Expropriation	N/A	+
H2c: Fear Expropriation → Democracy Pref	N/A	+
H3a: Income → Democracy Pref	-	+
H3b: Inequality → MV Democracy Pref	+	o
H3c: Inequality → (Income → Democracy Pref)	-	+

strength of relatively wealthy groups. Accordingly, higher inequality should be associated with ambivalence on the part of wealthier citizens toward universalistic redistributive spending.

Hypotheses H2a′ through H2c′ connect attitudes toward redistribution and expropriation to attitudes toward democracy. H2a′ suggests that for the relatively wealthy, concerns about expropriation are more salient than fears of redistribution. This means income is positively related to fears of expropriation (H2b′) – and fear of expropriation is positively related to preferences for democracy (H2c′).

Hypotheses H3a′ through H3c′ simply trace the elite-competition mechanism for preference formation about democracy. Higher-income individuals (provided they are not part of the autocratic elite) should more strongly favor democracy, since they stand to lose more from expropriation than poorer citizens. And because income inequality increases autocratic elites' incentive to predate, this preference for democracy should increase with aggregate inequality (H3c′). However, as per Hypothesis H3b′, it is not obvious that an increase in predation would threaten the relatively poorer median voter.

This section has produced a complicated array of hypotheses. To simplify their interpretation we set them out in Table 8.1. We now empirically test these hypotheses against each other. Section 8.3 examines preferences over redistribution, while Section 8.4 explores hypotheses about preferences for democracy.

8.3 PREFERENCES OVER REDISTRIBUTION: EMPIRICS

In this section, we put the redistributivist and elite-competition accounts of preference-formation under autocracy to the test. We do so conscious of an array of difficulties which make conclusive empirical testing difficult.

First, we seek to examine the preferences of citizens in autocracies with regard both to redistribution and democratization. These are contentious topics, and citizens in dictatorships may be understandably nervous about giving honest responses to survey questions. Moreover, questions about democracy and redistribution are likely questions about hypotheticals – hence wishful thinking or simple guesswork may be driving answers rather than rational materialist calculation of the marginal benefits and costs of different regimes. And as with most cross-national surveys, we lack panel data on individuals and thus cannot know how fluctuations in individuals' income over time might impact their preferences, and cannot fully separate out other time-invariant correlates of income such as social class, culture, or region from the impact of income itself.

Second, our theory distinguishes between the incumbent elite, who control the autocratic state, and rising elites, who push for democratization. Unfortunately, discerning the preferences of the incumbent elite is impossible. Members of this group are very unlikely to be sampled in surveys because of their small numbers and because of potential unwillingness to participate. Accordingly, we assume that all respondents are members of disenfranchised groups.

Finally, available survey questions about redistribution and expropriation are not entirely satisfactory as proxy measures for the theoretical mechanisms in either the redistributivist or elite-competition models. The World Values Surveys ask only about purely redistributive transfers and do not address the potential balance between universalistic and "club goods" government spending, and no question in cross-national surveys satisfactorily addresses fear of expropriation by the state. Hence we rely on a proxy question about state ownership of industry.

Despite these difficulties, the results we present below are strikingly at odds with predictions from the Meltzer-Richard model, and help adjudicate the relative merits of the redistributivist and elite-competition approaches. Combined with the empirical evidence presented in earlier chapters, analyses of individual-level data add further weight to the evidence in favor of an elite-competition view of regime change.

8.3.1 Data and Sample

To our knowledge there is only one source of cross-national public opinion data that asks respondents in autocracies about their preferences about redistribution: the World Values Surveys (WVS). Unfortunately, the WVS does not delve into great depth on this issue. Our core dependent variable is a ten-point scale: Respondents were asked to place themselves somewhere between one – "We need larger income differences as incentives" – and ten – "Incomes should be made more equal." We use this question (WVS variable *e035*) because, unlike most other WVS questions about redistribution or inequality, it is available across a wide range of autocracies.

The question does have a number of advantages. First, it suggests a trade-off – that equalizing incomes means potentially reducing individuals' incentives to work hard. Second, it connects inequality directly to redistribution in that the prompt "incomes should be made more equal" implies that someone – presumably the government – will redistribute incomes.

On the other hand, the question is far from perfect. For one, people might not believe that a relationship exists between income differentials and incentives to work hard, but they still might oppose redistributive taxing and spending. And even if a person agrees that incomes should be made more equal as a matter of principle, the question wording cannot tell us whether that person also believes that the government should tax and spend more to accomplish that goal. Finally, responses might vary, depending on the wording of the question. For example, responses might differ if the question had asked whether the respondent agreed that, "Incomes should be made more equal through a tax increase."

Despite these potential problems, this question is the best available for examining the core hypothesis of the redistributivist approach at the individual level in autocratic systems – and the results we report below certainly suggest that additional research would support our conjecture about the relationship between income, inequality, and preferences for redistribution and democracy.

We gathered data from the autocracies where the World Values Survey has been implemented – countries that failed to score a 6 or higher on the POLITY IV scale. This generates an initial sample of 29 countries and 43 surveys, as in the first column of Table 8.2. Unfortunately, the WVS did not ask question e035 in all of these countries, and other data necessary to test our argument also proved missing for some cases – particularly contemporaneous country-level Gini coefficients. This left us with a maximum N of 46,339 from 23 countries and 31 surveys implemented between 1990 and 2007, as indicated in the last two columns of the table.

Because the hypotheses about redistributive preferences apply both at the individual level within countries as well as cross-nationally, we employ multilevel modeling techniques. This requires gathering individual- and national-level information.

As independent variables at the individual level, our chief measures of interest are income and education; we explore the impact of each separately. Income is self-reported on a ten-point scale in that country's currency, then normalized across countries to create a ten-step scale that is cross-nationally comparable.[3]

---

[3] Individuals' current annual income, however might not reflect their lifetime expectation of earnings and, therefore, might only weakly reflect their preferences over redistribution. Because it is correlated with lifelong earnings potential and largely fixed for adults, we, therefore, also repeat our results in this section using education as a proxy for income. Education also avoids some of the measurement issues related to self-reported income in surveys, such as non-reporting and under/overestimation. We find the same effects as for income – education has a

TABLE 8.2. *Autocracies under Analysis*

Countries	Polity Score	Survey Year	Base Models	Full Models
Bosnia and Herzegovina	−10	1998	Yes	Yes
Bosnia and Herzegovina	−10	2001	Yes	Yes
Burkina Faso	0	2007	Yes	Yes
China	−7	1990		
China	−7	1995		
China	−7	2001		
China	−7	2007	Yes	Yes
Croatia	−5	1996	Yes	
Egypt	−6	2000	Yes	Yes
Egypt	−3	2008	Yes	Yes
Ethiopia	1	2007	Yes	Yes
Hungary	−7	1982		
Iran	3	2000	Yes	Yes
Iran	−6	2007	Yes	Yes
Iraq	−10	2004		
Iraq	−10	2006		
Jordan	−2	2001	Yes	Yes
Jordan	−3	2007		
Kyrgyzstan	−3	2003	Yes	Yes
Malaysia	3	2006	Yes	
Morocco	−6	2001	Yes	Yes
Morocco	−6	2007	Yes	
Nigeria	−5	1990	Yes	Yes
Nigeria	−6	1995	Yes	Yes
Nigeria	4	2000	Yes	Yes
Pakistan	−6	2001	Yes	Yes
Peru	1	1996	Yes	Yes
Russian Federation	0	1990	Yes	Yes
Russian Federation	3	1995	Yes	
Rwanda	−3	2007	Yes	Yes
Saudi Arabia	−10	2003		
Serbia and Montenegro	−7	1996		
Singapore	−2	2002	Yes	Yes
South Africa	4	1982		
South Africa	5	1990		
South Korea	−5	1982		
Tanzania	−1	2001	Yes	Yes
Thailand	−1	2007	Yes	Yes
Uganda	−4	2001	Yes	Yes
Vietnam	−7	2001	Yes	Yes
Vietnam	−7	2006	Yes	Yes
Zambia	5	2007	Yes	Yes
Zimbabwe	−4	2001	Yes	Yes

We also employ several individual-level control variables as potential predictors of preferences for redistribution. We control for education (a six-point index from incomplete elementary education through university graduate), employment status using a series of dummy variables (employed, unemployed, non-employed, retired, student); age; age squared; gender; number of children; and, following Scheve and Stasavage (2006), religiosity.[4]

At the national level, we use four variables to pick up contextual effects: (1) GDP per capita (from the 2010 World Development Indicators), (2) the Polity score (from Marshall, Jaggers, and Gurr 2003), (3) a measure of Ethno-Linguistic Fractionalization (from Alesina et al. 2003), and (4) our key independent variable, aggregate income inequality (from the 2010 World Development Indicators). Because this last measure does not distinguish between pre- and post-tax transfers, we acknowledge that – as in nearly every other study – our analysis only imperfectly tests the Meltzer-Richard conjecture.

Our approach does have particular advantages over existing research: As noted in Chapter 4, the Meltzer-Richard model requires that individuals know the true level of market inequality. The absence of information about pre-fisc inequality is particularly problematic for studies that test the median-voter model in wealthy democracies, where welfare-state spending is comparatively high, such as Finseraas (2009) and Kenworthy and McCall (2008). The higher the level of redistributive spending, the less likely will individuals possess accurate information about pre-fisc inequality. Moreover, average age in wealthy democracies is higher than the world average, and an aging population (rather than the median voter's income) tends to drive spending on pensions and healthcare (Lindert 2004). Finally and most importantly, studies of the sources of redistribution in wealthy democracies cannot eliminate the possibility that preferences today (i.e., those that scholars analyze from public-opinion surveys) have been shaped by the fact that welfare-state spending has been relatively high for decades. Individuals' preferences under democracy today are a function in part of electoral battles fought long ago, also under democracy.

In contrast, our sample of cases exhibits considerable variation in country-wealth; the average age is younger than in wealthier democracies; social-welfare spending levels tend to be lower; and, most importantly, preferences under autocracy about inequality and spending cannot be a function of the policy consequences of repeated past democratic elections. Consequently, our sample is especially useful for testing the Meltzer-Richard conjecture, because

---

negative effect on redistributive preferences at low levels of inequality but a null effect at high levels.

[4] Ideally, we would also code for ethnic minority status to pick up group-related preferences (as in Shayo 2009) but the World Values Survey does not provide a consistent framework for doing so. It also does not provide the kind of occupational data one would need to construct measures skill specificity, another factor often cited in the literature (Iversen and Soskice 2001).

it reduces – even if it cannot fully eliminate – the potential problem of endogeneity that bedevils research on this question.

As the hypotheses laid out in Section 8.2 suggest, we wish to explain cross-country variation in the effects of individual-level variables on redistributive preferences. That is, although Hypothesis 1a (1a′) is relatively straightforward, testing it cannot answer the question of whether preferences about redistribution change according to the societal level of inequality. Hypothesis 1b (1b′), therefore, seeks to answer the question of whether the median voter's preference for redistribution intensify – as all redistributivist models suggest they should – as one moves from an equal to an unequal society. Likewise, Hypothesis 1c (1c′) seeks to discover whether the individual effects of income and education on preferences for redistribution and democracy are accentuated in high inequality countries.

To test these hypotheses we use the "two-step" framework developed in Huber, Kernell, and Leoni (2005) and Jusko and Shively (2005), which takes into account how variation at the national level shapes variation at the individual level. In the first stage, using an ordered logit estimation, we generate estimates of individual-level preferences (in this case, for "making incomes more equal") for each country-year survey. We then save the estimated coefficients from the equation for each country-year for relevant individual-level variables (for example, individual income) and the constant term.

In the second stage, we use these country-year level estimates as dependent variables in a regression analysis with between 26 and 31 cases, with national-level variables such as the Gini coefficient as independent variables. Accordingly, in the second stage we are using national-level variables as predictors for coefficients estimated from individuals in the first stage. For example, in the second stage we use national-level economic inequality as a predictor of the first-stage effect of individual income on redistributive preferences within that country-year survey.[5]

8.3.2 Income, Inequality, and Redistributive Preferences

We begin by examining variation in the relationship between income and redistributive preferences across autocracies. Both Hypothesis 1a (redistributivist) and Hypothesis 1a′ (elite competition) suggest that individual income should be negatively associated with favorable attitudes about redistribution. However, the elite competition and redistributivist approaches differ in terms of the expected impact of national-level inequality on the connection between income and attitudes toward redistribution. Redistributivist Hypothesis 1c suggested that income should generate even stronger negative attitudes toward redistribution as national-level income inequality increases, since in such situations the rich have more to lose and the poor have more to gain. By contrast

---

[5] Further details about this estimation technique can be found in Section 8.6.

elite competition Hypothesis 1c' suggested that since inequality biases control of policymaking toward the interests of the elite, higher inequality should attenuate the connection between income and attitudes toward redistribution.

Hypotheses 1a and 1a' receive strong support in our first-stage analyses, since individual income is negatively related to preferences about redistribution, and statistically significant at the 5 percent level, in the majority of surveys analyzed. However, this finding alone is an insufficient test of the redistributivist model, which implies that the effect of income on attitudes toward democracy depends on variation in *national*-level inequality. And once we examine the second stage results, support for Hypothesis 1c evaporates. Indeed, the second-stage coefficient on the Gini index is *positive* and statistically significant at between the 4 and 10 percent level, depending on the estimation model used. This suggests that as inequality increases crossnationally the poor no longer favor redistribution and the rich are ambivalent or even positive toward it. This counterintuitive finding confounds the Meltzer-Richard logic, but fits with our elite-competition hypothesis H1c', which suggested that wealthier citizens (in both autocracies and democracies) will grow more supportive of public spending as societal inequality rises, as they are able to exert more influence over public finances.

To explore these findings we use both tabular and graphical presentation. Table 8.3 displays the second-stage regression results. Models 1 and 2 use a basic first-stage specification predicting individual redistributive preferences solely from individual income. We do not report results from the 31 separate first-stage regressions. Rather, we display the second-stage regressions where

TABLE 8.3. *The Effect of Income on Redistributive Preferences*

	(1) Basic	(2) Basic	(3) Full	(4) Full	(5) Weighted	(6) Weighted
Gini	0.521*	0.482[†]	0.444**	0.406*	0.474**	0.439*
	(0.261)	(0.296)	(0.208)	(0.209)	(0.213)	(0.216)
Log GDP p.c.		0.003		0.002		−0.000
		(0.016)		(0.013)		(0.013)
Polity		0.001		0.001		0.000
		(0.004)		(0.004)		(0.004)
ELF		0.047		0.030		0.036
		(0.064)		(0.057)		(0.056)
Constant	−0.293***	−0.321	−0.232**	−0.242	−0.242**	−0.245
	(0.104)	(0.214)	(0.085)	(0.157)	(0.087)	(0.157)
Observations	31	31	27	27	27	27
Countries	23	23	21	21	21	21

Standard errors in parentheses
[†] $p < 0.12$, * $p < 0.10$, ** $p < 0.05$, *** $p < 0.01$

the survey estimates for the coefficient on individual income are used as the dependent variable and regressed on country-level independent variables. The coefficients on individual-level income across countries are positively related to societal-level income inequality at around the 10 percent statistical significance level in these first two models.

Models 3 and 4 add the remaining individual control variables in the first stage regression, which reduces the number of country-years under analysis from 31 to 27 (and from 23 to 21 countries). Models 5 and 6 apply sample population weights taken from the WVS to the first stage regression. These models improve the estimated precision of the effect of income inequality – the Gini index is positively related to the first-stage coefficient on individual income at around the 5 percent level. GDP per capita, regime type and ethnolinguistic heterogeneity have no clear relationship to the size of the income coefficient.[6]

How should we interpret the positive effect of national-level income inequality on the effect of individual income on preferences over redistribution? Figure 8.2, drawn from Model 6, eases interpretation by displaying, against national income inequality, the point estimates for the coefficient on income for each country and the ninety-five percent confidence interval for those estimates.

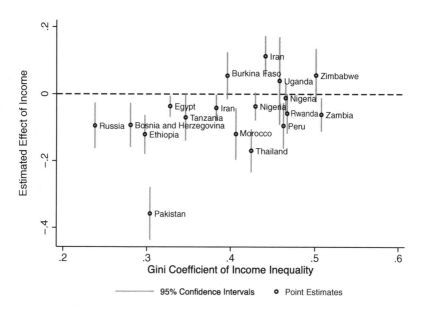

FIGURE 8.2. Effect of Income on Redistributive Preferences

---

[6] Using education as a proxy for income we find a very similar and slightly more statistically significant pattern.

Were Hypothesis 1c (the redistributivist prediction) correct, the trend line in Figure 8.2 would slope downward, as opposition to "making incomes more equal" would intensify as inequality increases. However, the trend line clearly slopes upward – the estimated effect of income moves from negative to positive (in at least a few cases) as income inequality rises. (Pakistan is an outlier, but even with this case removed, there is an upward trend overall.) Substantively, the implication is the following: in relatively equal countries the Meltzer-Richard model finds strong support, but the impact of individual-level income on preferences for redistribution is nonexistent in the most unequal countries – a finding certainly at odds with the model. By contrast, our own prediction is that where inequality is high, economic elites know they will have greater political control over policymaking and have little to fear from redistribution.

Let us provide an illustrative comparison. In Bosnia-Herzegovina (a comparatively equal country), as income rises, support for redistribution falls. This finding fits with the Meltzer-Richard model's expectations, and appears to confirm Hypothesis 1a. However, as Figure 8.2 reveals, relative to individuals in Bosnia-Herzegovina, preferences for redistribution in Zimbabwe actually *increase* with income – a finding certainly at odds with the Meltzer-Richard model's expectations.

8.3.3 "Typical" Redistributive Preferences and Inequality

We now move from examining the effects of societal-level inequality on individual-level variables like income to the direct effect of inequality on "typical" preferences for redistribution across countries. Here, we test redistributivist Hypothesis 1b – that the median voter more strongly supports redistribution in high-inequality countries – and elite competition Hypothesis 1b' – that the median voter's preferred level of redistribution decreases in unequal countries.

The successful extension of the Meltzer-Richard framework to the study of regime change hinges on the preferences of the would-be median voter under autocracy. Assessing preferences over redistribution cross-nationally, controlling for national-level per capita income, allows us to compare the relative intensity of the median voter's preferences for redistribution at different ratios of median to mean income – that is, at different national levels of inequality. This directly examines redistributivist models' underlying theoretical mechanism. We can also use this method to compare the preferences of individuals with different levels of income across countries with different levels of inequality, in order to further assess Hypotheses 1c and 1c'.

How can we estimate the median voter's preferences? To do so we estimate the constant term for the first-stage regressions, respecifying the independent variables such that zero is a meaningful quantity – the mean value for

TABLE 8.4. *Effects of Inequality on Citizens' Typical Redistributive Preferences*

	(1) 5th	(2) 25th	(3) Median	(4) 75th	(5) 95th
Gini	−7.078*	−6.508*	−5.969*	−4.984	−3.690
	(3.938)	(3.616)	(3.342)	(2.939)	(2.479)
Log GDP p.c.	0.064	0.054	0.033	0.034	−0.012
	(0.185)	(0.187)	(0.188)	(0.191)	(0.207)
Polity	−0.023	−0.021	−0.029	−0.034	−0.034
	(0.056)	(0.049)	(0.046)	(0.043)	(0.040)
ELF	1.164	1.229	1.348	1.436	1.518
	(1.143)	(1.059)	(1.022)	(0.953)	(0.893)
Constant	6.398**	6.078**	5.829**	5.259**	4.848**
	(2.517)	(2.390)	(2.281)	(2.126)	(2.001)
Observations	26	26	26	26	26
Countries	20	20	20	20	20

Standard errors in parentheses
* $p < 0.10$, ** $p < 0.05$, *** $p < 0.01$

continuous variables and zero for dummies.[7] We then regress these first-stage estimates on country-level characteristics in a second stage regression. We do so five times, creating different estimates of the constant term, by centering the individual income variable at the 5th, 25th, 50th, 75th, and 95th percentiles, respectively.

Putting this together, the constant term in each first-stage regression reflects the expected degree of support for redistribution for an employed male citizen with mean religiosity, education, number of children, and age, and who has an income at the 5th, 25th, 50th, 75th, or 95th percentile, depending on the model. The second stage regressions then examine the effects of macro-level variables such as aggregate inequality on the preferences for redistribution of this "typical" person at each of those percentiles.

Table 8.4 shows second stage regressions on the constant term at different levels of respondent income. Income inequality is not positively related to the constant term in any of the models. Instead, the coefficients on Gini are all negative, meaning that as national-level inequality increases, demand for redistribution *declines*. This relationship is statistically significant (at the 10% level) for citizens at the 5th, 25th, and median percentiles – meaning the demand for redistribution declines the most among the poorest citizens as societies become more unequal.

---

[7] To obtain estimates of the constant term for each country-year we must replace the ordered logit specification with a linear one. For the most part first-stage country-year linear regressions produce coefficients with similar substantive magnitude and statistical significance to the first-stage ordered logit specification. See 8.6 for further details.

This result sharply contrasts with the expectations of redistributivist Hypotheses 1b (for the median income citizen) and 1c (for the poorer groups). Indeed, although the Meltzer-Richard model predicts that opposition to redistribution should increase with income, these results suggest the opposite is true. The strongest negative coefficient is found at the 5th percentile, and the coefficients get smaller as we move up the income scale, eventually also becoming wholly insignificant – meaning that relatively wealthier citizens are relatively *less* opposed to redistribution as societal inequality increases. This confirms our own supposition in Hypothesis 1c'. Furthermore, the citizen with median income has lower demand for redistribution as inequality rises, supporting Hypothesis 1b'

This pattern can be seen in Figures 8.3a through 8.3e, which show estimates for all five of the income levels and which clearly reveal how the relationship between inequality and redistributive preferences weakens as income rises. Among richer citizens there is no clear connection between national-level inequality and redistributive preferences (the slope is negative but the coefficient insignificant), whereas among poorer citizens – including the would-be median voter under a potential future democracy-rising national-level inequality appears to reduce demand for redistribution.

These findings can be summarized simply: the interplay of individual income and societal inequality does not follow the core tenets of the redistributivist model. Income inequality does not accentuate redistributive divides between rich and poor – in fact, it moderates them. These results are far more

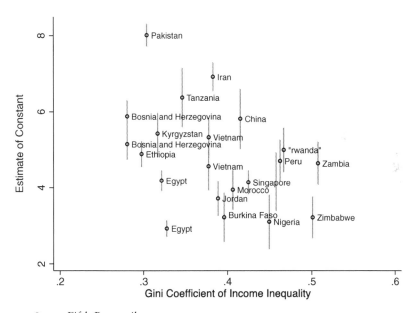

FIGURE 8.3A. Fifth Percentile

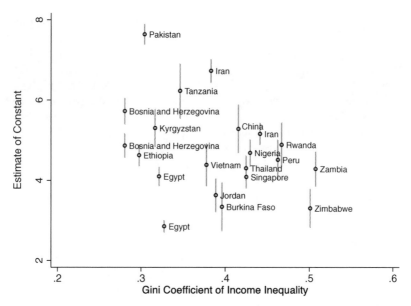

FIGURE 8.3B. Twenty-Fifth Percentile

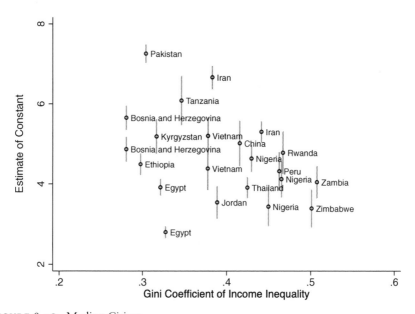

FIGURE 8.3C. Median Citizen

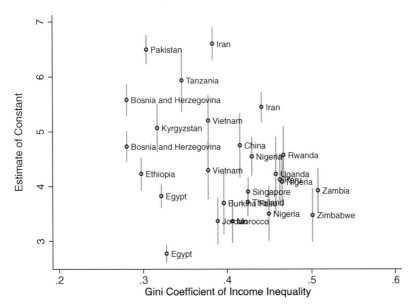

FIGURE 8.3D. Seventy-Fifth Percentile

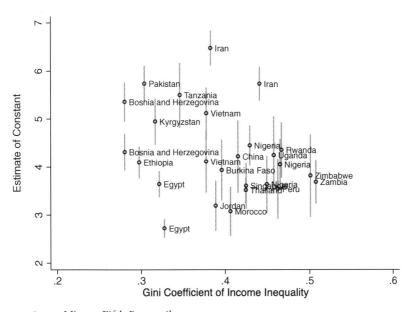

FIGURE 8.3E. Ninety-Fifth Percentile

supportive of our own understanding of the relationship between inequality and redistribution as developed in Chapter 7: rising inequality reduces the ability of the democratic median voter to control the distribution of public spending, because it politically empowers economic elites. In countries with high inequality the median voter supports redistribution less than in countries with low inequality, while elites are less antagonistic toward redistribution.

8.4 PREFERENCES OVER DEMOCRACY: EMPIRICS

The core mechanism of redistributivist models of regime change is that autocratic elites oppose democracy because they fear its redistributive consequences. Yet evidence from the world's autocracies suggests that a more unequal distribution of income *weakens* the predicted relationship between income and preferences over redistribution, implying that as societal-level inequality increases, wealthier people fear the poor relatively less. Fortunately this jibes with our elite-competition approach. An appreciation for the sociological significance of "income inequality" helps explain how inequality *reduces* the ability of the poor to obtain their preferred public-spending policies.

We now turn to preferences about democracy itself, and once more the empirical results challenge the redistributivist approach and support our own. We begin by showing that income strongly predicts preferences for private versus state ownership of the economy: richer citizens in autocracies not surprisingly support protecting private firms against nationalization and other state interference. Although not a perfect measure, this attitude is closely related to our core mechanism of preference formation – fear of expropriation by the state. Importantly, we also find that this relationship *increases* with national inequality.

We then turn to the determinants of support for democracy, examining the impact of individual income, opposition to state ownership, and support for redistribution. Our results again sharply contrast with redistributivist expectations: not only is income positively correlated with support for democracy, but opposition to redistribution is as well. Far from fearing democracy, "anti-redistributive" elites are its strongest proponents! Attitudes toward state ownership also strongly predict support for democracy: individuals who most oppose state ownership are the strongest supporters of democracy. We conclude by examining a second question tapping attitudes toward the economic consequences of democracy, which also generates results that support our elite-competition approach yet are difficult to reconcile with the redistributivist theory.

8.4.1 Attitudes toward State Ownership

Our elite-competition approach holds that high-income individuals who are not part of the incumbent elite are likely to support democratization, because it reduces the threat of state predation. Unfortunately, we know of no cross-national survey that directly taps attitudes on this question. The World Values Survey does not ask about taxes or the importance of the sanctity of contracts in autocratic regimes, for example. Nonetheless, question *e036* does get at concerns about the state's interference in the private sector. It asks,

How would you place your views on this scale? 1 means you agree completely with the statement on the left; 10 means you agree completely with the statement on the right... Private ownership of business should be increased vs Government ownership of business should be increased

An increase in this index implies potentially uncompensated seizure of private assets by the state. Of course, this question does not tap many other concerns individuals might have about state predation: corruption, punitive taxation, weak property rights enforcement, etc. To that end, and presuming these other concerns intensify with income, we expect income to affect preferences over democracy both through derived preferences over state ownership and net of these effects.

Before we examine preferences about democracy itself, however, it is important to verify that high income individuals are least supportive of state ownership and to examine the role of inequality in shaping that preference. Table 8.5 presents a series of hierarchical linear random effects estimations of the ten-point state ownership attitude scale.[8] We begin in Model 1 with a similar specification to those used in the first stage estimates of redistribution preferences in Section 8.3, albeit fully pooled across 26 countries. Not surprisingly, the effect of income on support for state ownership is strongly negative and very precisely estimated. This finding is robust to the inclusion of national-level variables in Model 2, strongly confirming Hypothesis H2b'. Importantly, national-level inequality is negatively related to support for state ownership in Model 2, suggesting – as our argument implies – that concerns about expropriation are higher in high-inequality countries.

Model 3 adds a cross-level interaction term between income and national-level inequality. Although the interaction term does not appear statistically significant at conventional levels, this is somewhat misleading. As Figure 8.4 demonstrates, the interacted model shows a clear pattern: individual income is only a statistically significant (at the $p > 0.05$ level) predictor of preferences over state ownership in countries with a Gini above .35, suggesting that only where income inequality is moderate to high are richer citizens particularly concerned about state expropriation.

8.4.2 Support for Democracy: Expectations

Having established the connection between income and concerns about state ownership, we now examine the determinants of preferences for democracy.

---

[8] Ordered logit estimation produces extremely similar results.

TABLE 8.5. *Preferences over State Ownership*

	(1)	(2)	(3)
Income	−0.082***	−0.076***	0.125
	(0.021)	(0.025)	(0.145)
Education	−0.163***	−0.171***	−0.169***
	(0.023)	(0.019)	(0.017)
Female	0.240***	0.256***	0.254***
	(0.058)	(0.063)	(0.063)
Children	0.024*	0.024	0.023
	(0.014)	(0.015)	(0.015)
Age	−0.005	−0.013	−0.013
	(0.010)	(0.011)	(0.011)
Age Sq.	0.000	0.000	0.000
	(0.000)	(0.000)	(0.000)
Gini		−5.104***	−2.924
		(1.883)	(2.162)
Log GDP p.c.		0.199	0.207
		(0.153)	(0.150)
ELF		−1.806***	−1.791***
		(0.623)	(0.620)
Polity		0.059***	0.065***
		(0.012)	(0.017)
Income X Gini			−0.498
			(0.367)
Constant	6.347***	8.302***	7.360***
	(0.247)	(1.600)	(1.435)
Observations	44672	37846	37846
Countries	26	23	23

We focus on the impact of three individual-level factors: income, preferences about state ownership, and preferences for redistribution, as well as national-level inequality.

The WVS asks a series of questions about how citizens understand democracy. We focus on two questions that assess citizens' opinions about democracy's desirability, and about its effects on the economy and redistribution. The first ($e117$ in the WVS) asks whether "Having a democratic political system is ... a very good, fairly good, fairly bad, or very bad way of governing the country." We use two versions of this variable – the full four point scale (with four equaling very good) and a binary version where one equals very good or fairly good, and zero equals fairly bad or very bad.

The second question concerns the predicted economic consequences of democracy. Question $e120$ asks, "Could you please tell me if you agree

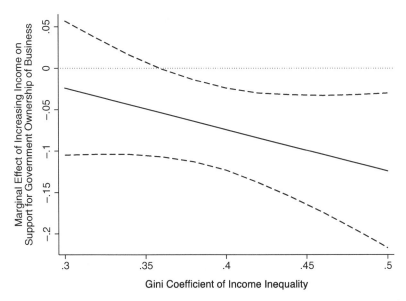

FIGURE 8.4. Effect of Income on State Ownership Preferences at Varying Levels of Inequality

strongly, agree, disagree, or disagree strongly" with the following: "In democracy, the economic system runs badly." We recoded this as a binary variable, where zero equals "strongly agree" or "agree" that the economy runs badly in democracies, and one equals "disagree" or "disagree strongly" with that statement.

Let us recap the elite-competition and redistributivist hypotheses relating income to preferences about democracy. Recall that all our surveys were taken in autocratic systems, and are thus asking respondents to think about a hypothetical democracy both in terms of its general desirability and its economic consequences. Both the redistributivist and elite-competition approaches presume that actors' attitudes toward democracy are shaped by material concerns: fear of redistribution under democracy, and fear of expropriation under autocracy. Hence attitudes toward democracy's economic consequences ought to be similar to attitudes toward democracy itself.

We begin with redistributivist hypotheses H2a and H3a through H3c. Hypothesis 2a stated that attitudes regarding redistribution should predict preferences for democracy, with citizens who support redistribution also supporting democracy. Hypotheses H3a through H3c extend this logic, suggesting that as individual income increases, support for democracy should decline (due to fear of redistribution), and that aggregate income inequality should accentuate the negative impact of income (as well as have a negative direct average effect).

By contrast, our elite-competition Hypotheses H2a' and H2c' suggest that fear of expropriation has more impact than fear of redistribution. We proxy for fear of expropriation with attitudes toward state ownership, where negative attitudes toward state ownership are assumed to reflect fear of expropriation by the state. We also connect individual income to preferences for democracy in Hypotheses H3a', H3b', and H3c'. Higher-income individuals should more strongly support democracy, since they have more at risk from expropriation. This effect should increase with aggregate income inequality, because higher Ginis indicate relatively more wealthy individuals from whom to expropriate. However, since the median voter is unlikely to be the core target of expropriation we do not expect income inequality to impact average voters' preferences for democracy.

8.4.3 Attitudes toward Democracy

We examine support for democracy in Tables 8.6a and 8.6b, which cover up to 23 countries and 40,000 respondents. Table 8.6a reports probit analyses of the dummy measure for support for democracy, whereas Table 8.6b reports ordered probit analyses of the four-point scale.[9]

Beginning with Table 8.6a, Model 1 is the baseline, and excludes country-level characteristics. It is immediately apparent that individual income is *positively* related to support for democracy. This finding is paradoxical for the redistributivist approach, but supports our elite-competition argument – or rather, it disconfirms redistributivist Hypothesis H3a and is in line with the elite-competition Hypothesis H3a'. It is true that average support for democracy (whether that support is intense or weak) is high (over 90%), meaning that the magnitude of the effect of income on preferences is subject to ceiling effects. Nonetheless, moving from the poorest to the richest group is estimated to increase support for democracy by about four percent points, or 1.5 times the standard deviation of this variable.

The effect of individual income is robust to the inclusion of country-level characteristics such as inequality, income, ethnic heterogeneity, the Polity score, and individual-level controls for preferences over state ownership (Model 3) and redistribution (Model 4).[10] Importantly, income inequality is not statistically significant in any model and its sign is negative, disconfirming redistributivist Hypothesis 3b, which had expected a robust positive effect of inequality on average support for democracy.

---

[9] All models include sample weights and standard errors clustered by country.

[10] Adding the country-level characteristics reduces the number of countries in the sample by two and the number of respondents by around 10%. None of the country-level variables reach significance in Models 2 through 5, though country-level income per capita appears negatively related in the ordered probit analyses in Table 8.6b.

TABLE 8.6A. *Views on Whether Democracy Is Desirable: Binary*

	(1)	(2)	(3)	(4)	(5)
Income	0.027**	0.021**	0.018**	0.018**	−0.038
	(0.011)	(0.009)	(0.009)	(0.009)	(0.056)
Education	−0.011	−0.005	−0.010	−0.007	−0.012
	(0.016)	(0.016)	(0.017)	(0.017)	(0.017)
Female	−0.130*	−0.117***	−0.109**	−0.120***	−0.114***
	(0.068)	(0.045)	(0.042)	(0.044)	(0.042)
Children	0.036	0.053**	0.056***	0.052**	0.053***
	(0.022)	(0.021)	(0.021)	(0.020)	(0.020)
Age	−0.000	−0.007	−0.008	−0.007	−0.007
	(0.007)	(0.010)	(0.009)	(0.009)	(0.009)
Age Sq.	−0.000	0.000	0.000	0.000	0.000
	(0.000)	(0.000)	(0.000)	(0.000)	(0.000)
Gini		−1.967	−2.035	−2.188	−2.709
		(1.420)	(1.451)	(1.437)	(1.660)
Log GDP p.c.		−0.013	0.002	−0.015	0.004
		(0.053)	(0.054)	(0.051)	(0.052)
ELF		−0.109	−0.219	−0.052	−0.159
		(0.447)	(0.414)	(0.443)	(0.412)
Polity		−0.024	−0.030	−0.026	−0.032
		(0.023)	(0.024)	(0.023)	(0.024)
State Ownership			−0.035***		−0.036***
			(0.011)		(0.010)
Redis. Prefs				−0.024**	−0.029***
				(0.011)	(0.011)
Income X Gini					0.133
					(0.140)
Constant	1.314***	2.337***	2.520***	2.526***	2.883***
	(0.185)	(0.867)	(0.881)	(0.874)	(0.920)
Observations	40151	36080	32563	35157	32337
Countries	23	21	21	21	21

Model 3 shows that preferences over state ownership are *negatively* related to attitudes toward democracy. Thus, on the assumption that the state owner-ship variable proxies adequately for fears about arbitrary state expropriation, we have support for elite-competition Hypothesis 2c' – citizens who support state ownership less (who are more concerned about expropriation) are more favorable toward democracy. This effect is comparable in magnitude for that found for income: citizens most supportive of private ownership are four and a half percent more supportive of democracy than those most supportive of state ownership.

Model 4 also shows that redistributive preferences are *negatively* related to support for democracy. This result suggests – bizarrely, for the Meltzer-Richard

TABLE 8.6B. *Views on Whether Democracy Is Desirable: Ordered*

	(1)	(2)	(3)	(4)	(5)
Income	0.015*	0.010	0.028**	0.048**	−0.044
	(0.009)	(0.009)	(0.014)	(0.022)	(0.045)
Education	−0.014	−0.022	−0.022	−0.023	−0.022
	(0.026)	(0.027)	(0.027)	(0.027)	(0.027)
Female	−0.127***	−0.123***	−0.124***	−0.124***	−0.122***
	(0.042)	(0.042)	(0.042)	(0.042)	(0.042)
Children	0.036*	0.036*	0.036*	0.036*	0.036*
	(0.021)	(0.020)	(0.020)	(0.020)	(0.020)
Age	−0.001	−0.001	−0.001	−0.002	−0.001
	(0.008)	(0.008)	(0.008)	(0.008)	(0.008)
Age Sq.	−0.000	−0.000	−0.000	−0.000	−0.000
	(0.000)	(0.000)	(0.000)	(0.000)	(0.000)
Gini	−1.981	−2.083	−2.066	−2.050	−2.709*
	(1.395)	(1.425)	(1.429)	(1.431)	(1.457)
Log GDP p.c.	−0.142***	−0.125**	−0.124**	−0.124**	−0.125**
	(0.051)	(0.050)	(0.050)	(0.050)	(0.050)
ELF	−0.265	−0.300	−0.297	−0.293	−0.303
	(0.371)	(0.345)	(0.343)	(0.344)	(0.345)
Polity	−0.000	−0.008	−0.008	−0.008	−0.008
	(0.021)	(0.024)	(0.024)	(0.024)	(0.024)
Redis. Prefs		−0.024***	−0.006	−0.006	−0.025***
		(0.009)	(0.013)	(0.013)	(0.009)
State Ownership		−0.025***	−0.025***	−0.009	−0.025***
		(0.009)	(0.009)	(0.011)	(0.009)
Income X Redis			−0.004*	−0.004*	
			(0.002)	(0.002)	
Income X Own.				−0.003	
				(0.002)	
Income X Gini					0.137
					(0.116)
Observations	36080	32337	32337	32337	32337
Countries	21	21	21	21	21

model – that individuals who strongly favor government action to reduce inequalities are *less* supportive of democracy than those who oppose it. This effect is comparable in magnitude to that of income, but in the reverse direction, and thus disconfirms redistributivist Hypothesis H2a while supporting our Hypothesis H2a' that no positive connection between redistributive preferences and democratic preferences exists.

Finally, Model 5 adds the interaction of income and national-level inequality. There is no strong evidence of a conditional effect here, although the interactive coefficient is positive. At a minimum, this again confounds redistributivist expectations (H3c) that as societal inequality increases we should observe a more strongly negative relationship between income and the demand for democracy. The elite-competition equivalent hypothesis H3c' is not confirmed, although the coefficient points in the expected direction.

Table 8.6b examines a series of ordered logit estimations using the four-point support for democracy scale as the dependent variable. Model 1 shows that the effect of income is slightly weaker than in the binary models but still positive and significant at the 10 percent level. This effect of income loses statistical significance in Model 2 when state ownership and redistributive preferences are included, but these preferences are still robustly negatively related to support for democracy as in Table 8.6b.

The next three models examine interactive relationships with individual income. Model 3 reveals an apparent conditional relationship between redistributive preferences and income, with income mattering less among those who strongly support redistribution and, symmetrically, redistributive preferences only mattering among those with high incomes.[11] Model 4 adds a similar interactive effect with individual income and state ownership – which is again negative, though not quite significant at the 10 percent level. Finally Model 5 includes an interaction of income inequality and individual income, again showing that although this relationship is not statistically significant it is positively signed, in sharp contrast to redistributivist expectations.

To illustrate our results, Tables 8.6c and 8.6d set out predicted probabilities of believing democracy is very desirable (the highest score on the four point indicator) for individuals arrayed by (a) income and by redistributive preferences, and (b) income and state ownership preferences. Both sets of predictions are drawn from Model 4 of Table 8.6b.

We begin with Table 8.6c. Examining across the rows first, individual income only appears to matter among citizens who oppose redistribution: low-income individuals have a probability of 0.56 of strongly supporting democracy, while the probability among high-income individuals is 0.64. (This

TABLE 8.6C. *Probability of Believing Democracy Is Very Desirable: Effects of Income and Redistribution Preferences*

	Low Income	Medium Income	High Income
Anti-Redistribution	0.56	0.60	0.64
Ambivalent	0.54	0.55	0.56
Pro-Redistribution	0.52	0.50	0.48

[11] No such interactive effect exists with regard to the binary model – the effects of income and redistributive preferences are unconditional in Model 4.

TABLE 8.6D. *Probability of Believing Democracy Is Very Desirable:*
Effects of Income and State Ownership Preferences

	Low Income	Medium Income	High Income
Anti-State Ownership	0.57	0.61	0.65
Ambivalent	0.55	0.56	0.58
Pro-State Ownership	0.52	0.52	0.51

difference is statistically significant at the $p < 0.05$ level.) In contrast, for individuals who are more ambivalent or who favor redistribution, the effect of income actually declines, and then reverses.

Examining the columns, here we see that the effects of redistributive preferences on support for democracy are higher as citizens' incomes go up, and that they are always downward sloping: that is, citizens who desire more redistribution tend to support democracy *less*, and the magnitude of this effect increases as incomes goes up. Low-income individuals have very similar levels of "strong" support for democracy, regardless of their redistributive preferences – around 0.54 probability. High-income individuals, by contrast, vary in their support according to their redistributive preferences. Those who support redistribution only have a 0.48 chance of strongly supporting democracy whereas the probability for high-income individuals who oppose redistribution is 0.64. This finding is precisely the reverse of what redistributivist approaches would expect, but is in line with our own expectations: richer citizens with stronger concerns about taxation will more strongly support democratization.

Examining Table 8.6d we find extremely similar results. Once more, income accentuates the effect of attitudes toward state ownership, and only in the case of citizens who oppose state ownership does income have a clear effect. That is, individuals who most strongly support democracy are those with high income and who oppose state ownership, whereas those most ambivalent toward democracy are citizens who support state ownership.

The patterns the data reveal are wholly at odds with redistributivist expectations, but in line with ours. The chief advocates of democracy are high-income individuals who both oppose redistribution and state ownership, not the allegedly pro-redistribution/pro-nationalization poor.

We conclude by examining citizens' opinions about the consequences of democracy for the economy. As noted, since both the elite-competition and redistributivist approaches hold materialist conceptions of democracy, when asked about the material consequences of democracy, both expect citizens to act in line with their hypothesized preferences about democracy itself. In other words, to the degree that we find similar results for democracy's economic consequences and for democracy itself, we can be sure that material motivations are key to understanding attitudes toward democracy, as opposed to psychological, cultural, or other motivations.

TABLE 8.7. *Views on Whether Democracy Is Good for the Economy*

	(1)	(2)	(3)	(4)	(5)
Income	0.048***	0.042***	0.034**	0.039***	0.022
	(0.010)	(0.013)	(0.014)	(0.013)	(0.052)
Education	0.009	0.026	0.018	0.021	0.026
	(0.025)	(0.025)	(0.027)	(0.026)	(0.025)
Female	−0.138**	−0.128**	−0.118**	−0.127**	−0.128**
	(0.060)	(0.052)	(0.053)	(0.051)	(0.052)
Children	0.022	0.030	0.033**	0.025	0.030
	(0.018)	(0.018)	(0.017)	(0.016)	(0.018)
Age	−0.002	−0.007	−0.007	−0.005	−0.007
	(0.007)	(0.008)	(0.008)	(0.008)	(0.008)
Age Sq.	0.000	0.000	0.000	0.000	0.000
	(0.000)	(0.000)	(0.000)	(0.000)	(0.000)
Gini		0.473	0.542	0.210	0.256
		(0.990)	(1.100)	(0.996)	(1.286)
Log GDP p.c.		−0.030	−0.003	−0.033	−0.030
		(0.094)	(0.111)	(0.099)	(0.094)
ELF		−0.131	−0.216	−0.043	−0.136
		(0.314)	(0.308)	(0.292)	(0.322)
Polity		−0.046***	−0.052**	−0.044***	−0.046***
		(0.016)	(0.023)	(0.015)	(0.016)
State Ownership			−0.027**		
			(0.011)		
Redis. Prefs				−0.032***	
				(0.012)	
Income X Gini					0.050
					(0.115)
Constant	0.267	0.269	0.280	0.486	0.360
	(0.200)	(1.051)	(1.184)	(1.101)	(1.183)
Observations	22804	18349	15665	17709	18349
Countries	18	14	14	14	14

Table 8.7 shows that higher levels of income are associated with stronger beliefs that democracy is good for the economy. This effect is of similar magnitude regardless of whether we introduce national-level characteristics (Model 2), state ownership preferences (Model 3), or redistributive preferences (Model 4). Finally, Model 5 examines whether any interactive effect exists between income and national level inequality, but no relationship appears.

These findings are consistent with those found in Table 8.6a, where income predicted support for democracy, and support for redistribution or state ownership led to less support for democracy – but again sharply conflict with redistributivist expectations, which presume wealthier citizens fear the economic consequences of democratization. By contrast, our elite-competition approach presumes that richer citizens, especially new elites, will expect better economic conditions under democracy since democracies will not engage in expropriation or other arbitrary predatory behavior that has negative economic consequences.

8.5 CONCLUSION: INTERPRETING OUR RESULTS

This chapter searched for empirical support for the preference-formation mechanisms underlying the elite-competition and redistributivist theories of regime change. Both arguments connect individual-level income and societal-level inequality to preferences toward democracy, but they do so through contrasting mechanisms.

Redistributivist arguments contend that wealthy citizens in autocracies fear democracy because they would face higher redistributive taxes. Likewise, such arguments presume that poor citizens favor democracy because they would benefit from such redistribution. These clashing preferences should be accentuated where inequality is relatively higher.

Our elite-competition approach, by contrast, suggests the opposite relationship between income and attitudes toward democracy should hold. High-income individuals, unless they are part of the ruling elite, have a great deal to fear from the autocratic state, for they have more property and income that can be expropriated. Their fear should increase where societal inequality is higher, because inequality signifies a fatter chicken for the autocratic elite to pluck. Furthermore, while our theory does not dispute the preferences of the poor and rich for and against (universalistic) redistribution, we argue that (a) inequality *reduces* the impact of income on preferences over such redistribution, and that (b) citizens who prefer such redistribution do not necessarily prefer democracy.

Results in this chapter strongly support our elite-competition hypotheses, undermining confidence in the redistributivist argument. Where income inequality is higher, the negative effect of income on redistributive preferences disappears. This is in sharp contrast to the Meltzer-Richard hypothesis, but follows our claims in Chapters 4 and 7 that income inequality tends to bias public spending away from the desires of the poor. In high inequality countries the poor appear skeptical that increased taxation and spending would benefit them.

Moreover, high-income individuals may dislike universalistic redistribution, but they hold the strongest preferences for democracy – while individuals who prefer universalistic redistribution do not appear to be fond of democracy at all. Instead, as we hypothesized, those who fear expropriation and have high enough incomes to be juicy targets for expropriation most strongly support democracy.

The plausibility of theories of regime change depends on whether their underlying causal mechanisms of preference formation actually hold up to empirical scrutiny. This chapter offers the first examination of how individuals in autocratic societies feel about democracy and redistribution. We find ample support for our elite-competition argument, which focuses on the incentives of rising elites to protect their newfound wealth, but precious little support for a view that centers on the redistributive demands of the poor. Once more, intra-class grievances not inter-class conflict drive democratization forward.

8.6 APPENDIX: ESTIMATION TECHNIQUE FOR TWO-STAGE ANALYSIS

The two-step process produces more consistent and precise estimates of conditional effects than simple pooled models; it is also relatively efficient as compared to MLE and Bayesian random effects models–but considerably less computationally intensive, particularly when using large clusters and ordered probit models (as we are here) (Leoni 2009). A further advantage comes from the ability to graphically represent first-stage estimations and their confidence intervals against second-stage variables like inequality.

We implement the two-step regression by firstly generating survey-by-survey estimates of the effects of individual-level variables: these are the first-stage regressions. Since some countries have multiple surveys we should clarify that the second level of our analysis is "country-year." For each country-year, indexed j, we estimate the following model: $Y_{ij}^* = v_j + \beta_{1j}X_{1ij} + \beta_{2j}X_{2ij} + \ldots \beta_{Nj}X_{Nij} + \epsilon_{ij}$, where Y_{ij}^* is the unobserved (latent) support for redistribution for individual i, v_j is a country-year specific effect, X_{1ij} through X_{Nij} are N individual level observations on the N independent variables for person i in country-year j, β_{1j} through β_{Nj} are the N coefficient estimates for country-year j, and ϵ_{ij} is an independently drawn error term. We then estimate these parameters predicting unobserved Y_{ij}^* using our observed ten-point ordered scale Y_{ij} and an ordered logit estimation procedure that produces estimates of nine country-year cut-points τ_{1j} through τ_{9j} but drops the country-year constant v_j. Since these cut-points are difficult to interpret in the cross-national context, we also run a linear model directly on the ten-point WVS scale (i.e., we assume $Y_{ij}^* = Y_{ij}$) and directly extract the country-year constant terms v_j.[12]

In the second stage of the analysis we regress these estimated quantities from the first stage on national level variables. As an example, assume that X_{1ij} is individual i's income in country-year j. Accordingly, β_{1j} is the coefficient

---

[12] To be precise, we use the coefficients from ordered logit analysis for the estimates pertaining to the effects of education and income. For the constant term analysis, discussed below, we use a linear regression since the ordered logit estimation technique does not produce a conventional constant term but nine cut-points that are less interpretable in the cross-country context (since the position of all nine cutpoints changes across countries). Since the dependent variable has eleven points, the move to a linear model does not produce dramatically different estimates of coefficients' statistical significance.

estimate for the impact of individual income on preferences over redistribution in country-year j. The second stage regression can then be written out as $\beta_j = \alpha_0 + \gamma_1 z_{1j} + \gamma_2 z_{2j} + \ldots \gamma_M z_{Mj} + u_j$, where the coefficients from the first-stage for each country-year survey j are regressed on M country-level independent variables z_{1j} through z_{Mj}, with a single intercept α_0 and error term u_j. The coefficients γ_1 through γ_M demonstrate the effects of national variables, such as inequality or democracy, in the second stage on the estimated coefficient for individual income β_{1j}, from the first stage.

As our second-stage estimation procedure we use both an OLS, with country-clustered standard errors, and the sampled dependent variable (SDV) technique developed in Lewis and Linzer (2005), and adapted by Leoni (2009), which adjusts standard errors to reflect the fact that the dependent variables are themselves produced by an estimation procedure. We cluster the standard errors of this regression by country (since six countries have multiple samples) and use the weighting scheme developed by Borjas and Sueyoshi (1994) to adjust for the precision of our estimates by country-year.

9

Conclusion

What explains the emergence of democracy? We offered a new answer to this question, by reinterpreting the relationship between economic development, patterns of inequality, and pressures for regime change.

Historically, conservatives have feared the consequences of modernization, while progressives have been more hopeful. Both sides agree that economic development brings about wholesale social, cultural, and political change. Scholars have long sought to identify more precisely the causal connection between political and economic development. Recent scholarship has shifted from the hypothesized impact of economic growth per se to the question of the political consequences of different patterns – equal or unequal – of growth.

Redistributivist approaches to regime change share the assumption that a tension necessarily exists between democracy and property, and share the inference that the wider the suffrage and the greater the economic inequality, the greater the danger to property. The notion that economic equality would inevitably follow political equality has long haunted the nightmares of those on the right and inspired the dreams of those on the left, and finds continued resonance in politics as in academia. We are hardly the first to shine a light on this ironic juxtaposition of Marxist and libertarian-conservative ideas; Karl Polanyi (1944), for example, noted that left- and right-wing interpretations of the world mirror each other, with both sides seeing politics as fundamentally characterized by conflict between rich and poor. Seeing politics as dominated by a war between opposing classes, Polanyi noted, radicals and reactionaries ironically end up holding identical views of the world (see also Hirschman 1991).

And yet, despite its broad appeal, and despite the fact that many countries do have large welfare states, theoretical support for the redistributive argument's assumptions as well as empirical evidence in its favor remain strikingly ambiguous. No clear and consistent cross-national relationship exists between democracy, inequality, and redistribution. In fact, although the idea that democracy and redistribution go hand in hand persists, no intellectual or political consensus has ever really existed that democracy and property are incompatible. If democracy and property were indeed necessarily in tension, then the redistributivist argument would find greater empirical support. Yet if our intuition that democracy and property are fundamentally compatible is instead correct, then transitions to democracy are unlikely to have much to do with autocratic elites' fear of the poor. Instead, they are far more likely to be about rising elites' fear of the state.

Our focus on fear of the state is philosophically rooted in the Enlightenment liberal idea of "protective" democracy. In this book, we have sought to reintroduce the importance of liberalism's core principles for understanding regime change, and to highlight the connection between liberal political thought, Modernization Theory, and arguments for "endogenous" democratization. Enlightenment liberalism emerged in the context of the socio-cultural transformations wrought by the gradual decline of feudalism and the more rapid rise of commercial and industrial capitalism in Western Europe – that is, in the context of "Modernization." Thus, it represented an intellectual search for the form of government most suited to societies undergoing such change.

 liberals

Liberals hewed to a belief that politics should be reformed to accommodate the characteristics and requirements of a modern commercial and industrial economy. Most fundamentally, building on Hobbes and Locke, liberals such as James Madison, Jeremy Bentham, Adam Smith, James Mill, and David Ricardo argued that the purpose of government is the protection of life, liberty, and property. Their arguments found echo in rising economic groups' growing demands for limited government, and equated an expanded suffrage with *protection* of property. Indeed, according to this view, the wider the suffrage, the greater the limits on arbitrary exercise of government power.

neo-institution

Contemporary neo-institutionalist research in the social sciences provides a modern spin on these classic ideas. And just as Boix and Acemoglu and Robinson did for Meltzer and Richard, we seek to place the ideas of North and Weingast (1989) and others working in this vein front and center in the comparative study of regime change. North and Weingast focused on the political sources of economic development, not regime change; we seek to connect classical liberal thought to contemporary neo-institutionalist research, and both of these to the study of the economic origins of democracy.

We recognize that liberalism is not exclusively concerned with the defense of property rights. The massive socioeconomic changes in the 17th–19th centuries that altered conceptions of property and generated increasing demand for protection from arbitrary government also brought about wider and greater demands for religious tolerance, freedom of speech and assembly, and other individual liberties. The contemporary definition of human rights has moved beyond early liberal conceptions of property, but protection of rights to property has always been central to liberal thought. Property rights have always been central to the emergence of democracy – and they should be central to the *study* of the emergence of democracy. After all, as (Dunn 1979, 25) noted, James Mill's intuitions about the symbiotic relationship between capitalism and a wide suffrage ultimately proved more prescient than Marx's later claim that democracy and property were naturally incompatible.

Classical liberals held that wherever aristocratic landowners retain their privilege and power, they must be opposed, because they embody illegitimate authority and would use their power to undermine the public good – to retard the forces of "progress." Yet while they also shrugged their shoulders at the notion of a redistributive threat from the poor, they somewhat ironically agreed with Marx that the urban "middle" classes – the bourgeoisie, white-collar and even industrial workers – drive political change in a modernizing society. These notions resonate with our elite-competition approach to regime change, which distinguishes between the political consequences of land and income inequality. These social-structural factors can vary considerably across time and space, are not necessarily correlated with each other, and have distinct effects on the likely emergence of democracy.

Because land and income inequality are not proxies for each other, to understand patterns of regime change one cannot include the one in empirical analysis without controlling for the other. Countries can have high land inequality and low income inequality – or vice versa, or some other combination. The reason for the lack of tighter correlation between these two variables is that high land inequality is often correlated with low income inequality *in the rural sector* – and both can coexist with either low *or* high income inequality in the urban environment. High land inequality means a highly *inegalitarian* society in that the elites dominate the rural poor economically, socially and politically, but that same rural context will not be "unequal" in having a high Gini coefficient, simply because nearly everyone will be relatively equally poor. As a country begins to develop and the industrial sector grows, overall income inequality will rise – a function of the emergence of the urban bourgeoisie, middle, and working classes.

Regardless, we agree that if we know anything with near certainty about the social-structural sources of democratization, it is that land inequality works against it Mahoney (2003, 147). Land inequality empowers a small caste of landowners who share homogenous political interests and who are willing and able to wield their wealth to dominate politics, whether through lobbying or repression.

We sense, however, that in some cases scholars have failed to heed the lesson of the dog that did not bark – that is, to appreciate the political implications for regime change of weak or nonexistent landed elites, regardless of the level of overall income inequality. If we believe that land inequality and a strong landed aristocracy retard democracy's emergence, then we should be equally confident that relative equality of landholdings and a weak landed elite help pave a relatively smooth road to democracy.

For example, as Kopstein (2003, 246) suggested, one of the ironies of the Leninist legacy in East-Central Europe is that the region has greater affinity for democracy today than in the inter-war years, when landed elites retained considerable economic and cultural influence. Communist land reforms in Eastern Europe had the same effects as right-wing land reforms in Taiwan and South Korea; in these countries as elsewhere, the political legacy of such transformations in the countryside may have included the social preconditions for democracy.

Our argument about the political consequences of income inequality departs substantially from the conventional wisdom. We start with an effort to rethink the way scholars relate qualitative evaluations of social-class structure to quantitative measures of income inequality. Doing so generates profound implications for how we think about the study of the relationship between 'inequality' and regime change.

As we saw in Chapter 2, social tables help us interpret a crucial theoretical question: the political implications of the relative size and location of different social classes on the income distribution. As a simple matter of historical fact, incumbent autocratic elites are typically found in the top 1–2 percent (or even less), and the middle classes, defined by sociological and cultural attributes – are typically found in the top decile of the income distribution, or at most the top quartile. That is, "middling" groups – *including the working class* – historically, are located far above the median voter's location in the income distribution. Once we have considered social tables, and related them to Gini coefficients, we begin to see that a low Gini coefficient in a developing autocracy does not imply a large middle class, and a high Gini coefficient does not imply the opposite. Research on regime change has largely ignored the connection between modernization, the emergence of groups demanding political change, and an *increase* in income inequality.

Our use of classic "dual sector" models of economic growth (Harris and Todaro 1970; Lewis 1954) then helps us explain why different types of inequality have distinct political consequences. In these models, emerging economic groups appropriate most of the gains from modernization. As Simon Kuznets famously explained, income inequality tends to increase with the onset of industrialization because production increases rapidly in urban industrial and commercial sectors. This causes wage differentials between industrial and agricultural sectors and huge income gains among rising urban elites, all of which generates rising income inequality. To the extent that inequality increases with economic development, we gain a new way of thinking about the connection between growth, the distributional consequences of growth, and pressures for political change.

Gaining a proper understanding of how different class structures correspond to different Gini coefficients returns us to the crucial question of "who matters" for regime change, and explains why income inequality is positively related to pressures for democratization. Our approach flips the redistributive approach on its head in terms of who matters and why. Redistributivist arguments exaggerate the political relevance of the median voter and all those below him or her on the income distribution. These are Marx's famous "potatoes in a sack" – politically ignorant and inert, and unlikely to constitute a threat to those who control the coercive power of the state.

It is theoretically and empirically more fruitful to begin with the notion that the principal threat to incumbent elites in an autocracy comes from other elites – disenfranchised yet newly wealthy citizens who fear expropriation of their wealth and property, and who have powerful incentives to organize and mobilize in defense of their interests. This dynamic, of elite competition, is far more common historically than are battles between autocratic elites and the poor (e.g., Collier 1999; Haggard and Kaufman 2012).

Contemporary debates about regime change seek to claim the mantle of Barrington Moore (1966). Moore broke with Modernization Theory's original sin of teleology, explaining how and why economic development is not an engine barreling down a single historical track of political development. Although Moore's language is methodologically Marxist in his focus on classes, class coalitions, and actors' material interests, his argument is not redistributivist. Fear of the poor plays little role in Moore's account, and he says virtually nothing about any group's redistributive demands.

Moore's "no bourgeoisie, no democracy" hypothesis actually suggests that all of the important action occurs near the top of the income distribution, in a struggle between the landed elite's defense of the status quo against the bourgeoisie's demands for protection against arbitrary government authority.[1] And instead of fear of redistribution, key actors' preferences for or against democracy are a function of the political consequences of the commercialization of agriculture and the rise of industry. The key exogenous factor shaping actors' endogenous power is changes in the nature of both urban and rural property rights and in the relative demand for manual labor in both sectors as economic modernization advances. Thus, like North and Weingast, Moore highlights growing demands to rein in royal prerogative over taxing and spending (e.g. 13n22, 33) among both voters and nonvoters, and in both rural and urban areas. Where aspiring economic elites were numerous and strong enough, democracy prevailed. Although Moore's methodological script is Marxist, the interests of the main actors in his drama are fundamentally Lockean. We employ different tools to tell this tale, but Moore's story resonates with our own.

---

[1] Moore does acknowledge that to some extent a common social apprehension of the "lower orders" united modernizers and traditionalists. This meant that under some circumstances, the attitude of rising economic elites toward state authority was ambivalent. However, he also notes that the lower orders remained powerless in the face of the wealth and influence of old landowners and new commercial interests. The point is that economic elites had a cultural aversion to, rather than an economic fear of, the poor.

Our findings should encourage a reconsideration of the relationship between democracy and development. A crucial takeaway is that the search for "endogenous" effects of economic growth per se may be chimerical, as the distributional consequences of economic growth appear to have far more consistent and substantively important political consequences. Still, we do place clear scope conditions on our claims. Our model suggests – and our empirical results confirm – that land and income inequality should have the strongest effects in transitions from autocracy to partial rather than full democracy. Moreover, land and income inequality matter, but not always, and not always to the same degree: land inequality will matter more where landed elites tend to be stronger, in lower-income autocracies. Meanwhile, income inequality will matter more where urban elites have grown in prominence, in higher-income regimes. And of course, socioeconomic factors are never the only source of regime change. Our results also support the intuition, missing from Przeworski et al. (2000), that when international factors matter a great deal (as in the Cold War), "endogenous" socioeconomic factors will matter much less.

In any case, our findings suggest that recent scholarly focus on redistributive pressures from the poor median voter is misplaced; much work, however remains to be done exploring key actors' relative fear of the state as an engine driving regime change.

One interesting question we left entirely on the table is whether different "types" of autocratic regimes are more or less likely to break down given different degrees of land and income inequality (Geddes 2007; Svolik 2012), perhaps because certain types of dictators are more or less likely to endogenize equality or inequality. Still, even in systems where the wealthy are creatures of the regime, demand for economic and political rights may emerge due to questions of moral hazard.

Another prominent issue we only briefly considered is the impact of asset-specificity on regime change. We suggested that the conventional wisdom – that countries where mobile assets are relatively more important are more likely to democratize – is likely right, but for the wrong theoretical reasons. The Meltzer-Richard model assumes that they key issue is fear of the poor, and assumes that *no* assets are taxed under autocracy. By focusing on fear of the state and allowing autocracies to tax, it is simple to perceive that holders of immobile assets have relatively greater reasons to fear the autocratic state – and, thus, stronger incentives to demand democracy. Yet where mobile assets dominate an economy, an autocratic regime has greater incentives to grant concessions, to gain revenue. Asset-mobility may lead to democracy – not because of demand from rising elites, but because of the state's need for revenue. Separating out these potential mechanisms should be a focus of future work.

Other questions we did not consider include the relationship between domestic and international factors, whether land and income inequality impact the stability or quality of democracy, and the role of violence in fostering or impeding democratization. Regarding this last issue, we only note that it appears futile to correlate economic inequality with revolution. The major cases of social revolution in world history have occurred under conditions of high land but low or average income inequality – hardly those that we predict lead to democracy. Perhaps for this reason, Skocpol (1979) noted that the key factors include state weakness, loss in war, and the international context. Nonetheless, violence may play an unappreciated role in fostering or impeding regime change, given different levels of land and income inequality.

In terms of the stability or quality of democracy, we recognize that suggesting that income inequality is associated with pressures for democratization has somewhat discomfiting implications. We are certainly not advocating income inequality to promote democracy, but our argument does imply that in relatively new, developing democracies land inequality should be destabilizing, but income inequality should have a salutary and opposite effect. However, our findings in Chapter 7 also imply that one should not expect substantial redistributivist pressures from below in most new democracies – particularly those that transition under conditions of high income inequality. The political consequences of inequality for governance and regime stability merit further consideration.

Taken together, our argument and findings about (1) the conditions that foster regime change; (2) the relationship between inequality, regime type, and public spending, and (3) the preferences of citizens under autocracy suggest that what matters is not a fear of the downtrodden masses, but competition between economic elites for control over the expropriative authority of the State. The notion that democracy is fundamentally about battles for taxation with representation is a fruitful starting point for the comparative study of regime change and the contemporary effort to understand the interplay between growth, inequality, and the politics of democratization across time and space.

Bibliography

Acemoglu, Daron, Simon Johnson, and James A. Robinson. 2000. "The Colonial Origins of Comparative Development: An Empirical Investigation." http://www.nber.org/papers/w7771.

———. 2008. "Income and Democracy." *The American Economic Review* 98 (3):808–842.

Acemoglu, Daron, Simon Johnson, James Robinson, and Pierre Yared. 2005. "Income and Democracy." National Bureau of Economic Research.

Acemoglu, D. and J.A. Robinson. 2000. "Why Did the West Extend the Franchise? Democracy, Inequality, and Growth in Historical Perspective." *The Quarterly Journal of Economics* 115 (4):1167–1199.

———. 2001. "A Theory of Political Transitions." *American Economic Review* 91 (4):938–963.

———. 2006. *Economic Origins of Dictatorship and Democracy*. New York: Cambridge University Press.

Aghion, Phillippe and Jeffrey Williamson. 1998. *Growth, Inequality and Globalization: Theory, History, and Policy*. Cambridge: Cambridge University Press.

Ahlquist, J.S. and E. Wibbels. 2012. "Riding the Wave: World Trade and Factor-Based Models of Democratization." *American Journal of Political Science* 56 (2):447–464.

Aidt, T.S., M. Daunton, and J. Dutta. 2010. "The Retrenchment Hypothesis and the Extension of the Franchise in England and Wales." *The Economic Journal* 120 (547):990–1020.

Aidt, T.S., J. Dutta, and E. Loukoianova. 2006. "Democracy Comes to Europe: Franchise Extension and Fiscal Outcomes 1830–1938." *European Economic Review* 50 (2):249–283.

Aidt, T.S. and P.S. Jensen. 2011. "Workers of the World, Unite! Franchise Extensions and the Threat of Revolution in Europe, 1820–1938." *Discussion Papers of Business and Economics*.

Albertus, M. and V. Menaldo. 2012. "If You're Against Them You're With Us: The Effect of Expropriation on Autocratic Survival." *Comparative Political Studies* 45 (8), 973–1003

Alesina, A., A. Devleeschauwer, W. Easterly, S. Kurlat, and R. Wacziarg. 2003. "Fractionalization." *Journal of Economic Growth* 8 (2):155–194.

Alesina, A. and E.L. Glaeser. 2005. *Fighting Poverty in the US and Europe: A World of Difference*. New York: Oxford University Press.

Alesina, A. and E. La Ferrara. 2005. "Preferences for Redistribution in the Land of Opportunities." *Journal of Public Economics* 89 (5):897–931.

Alesina, A. and D. Rodrik. 1994. "Distributive Politics and Economic Growth." *The Quarterly Journal of Economics* 109 (2):465–490.

Alesina, A. and E. Spolaore. 2005. *The Size of Nations*. Cambridge, MA: MIT Press.

Amsden, A.H. 1992. *Asia's Next Giant: South Korea and Late Industrialization*. New York: Oxford University Press.

Anderson, Christopher J. and Pablo Beramendi. 2012. "Left Parties, Poor Voters, and Electoral Participation in Advanced Industrial Societies." *Comparative Political Studies* 45 (6):714–746.

Anderson, Margaret Lavina. 1993. "Voter, Junker, Landrat, Priest: The Old Authorities and the New Franchise in Imperial Germany." *The American Historical Review* 98 (5):1448–1474.

———. 2000. *Practicing Democracy: Elections and Political Culture in Imperial Germany*. Princeton, NJ: Princeton University Press.

Angrist, Joshua and Alan B Krueger. 2001. "Instrumental Variables and the Search for Identification: From Supply and Demand to Natural Experiments." Tech. rep., National Bureau of Economic Research.

Ansell, B. W. 2010. *From the Ballot to the Blackboard: the Redistributive Political Economy of Education*. New York: Cambridge University Press.

Ansell, B. W. and J. Lindvall. 2013. "The Origins of Primary Education Regimes: Ideology, Institutions, and Interdenominational Conflict in an Era of Nation-Building." *American Political Science Review* (3):1–22.

Ardañaz, Martin and Isabela Mares. 2012. "Rural inequality, labor mobility and democratic reforms." Working Paper, Columbia University.

Atkinson, Anthony. 2007. "The Distribution of Top Incomes in the United Kingdom 1908–2000." In A.B. Atkinson and T. Piketty (eds.), *Top Incomes over the Twentieth Century: A Contrast between Continental European and English-Speaking Countries*, New York: Oxford University Press, 82–140.

Atkinson, A.B. and A. Brandolini. 2001. "Promise and pitfalls in the use of "secondary" data-sets: Income inequality in OECD countries as a case study." *Journal of Economic Literature* 39 (3):771–799.

Atkinson, Anthony, Thomas Piketty and Emmanuel Saez. 2011. "Top Incomes in the Long Run of History." *Journal of Economic Literature* 49 (1):3–71.

Babones, S.J. and M.J. Álvarez-Riva dulla. 2007. "Standardized Income Inequality Data for Use in Cross-National Research." *Sociological Inquiry* 77 (1):3–22.

Bagehot, Walter. 1865. "The English Constitution." *Fortnightly Review* 1:1–331.

Banerjee, A.V. and E. Duflo. 2003. "Inequality and Growth: What Can the Data Say?" *Journal of Economic Growth* 8 (3):267–99.

———. 2008. "What Is Middle Class about the Middle Classes Around the World?" *Journal of Economic Perspectives* 22 (2):3–28.

Barro, R.J. 1991. "A Cross-country Study of Growth, Saving, and Government." In B.D. Bernheim and J.D. Shoven. (eds.) *National saving and economic performance*. Chicago: University of Chicago Press, pp. 271–304.

Bartels, L.M. 2010. *Unequal Democracy: The Political Economy of the New Gilded Age*. Princeton, NJ: Princeton University Press.

Bastiat, Frédéric. 1850. *La Loi*. Ludwig von Mises Institute. Auburn, Alabama. 2007.

Bates, R.H. and D.H. Lien. 1985. "A Note on Taxation, Development, and Representative Government." *Politics & Society* 14 (1):53.

Baumol, W.J. 1967. "Macroeconomics of Unbalanced Growth: The Anatomy of Urban Crisis." *The American Economic Review* 57 (3):415–426.

Baxter, R. Dudley. 1868. *National Income: The United Kingdom*. London: MacMillan and Co.

Béja, J.P. 2009. "The Massacre's Long Shadow." *Journal of Democracy* 20 (3):5–16.

Benabou, Roland. 1996. "Inequality and Growth." In *NBER Macroeconomics Annual Volume 11*. Cambridge, MA: MIT Press, 11–92.

———. 2000. "Unequal Societies: Income Distribution and the Social Contract." *The American Economic Review* 90 (1):96–129.

Benabou, R. and E.A. Ok. 2001. "Social Mobility and the Demand for Redistribution: The POUM Hypothesis." *Quarterly Journal of Economics* 116 (2):447–487.

Benjamin, Dwayne. 2008. "Income Inequality During China's Economic Transition." In Loren Brandt and Thomas Rawski (eds.), *China's Great Economic Transformation*. New York: Cambridge University Press, 729–775.

Berlinski, Samuel and Torun Dewan. 2011. "The Political Consequences of Franchise Extension: Evidence from the Second Reform Act." *Quarterly Journal of Political Science* 6 (3-4):329–376.

Berry, Albert. 1990. "International Trade, Government and Income distribution in Peru since 1870." *Latin American Research Review* 25 (2):31–59.

Blackbourn, David and Richard J. Evans, (eds.) 1991. *The German Bourgeoisie: Essays on the Social History of the German Middle Class from the Late Eighteenth to the Early Twentieth Century*. London: Routledge.

Boix, Carles. 2001. "Democracy, Development, and the Public Sector." *American Journal of Political Science* :1–17.

———. 2003. *Democracy and Redistribution*. New York: Cambridge University Press.

———. 2011. "Democracy, Development, and the International System." *American Political Science Review* 105 (4):809–28.

Boix, Carles and Sebastian Rosato. 2001. "A Complete Data Set of Political Regimes, 1800–1999." *Chicago: Department of Political Science, University of Chicago*.

Boix, Carles and Susan C. Stokes. 2003. "Endogenous Democratization." *World Politics* 55 (4):517–549.

Bollen, K.A. and R.W. Jackman. 1985. "Political Democracy and the Size Distribution of Income." *American Sociological Review* 50 (4):438–457.

———. 1989. "Democracy, Stability, and Dichotomies." *American Sociological Review* 54 (4):612–621.

———. 1995. "Income Inequality and Democratization Revisited: Comment on Muller." *American Sociological Review* 60 (6):983–989.

Bomhoff, Eduard and Mary Man Li Gu. 2011. "Chinese Culture and Modernization: Testing the Value Shift Hypothesis." Available at: ssrn.com/abstract=1740169.

Booth, Anne. 1998. "Living Standards and the Distribution of Income in Colonial Indonesia." *Journal of Southeast Asia Studies* 19 (2):310–334.

Borjas, G.J. and G.T. Sueyoshi. 1994. "A Two-stage Estimator for Probit Models with Structural Group Effects." *Journal of Econometrics* 64:165–182.

Bourguignon, Francois and Christian Morrisson. 1998. "Inequality and Development: The Role of Dualism." *Journal of Development Economics* 57:233–257.

———. 2002. "Inequality among World Citizens: 1820–1992." *The American Economic Review* 92 (4):727–744.

Boyer, George. 1986. "The Old Poor Law and the Agricultural Labor Market in Southern England: An Empirical Analysis." *Journal of Economic History* 46: 113–135.

Bradley, D., E. Huber, S. Moller, F. Nielsen, and J.D. Stephens. 2003. "Distribution and Redistribution in Postindustrial Democracies." *World Politics* 55 (2):193–228.

Capoccia, G. and D. Ziblatt. 2010. "The Historical Turn in Democratization Studies: A New Research Agenda for Europe and Beyond." *Comparative Political Studies* 43 (8–9):931–968.

Caramani, D. 2000. The Societies of Europe: *Elections in Western Europe since 1815.* London: Palgrave Macmillan.

Cheibub, J.A. 1998. "Political Regimes and the Extractive Capacity of Governments: Taxation in Democracies and Dictatorships." *World Politics* 50:349–376.

China Digital Times 2013. "China Lets Gini Out of the Bottle." URL chinadigitaltimes. net/2013/01/china-lets-gini-out-of-the-bottle/.

Cho, Seok Kon. 2001. "Changes in Korean Land Tenure in the 20th Century – An Ideology of Land Ownership for Farmers." *In History of Korean Economic Development.* Seoul: National University Press, 329–364.

Choi, Chang Jip. 1993. "Political Cleavages in South Korea." In Hagen Koo (ed.), *State and Society in Contemporary Korea.* Ithaca: Cornell University Press, 13–50.

CIA. 2014. "The World Factbook: Gini Index." https://www.cia.gov/library/ publications/the-world-factbook/fields/2172.html, accessed July 27, 2014.

Clark, G. 2008. *A Farewell to Alms: A Brief Economic History of the World.* Princeton, NJ: Princeton University Press.

Clark, Kitson. 1962. *The Making of Victorian England.* Cambridge, MA: Harvard University Press.

Collier, D. and R. Adcock. 1999. "Democracy and Dichotomies: A Pragmatic Approach to Choices about Concepts." *Annual Review of Political Science* 2 (1):537–565.

Collier, D. and S. Levitsky. 1997. "Democracy with Adjectives: Conceptual Innovation in Comparative Research." *World Politics* 49 (3):430–451.

Collier, Paul, Anke Hoeffler, and Nicholas Sambanis. 2005. "The Collier-Hoeffler Model of Civil War Onset and the Case Study Project Research Design." In Paul Collier and Nicholas Sambanis (eds.), Understanding Civil War: Evidence and Analysis. Washington, DC: World Bank Publications, 1–35.

Collier, R.B. 1999. *Paths toward Democracy: The Working Class and Elites in Western Europe and South America.* Cambridge, MA: Cambridge University Press.

Collini, Stefan, Donald Winch, and John Burrow. 1983. *That Noble Science of Politics: A Study in Nineteenth-Century Intellectual History.* Cambridge, UK: Cambridge University Press.

Coppedge, Michael. 2012. *Democratization and Research Methods: Strategies for Social Inquiry.* New York: Cambridge University Press.

Cowling, Maurice. 1967. *Disraeli, Gladstone and Revolution: The Passing of the Second Reform Bill.* Cambridge, UK: Cambridge University Press.

Cutright, Phillips. 1965. "Political Structure, Economic Development, and National Social Security Programs." *American Journal of Sociology* :537–550.

Dahl, R.A. 1971. *Polyarchy: Participation and Opposition*. New Haven, CT: Yale University Press.

Deininger, K. and L. Squire. 1996. "A New Data Set Measuring Income Inequality." *The World Bank Economic Review* 10 (3):565–591.

Diamond, Jared M. and Doug Ordunio. 1997. *Guns, Germs, and Steel*. New York: Norton.

Diamond, J.M. and J.A. Robinson. 2010. *Natural Experiments of History*. Cambridge, MA: Belknap Press.

Diamond, L. 2012. "The Coming Wave." *Journal of Democracy* 23 (1):5–13.

Dincecco, Mark and Mauricio Prado. 2010. "War, Democracy, and Government Size Over the Long Run: A Structural Breaks Analysis." *Unpublished, IMT Luca Institute for Advanced Studies*.

Dunn, John. 1979. *Western Political Theory in the Face of the Future*. Cambridge, UK: Cambridge University Press.

Dunning, T. 2008a. *Crude Democracy: Natural Resource Wealth and Political Regimes*. New York: Cambridge University Press.

———. 2008b. "Model Specification in instrumental-variables Regression." *Political Analysis* 16 (3):290.

Easterly, William. 2001. "The Middle Class Consensus and Economic Development." *Journal of Economic Growth* 6 (4):317–335.

Easterly, W. and S. Rebelo. 1993. "Fiscal Policy and Economic Growth." *Journal of Monetary Economics* 32 (3):417–458.

Eddie, Scott M. 2008. *Landownership in Eastern Germany Before the Great War: A Quantitative Analysis*. New York: Oxford University Press.

Eley, Geoff. 1991. "Liberalism, Europe and the Bourgeoisie 1860–1914." In D. Blackbourn and RJ Evans (eds.), *The German Bourgeoisie: Essays on the Social History of the German Middle Class from the Late Eighteenth to the Early Twentieth Century*. New York: Routledge, 293–317.

Elkins, Z. 2000. "Gradations of Democracy? Empirical Tests of Alternative Conceptualizations." *American Journal of Political Science* 44 (2):193–200.

Epstein, D.L., R. Bates, J. Goldstone, I. Kristensen, and S. O'Halloran. 2006. "Democratic Transitions." *American Journal of Political Science* 50 (3):551–569.

Fang, Xuyan and Lea Yu. 2012. "Gov't Refuses to Release Gini Coefficient." From Caixin Online, http://english.caixin.com/2012-01-18/100349814.html, Accessed June 23 2014.

Fearon, James D. 2008. "Economic development, insurgency, and civil war." In Elanan Helpman (ed.), *Institutions and Economic Performance*. Cambridge, MA: Harvard University Press, 292–328.

Fields, Gary S. 1993. "Inequality in Dual Economy Models." *The Economic Journal* 103 (420):1228–1235.

———. 2004. "Dualism in the Labor Market: A perspective on the Lewis Model after Half a Century." *The Manchester School* 72 (6):724–735.

Finseraas, H. 2009. "Income Inequality and Demand for Redistribution: A Multilevel Analysis of European Public Opinion." *Scandinavian Political Studies* 32 (1):94–119.

Frankema, E. 2010. "The Colonial Roots of Land Inequality: Geography, Factor Endowments, or Institutions?" *The Economic History Review* 63 (2):418–451.

Franzese, R.J. 1998. "Political Participation, Income Distribution, and Public Transfers in Developed Democracies." Unpublished, University of Michigan.

Fraser, Derek. 1976. *Urban Politics in Victorian England.* Leicester, UK: Leicester University Press.

Freeman, J.R. and D.P. Quinn. 2010. "The Economic Origins of Democracy Reconsidered." *American Political Science Review* 106 (1):1–23.

Frye, T. and A. Shleifer. 1997. "The Invisible Hand and the Grabbing Hand." *American Economic Review* 87 (2): 354–358.

Geddes, B. 2007. "What Causes Democratization?" Unpublished, UCLA Department of Political Science.

Gehlbach, Scott and Philip Keefer. 2011. "Investment without Democracy: Ruling-party Institutionalization and Credible Commitment in Autocracies." *Journal of Comparative Economics* 39 (2):123–139.

Gerschenkron, Alexander. 1943. *Bread and Democracy in Germany.* Berkeley: University of California Press.

Gibbons. 1990. *Victorian Liberalism.* London: Routledge.

Gilens, M. 2000. *Why Americans Hate Welfare: Race, Media, and the Politics of Antipoverty Policy.* Chicago, IL: University of Chicago Press.

———. 2012. *Affluence and Influence: Economic Inequality and Political Power in America.* Princeton, NJ: Princeton University Press.

Goertz, G. 2006. *Social science concepts: A user's guide.* Princeton, NJ: Princeton University Press.

Gold, T.B. 1990. "The Resurgence of Civil Society in China." *Journal of Democracy* 1 (1):18–31.

Goldman, M. 1990. "China's Great Leap Backward." *Journal of Democracy* 1 (1):9–17.

Gottschalk, P. and T.M. Smeeding. 1997. "Cross-national Comparisons of Earnings and Income Inequality." *Journal of Economic Literature* 35 (2):633–687.

Grant, Oliver. 2002. "Does Industrialisation Push Up Inequality? New Evidence on the Kuznets Curve from Nineteenth Century Prussian Tax Statistics." Working paper, Oxford University Department of History.

———. 2005. *Migration and Inequality in Germany, 1870–1913.* New York: Oxford University Press.

Green, D.P., S.Y.H. Kim, and D. Yoon. 2001. "Dirty Pool." *International Organization* 55 (2):441–468.

Greene, W. 2004. "Fixed Effects and Bias Due to the Incidental Parameters Problem in the Tobit Model." *Econometric Reviews* 23 (2):125–147.

Grossman, Gene and Elhanan Helpman. 1996. "Electoral Competition and Special Interest Politics." *Journal of Public Economics* 63 (2):265–286.

———. 2002. *Special Interest Politics.* Cambridge, MA: MIT Press.

Grossman, Herschel and Suk Jae Noh. 1994. "Proprietary Public Finance and Economic Welfare." *Journal of Public Economics* 53:187–204.

Grossmann, V. 2003. "Income inequality, voting over the size of public consumption, and growth." *European Journal of Political Economy* 19 (2):265–287.

Gurr, T.R. 1970. *Why Men Rebel.* Princeton, NJ: Princeton University Press.

Haggard, S. and R.R. Kaufman. 1995. *The Political Economy of Democratic Transitions.* Princeton, NJ: Princeton University Press.

———. 2012. "Inequality and Regime Change: Democratic Transitions and the Stability of Democratic Rule." *American Political Science Review* 106 (3):495–516.

Haggard, Stephan and Chung in Moon. 1993. "The State, Politics, and Economic Development in Postwar South Korea." In Hagen Koo (ed.), *State and Society in Contemporary Korea*. Ithaca: Cornell University Press, 51–93.

Harms, P. and S. Zink. 2003. "Limits to Redistribution in a Democracy: A Survey." *European Journal of Political Economy* 19 (4):651–668.

Harris, John R. and Michael P. Todaro. 1970. "Migration, unemployment and development: a two-sector analysis." *American Economic Review* 60 (1): 126–142.

Harrison, Royden. 1965. *Before the Socialists: Studies in Labour and Politics 1861-1881*. London: Routledge and Kegan Paul.

Heckman, J.J. 1987. "The Incidental Parameters Problem and the Problem of Initial Conditions in Estimating a Discrete Time-Discrete Data Stochastic Process and Some Monte Carlo Evidence." In Charles Manski (ed.), *Structural Analysis of Discrete Data*. Cambridge, MA: MIT Press, 179–195.

Held, David. 1987. *Models of Democracy*. Cambridge, UK: Polity Press.

Herb, M. 2003. "Taxation and Representation." *Studies in Comparative International Development* 38 (3):3–31.

———. 2005. "No Representation without Taxation? Rents, Development, and Democracy." *Comparative Politics* 37 (3):297–316.

Himmelfarb, Gertrude. 1966. "The Politics of Democracy: The English Reform Act of 1867." *Journal of British Studies* 6 (1):97–138.

Hirschman, A.O. 1970. *Exit, Voice, and Loyalty: Responses to Decline in Firms, Organizations, and States*, Cambridge, MA: Harvard University Press.

———. 1991. *The Rhetoric of Reaction*. Princeton, NJ: Princeton University Press.

Hirshleifer, J. 1995. "Anarchy and Its Breakdown." *The Journal of Political Economy* 103 (1):26–52.

———. 2001. *The Dark Side of the Force: Economic Foundations of Conflict Theory*. Cambridge University Press.

Hobsbawm, Eric. 1978. "The Forward March of Labour Halted?" *Marxism Today* (September):279–286. See http://www.amielandmelburn.org.uk/collections/mt/pdf/78_09_hobsbawm.pdf

———. 1985. *Workers: Worlds of Labour*. New York: Pantheon.

Hochschild, J.L. 1996. *Facing up to the American Dream: Race, Class, and the Soul of the Nation*. Princeton, NJ: Princeton University Press.

Hoppen, K. Theodore. 1998. *The Mid-Victorian Generation, 1846–1886*. Oxford: Clarendon Press.

Houle, C. 2009a. "Inequality and Democracy: Why Inequality Harms Consolidation but Does Not Affect Democratization." *World Politics* 61 (04):589–622.

———. 2009b. "Inequality, Economic Development and Democratization." Unpublished manuscript, University of Rochester.

Huber, J.D., G. Kernell, and E.L. Leoni. 2005. "Institutional Context, Cognitive Resources and Party Attachments across Democracies." *Political Analysis* 13 (4):365–386.

Huber, J. and P. Stanig. 2009. "Individual Income and Voting for Redistribution across Democracies." Unpublished. Columbia University.

Hunt, James. 1974. "Peasants, Grain Tariffs and Meat Quotas: Imperial German Protectionism Reexamined." *Central European History* 7 (4):311–331.

Hunt, Shane J. 1985. "Growth and Guano in the Nineteenth Century." In Conde, R.C. et al., *Latin American Economies: Growth and the Export Sector, 1880–1930.* Teaneck, NJ: Holmes and Meier Publishers.

Huntington, S.P. 1991. *The Third Wave: Democratization in the Late Twentieth Century.* Norman, OK: University of Oklahoma Press.

Hwang, Han Sik. 1985. "Agriculture under the American Military Government and Land Reform Policy." in *Contemporary Korean Politics* 2. Seoul: Hankilsa, 284–329.

ILO. 1933. *International Survey of Social Services.* Geneva: International Labour Office.

———. 1936. *International Survey of Social Services (2 volumes).* Geneva: International Labour Office.

Inglehart, Ronald and Christian Welzel. 2009. "How Development Leads to Democracy - What We Know about Modernization." *Foreign Affairs* 88:33–48.

Iversen, T. and D. Soskice. 2001. "An Asset Theory of Social Policy Preferences." In *American Political Science Review* 95(4):875–893.

———. 2006. "Electoral Institutions and the Politics of Coalitions: Why Some Democracies Redistribute More than Others." *American Political Science Review* 100 (2):165–181.

Jackman, R. 1974. "Political Democracy and Social Inequality." *American Sociological Review* 39 (1):29–45.

Jang, Sang Hwan. 1985. "Empirical Research on the Process of Land Reform." in *Contemporary Korean Politics* 2. Seoul: Hankilsa, 330–401.

Jazairy, Idriss, Mohuiddin Alamgir, and Theresa Panuccio. 1992. *The State of World Poverty: An Inquiry into Its Causes and Consequences.* New York: NYU Press.

Jeon, Y.D. and Y.Y. Kim. 2000. "Land Reform, Income Redistribution, and Agricultural Production in Korea." *Economic Development and Cultural Change* 48 (2):253–268.

Jones, H. Stuart. 1990. *Victorian Political Thought.* New York: St. Martins.

Jones, R.W. 1971. "A Three-Factor Model in Theory, Trade, and History." *Trade, Balance of Payments, and Growth* 1:3–21.

Jusko, K.L. and W.P. Shively. 2005. "Applying a Two-Step Strategy to the Analysis of Cross-national Public Opinion Data." *Political Analysis* 13 (4):327–344.

Justman, M. and M. Gradstein. 1999. "The Industrial Revolution, Political Transition, and the Subsequent Decline in Inequality in 19th-century Britain." *Explorations in Economic History* 36 (2):109–127.

Kalyvas, S.N. 1996. *The Rise of Christian Democracy in Europe.* Ithaca: Cornell University Press.

Kang, Man Kil. 2000. *History of Korean Capitalism.* Seoul: Yeoksabipyung.

Katznelson, Ira. 1985. "Working Class Formation and the State: Nineteenth Century England in American Perspective." in Evans et al. (eds.), *Bringing the State Back In. New York: Cambridge University Press*, pp. 257–284.

Kenworthy, L. 2008. *Jobs with Equality.* New York: Oxford University Press.

Kenworthy, L. and L. McCall. 2008. "Inequality, Public Opinion and Redistribution." *Socio-Economic Review* 6 (1):35–68.

Kenworthy, L. and J. Pontusson. 2005. "Rising Inequality and the Politics of Redistribution in Affluent Countries." *Perspectives on Politics* 3 (3):449–471.

Kim, S. 2000. *The Politics of Democratization in Korea: The Role of Civil Society.* Pittsburgh: University of Pittsburgh Press.

Kim, Tae Il. 1990. "Structural Change in Agricultural Society and Peasant Politics." In *Studies in Contemporary Korean Politics I.* Seoul: Nanam, 443–472.

King, G., M. Tomz, and J. Wittenberg. 2000. "Making the Most of Statistical Analyses: Improving Interpretation and Presentation." *American Journal of Political Science* 44 (2):347–361.

Kiser, Edgar. 1994. "Markets and Hierarchies in Early Modern Tax Systems: A Principal-agent Analysis." *Politics & Society* 22 (3):284–315.

Knight, J. 1992. *Institutions and Social Conflict.* New York: Cambridge University Press.

Knutsen, Carl. 2011. "Democracy, Dictatorship and Protection of Property Rights." *Journal of Development Studies* 47 (1):164–182.

Kohli, Atul. 2004. *State-Directed Development: Political Power and Industrialization in the Global Periphery.* New York: Cambridge University Press.

Koo, Hagen. 1993. "The State, Minjung, and the Working Class in South Korea." In *State and Society in Contemporary Korea.* Ithaca: Cornell University Press, 131–162.

———. 2002. "Engendering Civil Society: The Role of the Labor Movement." In Charles K. Armstrong (ed.), *Korean Society: Civil Society, Democracy and the State.* New York: Routledge, 109–131.

Kopstein, Jeffrey. 2003. "Postcommunist Democracy: Legacies and Outcomes." *Comparative Politics* 35 (2):231–250.

Krouse, Richard. 1982. "Two Concepts of Democratic Representation: James and John Stuart Mill." *Journal of Politics* 44 (2):509–537.

Kung, James Kai-sing, Xiaogang Wu, and Yuxiao Wu. 2012. "Inequality of land Tenure and Revolutionary Outcome: An Economic Analysis of China's Land Reform of 1946–1952." *Explorations in Economic History* 49 (4):482–497.

Kuznets, S. 1955. "Economic Growth and Income Inequality." *The American Economic Review* 45 (1):1–28.

Leblang, D.A. 1996. "Property Rights, Democracy and Economic Growth." *Political Research Quarterly* 49 (1):5–26.

Lee, W. and J.E. Roemer. 1998. "Income Distribution, Redistributive Politics, and Economic Growth." *Journal of Economic Growth* 3 (3):217–240.

Leoni, E.L. 2009. "Analyzing Multiple Surveys: Results from Monte Carlo Experiments." Unpublished manuscript, Columbia University.

Levi, M. 1989. *Of Rule and Revenue.* Berkeley: University of California Press.

Lewis, J.B. and D.A. Linzer. 2005. "Estimating Regression Models in Which the Dependent Variable Is Based on Estimates." *Political Analysis* 13 (4):345–364.

Lewis, W.A. 1954. "Economic Development with Unlimited Supplies of Labour." *The Manchester School* 22 (2): 139–191.

Li, C. 2012. "The End of the CCP's Resilient Authoritarianism? A Tripartite Assessment of Shifting Power in China." *The China Quarterly* 211 (1): 595–623.

Lie, J. 2000. *Han Unbound: The Political Economy of South Korea.* Stanford, CA: Stanford University Press.

Lindert, Peter and Jeffrey Williamson. 1983. "Reinterpreting Britain's Social Tables, 1688-1913." *Explorations in Economic History* 20:94–109.

———. 1985. "Growth, Equality, and History." *Explorations in Economic History* 22 (4):341–377.

Lindert, P.H. 1994. "The Rise of Social Spending, 1880–1930." *Explorations in Economic History* 31 (1):1–37.

———. 2004. *Growing Public: Social Spending and Economic Growth since the Eighteenth Century.* New York: Cambridge University Press.

Lippincott, Benjamin. [1938] 1974. *Victorian Critics of Democracy.* New York: Octagon Books.

Lipset, Seymour Martin. 1983. "Radicalism or Reformism: The Sources of Working-Class Politics." *American Political Science Review* 77 (1):1–19.

Lipset, S.M. 1959. "Some Social Requisites of Democracy: Economic Development and Political Legitimacy." *American Political Science Review* 53 (1):69–105.

Liu, Y. and D. Chen. 2012. "Why China Will Democratize." *The Washington Quarterly* 35 (1):41–63.

Lizzeri, A. and N. Persico. 2004. "Why Did the Elites Extend the Suffrage? Democracy and the Scope Of Government, with an Application to Britain's Age Of Reform." *Quarterly Journal of Economics* 119 (2):707–765.

Lott, J.R., Jr and L.W. Kenny. 1999. "Did Women's Suffrage Change the Size and Scope of Government?" *Journal of Political Economy* 107 (6):1163–1198.

Lübker, M. 2007. "Inequality and the Demand for Redistribution: Are the Assumptions of the New Growth Theory Valid?" *Socio-Economic Review* 5 (1):117–148.

Luebbert, G.M. 1991a. *Liberalism, Fascism, or Social Democracy: Social Classes and the Political Origins of Regimes in Interwar Europe.* New York: Oxford University Press.

———. 1991b. *Liberalism, Fascism or Social Democracy.* New York: Oxford University Press.

Maddison, A. 1997. "Monitoring the World Economy 1820–1992." *Review of International Economics* 5 (4):516–522.

Mahoney, James. 2003. "Knowledge Accumulation in Comparative Historical Research: The Case of Democracy and Authoritarianism." In J. Mahoney and D. Rueschemeyer (eds.), *Comparative Historical Analysis in the Social Sciences.* New York: Cambridge University Press, 131–176.

Marks, Gary, Heather Mbaye, and Hyung Min Kim. 2009. "Radicalism or Reformism? Socialist Parties before World War I." *American Sociological Review* 74:615–635.

Marshall, M.G., K. Jaggers, and T.R Gurr. 2003. *Polity IV Project.* College Park: Center for International Development and Conflict Management at the University of Maryland.

McClelland, Keith. 2000. "England's Greatness, the Working Man." in C. Hall (ed.), *Defining the Victorian Nation.* Cambridge, UK: Cambridge University Press.

McGuire, M.C. and M. Olson. 1996. "The Economics of Autocracy and Majority Rule: The Invisible Hand and the Use of Force." *Journal of Economic Literature* 34 (1):72–96.

Meltzer, A.H. and S.F. Richard. 1981. "A Rational Theory of the Size of Government." *The Journal of Political Economy* 89 (5):914–927.

Milanovic, B. 2000. "The Median-voter Hypothesis, Income Inequality, and Income Redistribution: An Empirical Test with the Required Data." *European Journal of Political Economy* 16 (3):367–410.

Milanovic, Branko, Peter H Lindert, and Jeffrey G Williamson. 2007. "Measuring Ancient Inequality." National Bureau of Economic Research.

Milanovic, Branko, Peter Lindert, and Jeffrey Williamson. 2011. "Pre-Industrial Inequality." *The Economic Journal* 121 (551):255–272.

Mill, James. [1820] 1992. "An Essay on Government." Reprinted in Terence Ball (ed.) *James Mill: Political Writings* 1–42. The Bath Press, Avon, UK.

Moene, K.O. and M. Wallerstein. 2001. "Inequality, Social Insurance, and Redistribution." In *American Political Science Review* 95:859–874.

———. 2003. "Earnings Inequality and Welfare Spending: A Disaggregated Analysis." *World Politics* 55 (4):485–516.

Montinola, Gabriela and Robert Jackman. 2002. "Sources of Corruption: A Cross-Country Study." *British Journal of Political Science* 32:147–170.

Moore, B. 1966. *Social Origins of Dictatorship and Democracy: Lord and Peasant in the Making of the Modern World.* Boston, MA: Beacon Press.

Moore, David Cresap. 1976. *The Politics of Deference: A Study of the Mid-19th Century English Political System.* Hassocks, UK: Harvester Press.

Moorhouse, H F. 1978. "The Marxist Theory of the Labour Aristocracy." *Social History* 3 (1):61–82.

Moriguchi, C. and E. Saez. 2006. *The Evolution of Income Concentration in Japan, 1886–2002: Evidence from Income Tax Statistics.* National Bureau of Economic Research.

Moselle, B. and B. Polak. 2001. "A Model of a Predatory state." *Journal of Law, Economics, and Organization* 17 (1):1–33.

Mueller, D.C. 2003. *Public Choice III.* New York: Cambridge University Press.

Muller, E.N. 1988. "Democracy, Economic Development, and Income Inequality." *American Sociological Review* 53 (1):50–68.

———. 1995a. "Economic Determinants of Democracy." *American Sociological Review* 60 (6):966–982.

———. 1995b. "Income Inequality and Democratization: Reply to Bollen and Jackman." *American Sociological Review* 60 (6):990–996.

Mulligan, Casey B, Ricard Gil, and Xavier Sala-i-Martin. 2004. "Do Democracies Have Different Public Policies than Nondemocracies?" *The Journal of Economic Perspectives* 18 (1):51–74.

Munck, G.L. and J. Verkuilen. 2002. "Conceptualizing and measuring democracy." *Comparative Political Studies* 35 (1):5–34.

Nafziger, Steven and Peter Lindert. 2011. "Russian Inequality on the Eve of the Revolution." Working Paper, Williams College.

Nathan, A.J. 2003. "Authoritarian Resilience." *Journal of Democracy* 14 (1):6–17.

———. 2013. "Foreseeing the Unforeseeable." *Journal of Democracy* 24 (1):20–25.

Nickell, S. 1981. "Biases in Dynamic Models with Fixed Effects." *Econometrica: Journal of the Econometric Society* 49 (6):1417–1426.

Niskanen, W.A. 1997. "Autocratic, Democratic, and Optimal Government." *Economic Inquiry* 35 (3):464–479.

Nohlen, D. 2005. *Elections in the Americas: North America, Central America, and the Caribbean,* vol. 1. New York: Oxford University Press.

North, Douglass. 1986. *Structure and Change in Economic History.* New York: WW Norton.

———. 1990. *Institutions, Institutional Change, and Economic Performance.* New York: Cambridge University Press.

North, Douglass and Barry Weingast. 1989. "Constitutions and Commitment: The Evolution of Institutions Governing Public Choice in Seventeenth-century England." *The Journal of Economic History* 49 (04):803–832.

Nossiter, T.J. 1975. *Influence, Opinion and Political Idioms in Reformed England: Case Studies from the North-east 1832–74*. Hassocks, UK: Harvester Press.

Oakley, S. 1966. *The Story of Sweden*. New York: Faber & Faber.

O'Brien, K.J. 2009. "Rural protest." *Journal of Democracy* 20 (3):25–28.

O'Donnell, G.A., P.C. Schmitter, and L. Whitehead. 1986. *Transitions from Authoritarian Rule: Comparative Perspectives*, vol. 3. Baltimore, MD: Johns Hopkins University Press.

Olson, Mancur. 1965. *The Logic of Collective Action*. Cambridge, MA: Harvard University Press.

———. 1982. *The Rise and Decline of Nations*. New Haven, CT: Yale University Press.

———. 1993. "Dictatorship, democracy, and development." *American Political Science Review* 87 (3):567–576.

Pack, Wolfgang. 1961. *Das parlamentarische Ringen um das Sozialistengesetz Bismarcks, 1878-1890*. Düsseldorf: Droste.

Pak, K.H. 1956. "Outcome of Land Reform in the Republic of Korea." *Journal of Farm Economics* 38 (4):1015–1023.

Pampel, F.C. and J.B. Williamson. 1992. *Age, Class, Politics, and the Welfare State*. New York: Cambridge University Press.

Peach, Terry. 2008. "Ricardo, David (1772–1823)." in *The New Palgrave Dictionary of Economics*. New York: Palgrave.

Pei, M. 2012. "Is CCP Rule Fragile or Resilient?" *Journal of Democracy* 23 (1):27–41.

Perotti, R. 1996. "Growth, Income Distribution, and Democracy: What the Data Say." *Journal of Economic growth* 1 (2):149–187.

Polanyi, Karl. 1944. *The Great Transformation*. Boston, MA: Beacon Press.

Pontusson, J. 2005. *Inequality and Prosperity: Social Europe vs. Liberal America*. Ithaca: Cornell University Press.

Przeworski, Adam. 1999. "Minimalist Democracy: A Defense." In Ian Shapiro and Casiano Hacker-Cordón (eds.), *Democracy's Value*. New York: Cambridge University Press, 23–55.

———. 2007. "Political Rights, Property Rights, and Economic Development." Presented at the Weatherhead Center for International Affairs, Harvard University.

———. 2009. "Democracy, Equality and Redistribution." in R. Bourke and R. Geuss (eds.), *Political Judgment: Essays for John Dunn*. New York: Cambridge University Press 281–312.

———. 2010. *Democracy and the Limits of Self-government*. New York: Cambridge University Press.

Przeworski, Adam, Jose A. Cheibub, Fernando Limongi, and Michael Alvarez. 2000. *Democracy and Development*. New York: Cambridge University Press.

Przeworski, Adam and John Sprague. 1986. *Paper Stones: A History of Electoral Socialism*. Chicago, IL: University of Chicago Press.

Przeworski, Adam and Michael Wallerstein. 1982. "The Structure of Class Conflict in Democratic Capitalist Societies." *American Political Science Review* 76 (2): 215–238.

Puhle, Hans-Jürgen. 1975. *Agrarische Interessenpolitik und preußischer Konservatismus im wilhelminischen Reich (1893-1914)*. Bonn-Bad Godesberg: Verlag Neue Gesellschaft.

Putterman, L. 1996. "Why Have the Rabble Not Redistributed the Wealth? On the Stability of Democracy and Unequal Property." In *IEA Conference Volume Series*, vol. 115. New York: The Macmillan Press Ltd, 359-389.

Rajan, R.G. 2009. "Rent Preservation and the Persistence of Underdevelopment." *American Economic Journal: Macroeconomics* 1 (1):178-218.

Ravallion, M. and S. Chen. 2007. "China's (uneven) Progress against Poverty." *Journal of Development Economics* 82 (1):1-42.

Rebelo, S. 1991. "Long-Run Policy Analysis and Long-Run Growth." *The Journal of Political Economy* 99 (3):500-521.

Ricardo, David. [1824] 1888. "Observations on Parliamentary Reform." in *The Works of David Ricardo* 5, 495-503. London: John Murray.

Rodrigiuez, FC. 1999. "Does Distributional Skewness Lead to Redistribution? Evidence from the United States." *Economics & Politics* 11 (2):171-199.

Rodriguez, F. and D. Ortega. 2006. "Are Capital Shares Higher in Poor Countries? Evidence from Industrial Surveys." Unpublished, *Wesleyan Economics Working Papers*.

Rodríguez Weber, Javier. 2009. *Los tiempos de la desigualdad. La distribución del ingreso en Chile, entre la larga duración, la globalización y la expansión de la frontera, 1860-1930*. Tesis de Maestría en Historia económica, Programa de Historia económica y social, Universidad de la República, Montevideo.

Rodrik, D. 1998. "Why Do More Open Economies Have Bigger Governments?" *The Journal of Political Economy* 106 (5):997-1032.

———. 1999. "Democracies Pay Higher Wages." *Quarterly Journal of Economics* 114 (3):707-738.

———. 2000. "Institutions for High-quality Growth: What They Are and How to Acquire them." *Studies in Comparative International Development* 35 (3):3-31.

Roemer, J.E. 1998. "Why the Poor Do Not Expropriate the Rich: An Old Argument in New Garb." *Journal of Public Economics* 70 (3):399-424.

———. 2005. "Will Democracy Engender Equality?" *Economic Theory* 25 (1):217-234.

Roine, J. and D. Waldenström. 2008. "The Evolution of Top Incomes in an Egalitarian Society: Sweden, 1903-2004." *Journal of Public Economics* 92 (1):366-387.

Rosenberg, Hans. 1967. *Grosse Depression und Bismarckzeit: Wirtschaftsablauf, Gesellschaft und Politik in Mitteleuropa*. Veröffentlichungen der Historischen Kommission zu Berlin. Berlin: Walter de Gruyter & Co.

Ross, M. 2006. "Is Democracy Good for the Poor?" *American Journal of Political Science* 50 (4):860-874.

Ross, M. 2004. "Does Taxation Lead to Representation?" *British Journal of Political Science* 34 (2):229-249.

Rothstein, Bo. 1998. "The State, Associations, and the Transition to Democracy: Early Coporatism in Sweden." In Dietriech Rueschemeyer et al. (eds.), *Participation and Democracy East and West: Comparisons and Interpretations*. Armonk, NY: M.E. Sharpe, 132-156.

Rowen, Henry. 2007. "When Will the Chinese People be Free?" *Journal of Democracy* 18 (3):38-53.

Rueschemeyer, D., E.H. Stephens, and J. Stephens. 1992. *Capitalist Development and Democracy*. Chicago: University of Chicago Press.

Rustow, D.A. 1970. "Transitions to Democracy: Toward a Dynamic Model." *Comparative Politics* 2 (3):337–363.

Scheve, K. and D. Stasavage. 2006. "Religion and Preferences for Social Insurance." *Quarterly Journal of Political Science* 1 (3):255–286.

———. 2009. "Institutions, Partisanship, and Inequality in the Long Run." *World Politics* 61 (2):215–253.

Scheve, Kenneth and David Stasavage. 2012. "Democracy, War and Wealth: Lessons from Two Centuries of Inheritance Taxation." *American Political Science Review* 106 (1):81–102.

Schlozman, K.L., S. Verba, and H.E. Brady. 2012. *The Unheavenly Chorus: Unequal Political Voice and the Broken Promise of American Democracy*. Princeton, NJ: Princeton University Press.

Schonhardt-Bailey, Cheryl. 2006. *From the Corn Laws to Free Trade: Interests, Ideas, and Institutions in Historical Perspective*. Cambridge, MA: MIT Press.

Scott, Franklin. 1988. *Sweden: A Nation's History (Enlarged Edition)*. Carbondale, IL: Southern Illinois University Press.

Scott, James C. 1985. *Weapons of the Weak: Everyday Forms of Peasant Resistance*. New Haven, CT: Yale University Press.

Sen, A. 1980. "Equality of what?" *Tanner lectures on human values* 1:195–220.

Shayo, M. 2009. "A Model of Social Identity with an Application to Political Economy: Nation, Class, and Redistribution." *American Political Science Review* 103 (2):147–174.

Shelton, C.A. 2007. "The Size and Composition of Government Expenditure." *Journal of Public Economics* 91 (11-12):2230–2260.

Shin, G.W. 1998. "Agrarian Conflict and the Origins of Korean Capitalism." *The American Journal of Sociology* 103 (5):1309–1351.

Shleifer, A. and R.W. Vishny. 2002. *The Grabbing Hand: Government Pathologies and Their Cures*. Cambridge, MA: Harvard University Press.

Skocpol, T. 1979. *States and Social Revolutions: A Comparative Analysis of France, Russia, and China*. New York: Cambridge University Press.

Slater, D. 2009. "Revolutions, Crackdowns, and Quiescence: Communal Elites and Democratic Mobilization in Southeast Asia." *American Journal of Sociology* 115 (1):203–254.

———. 2010. *Ordering Power: Contentious Politics and Authoritarian Leviathans in Southeast Asia*. New York: Cambridge University Press.

Slater, Dan and Ben Smith. 2012. "Economic Origins of Democratic Breakdown? Contrary Evidence from Southeast Asia and Beyond." Unpublished, University of Chicago.

Smith, B.B. 2007. *Hard Times in the Lands of Plenty: Oil Politics in Iran and Indonesia*. New York: Cornell University Press.

Smith, Francis. 1966. *The Making of the Second Reform Bill*. Cambridge, UK: Cambridge University Press.

Soderberg, J. 1991. "3. Wage Differentials in Sweden." *Income Distribution in Historical Perspective*. In Y. S. Brenner, Hartmut Kaelble, and Mark Thomas (eds.). New York: Cambridge University Press.

Statistisches Reichsamt. 1884. "Berufsstatistik der grösseren Verwaltungsbezirke." *Statistik des Deutschen Reichs* 2, N.F.

Stigler, G.J. 1970. "Director's Law of Public Income Redistribution." *Journal of Law and Economics* 13 (1):1–10.

Stürmer, Michael. 1974. *Regierung und Reichstag im Bismarckstaat 1871–1880*. Düsseldorf: Droste.

Svolik, Milan. 2012. *The Politics of Authoritarian Rule*. New York: Cambridge University Press.

Thomas, W. 1969. "James Mill's Politics: the 'Essay on Government' and the Movement for Reform." *Historical Journal* 12:249–294.

Thomson, Henry R. 2012. "The Strategic Determinants of Repression Costs: Structure and Agency in Bismarck's 'Second Founding' of the German Empire." APSA 2012 Annual Meeting Paper.

Thornton, John. 2008. "Long Time Coming: The Prospects for Democracy in China." *Foreign Affairs* 87 (2):2–18.

Tilly, C. 1990. *Coercion, Capital, and European States, AD 990–1990*. London: Blackwell.

Tilton, T.A. 1974. "The Social Origins of Liberal Democracy: The Swedish case." *American Political Science Review* 68 (2):561–571.

Tipton, Frank B. 1979. "Farm Labor and Power Politics: German, 1850–1914." *The Journal of Economic History* 34 (4):951–979.

Treier, S. and S. Jackman. 2008. "Democracy as a Latent Variable." *American Journal of Political Science* 52 (1):201–217.

Treisman, Daniel. 2000. "The Causes of Corruption: A Cross-national Study." *Journal of Public Economics* 76:399–457.

Tullock, G. 1983. "Further Tests of a Rational Theory of the Size of Government." *Public Choice* 41 (3):419–421.

UNDP. 2011. *Human Development Report 2011. Sustainability and Equity: A Better Future for All*. New York: UNDP.

University of Texas Inequality Project (UTIP). 2008 "Estimated Household Income Inequality Data Set (EHII)." Available at http://utip.gov.utexas.edu/data.html. June 23, 2014.

Vanhanen, T. 2000. "A New Dataset for Measuring Democracy, 1810–1998." *Journal of Peace Research* 37 (2):251.

Verba, Sidney, Kay Schlozman, and Henry Brady. 1994. *Voice and Equality: Civic Voluntarism in American Politics*. Cambridge, UK: Cambridge University Press.

Verney, Douglas. 1957. *Parliamentary Reform in Sweden, 1866–1921*. London: Clarendon Press.

Vollrath, D. and L. Erickson. 2007. "Land Distributiion and Financial System Development." IMF Working Paper. Washington DC: International Monetary Fund.

Wang, T. 2013. "Goodbye to Gradualism." *Journal of Democracy* 24 (1):49–56.

Weingast, Barry. 1997. "The Political Foundations of Democracy and the Rule of Law." *American Political Science Review* 91 (2): pp 245–263.

Welshman, John. 2006. *Underclass: A History of the Excluded, 1880–2000*. London: Continuum.

Whyte, M.K. 2010. *Myth of the Social Volcano: Perceptions of Inequality and Distributive Injustice in Contemporary China*. Stanford, CA: Stanford University Press.

Williamson, Jeffrey. 2009. "Five Centuries of Latin American Inequality." NBER Working Paper 15305.

Winters, J.A. 2011. *Oligarchy*. New York: Cambridge University Press.

Wooldridge, J.M. 2002. *Econometric Analysis of Cross Section and Panel Data.* Cambridge, MA: The MIT press.

———. 2005. "Simple Solutions to the Initial Conditions Problem in Dynamic, Nonlinear Panel Data Models with Unobserved Heterogeneity." *Journal of Applied Econometrics* 20 (1):39–54.

Wright, D G. 1970. *Democracy and Reform, 1815–1885.* London: Longman.

Wu, Ximing and Jeffrey Perloff. 2005. "China's Income Distribution, 1985–2001." *Review of Economics and Statistics* 87 (4):763–775.

Yao, Kevin and Aileen Wang. 2013. "China lets Gini out of the Bottle; Wide Wealth Gap." URL www.reuters.com/article/2013/01/18/us-china-economy-income-gap-idUSBRE90H06L20130118.

Zeitlin, Maurice. 1984. *The Civil Wars in Chile (or, the Bourgeois Revolutions That Never Were).* Princeton, NJ: Princeton University Press.

Zellner, A. and T.H. Lee. 1965. "Joint Estimation of Relationships Involving Discrete Random Variables." *Econometrica: Journal of the Econometric Society* 33 (2):382–394.

Ziblatt, D. 2008. "Does Landholding Inequality Block Democratization?: A Test of the 'Bread and Democracy' Thesis and the Case of Prussia." *World Politics* 60 (4):610–641.

Index

Allan Kornberg and Harold D. Clarke, *Citizens and Community: Political Support in a Representative Democracy*

Amie Kreppel, *The European Parliament and the Supranational Party System*

David D. Laitin, *Language Repertoires and State Construction in Africa*

Fabrice E. Lehoucq and Ivan Molina, *Stuffing the Ballot Box: Fraud, Electoral Reform, and Democratization in Costa Rica*

Mark Irving Lichbach and Alan S. Zuckerman, eds., *Comparative Politics: Rationality, Culture, and Structure, 2nd Edition*

Evan Lieberman, *Race and Regionalism in the Politics of Taxation in Brazil and South Africa*

Richard M. Locke, *Promoting Labor Standards in a Global Economy: The Promise and Limits of Private Power*

Pauline Jones Luong, *Institutional Change and Political Continuity in Post-Soviet Central Asia*

Pauline Jones Luong and Erika Weinthal, *Oil Is Not a Curse: Ownership Structure and Institutions in Soviet Successor States*

Julia Lynch, *Age in the Welfare State: The Origins of Social Spending on Pensioners, Workers, and Children*

Lauren M. MacLean, *Informal Institutions and Citizenship in Rural Africa: Risk and Reciprocity in Ghana and Côte d'Ivoire*

Beatriz Magaloni, *Voting for Autocracy: Hegemonic Party Survival and Its Demise in Mexico*

James Mahoney, *Colonialism and Postcolonial Development: Spanish America in Comparative Perspective*

James Mahoney and Dietrich Rueschemeyer, eds., *Comparative Historical Analysis in the Social Sciences*

Scott Mainwaring and Matthew Soberg Shugart, eds., *Presidentialism and Democracy in Latin America*

Isabela Mares, *The Politics of Social Risk: Business and Welfare State Development*

Isabela Mares, *Taxation, Wage Bargaining, and Unemployment*

Cathie Jo Martin and Duane Swank, *The Political Construction of Business Interests: Coordination, Growth, and Equality*

Anthony W. Marx, *Making Race, Making Nations: A Comparison of South Africa, the United States, and Brazil*

Doug McAdam, John McCarthy, and Mayer Zald, eds., *Comparative Perspectives on Social Movements*

Bonnie M. Meguid, *Party Competition between Unequals: Strategies and Electoral Fortunes in Western Europe*

Joel S. Migdal, *State in Society: Studying How States and Societies Constitute One Another*

Joel S. Migdal, Atul Kohli, and Vivienne Shue, eds., *State Power and Social Forces: Domination and Transformation in the Third World*

Scott Morgenstern and Benito Nacif, eds., *Legislative Politics in Latin America*

Kevin M. Morrison, *Nontaxation and Representation: The Fiscal Foundations of Political Stability*

Layna Mosley, *Global Capital and National Governments*

39725325R00142

Made in the USA
Middletown, DE
23 January 2017